SEALED

ETERNAL SECURITY!

CAN ONE LOSE ONE'S SALVATION?

by alfred g. lara

CONTENTS

THE CONTROVERSY!

The controversy of whether a person can or cannot lose their salvation after conversion is by far one of the most mind-boggling, significant, and at the same time, blurred unanswered questions asked by today's *faithful* throughout Christianity's spectrum. And all for a good reason, I might add, but asked with a hint of confusion!

If you were to take to social media in search of answers, you'd come across some pretty heated arguments, which more than likely would lead you right back to square one, inflamed, dazed, and confused, and I think it's the same all around the world when it comes to this obscured topic.

We are probably experiencing an equal sensation no matter where we turn. Whether someone believes in eternal security or not, the suspense remains pretty much the same in trying to figure out who's right or who's wrong on this most controversial and crucial subject of biblical implications that has sparked some unavoidable heated arguments over time, ones that should be filtered by an exponential and factual truth, and to what is the scriptural substance that eternal security stands on...or doesn't?

I guess that depends on where you began your biblical journey once upon a time, which will, in the end, dictate your theology altogether or at least shape some resolutions thereof, which set your biblical views to a point.

And the million-dollar question remains: Can you lose your salvation after conversion?

In my opinion, the answer to that question is quite obvious, as stated throughout Scripture. But only when sought out with diligence and not simply intent. It's also alimentally stated in Scripture that you can. The thing is, it must be viewed as intended, biblically speaking. And that would be a yes—yes, you can. Let me show you why that is!

It's not a secret Adam and Eve lost their place in Eden immediately after they sinned. It's not a secret Israel lost their place with God as they put to death the Messiah who came to save them, and to think Gentiles cannot lose their salvation after clearly knowing these events took place is mind-boggling, to say the least, since we know a third of the angels also lost their place in heaven, and it happened for the same reason the Garden of Eden was closed for business: sin!

Some may not understand that "where sin is, grace abides the more" discourse out of the pages of Romans, chapters five and six, which must be looked at outside of intent as I mentioned earlier and in pure content for authenticity as well as clarity. Let's engage in the other approach while exposing the former. Romans 5:19 gives us the reason sin came into existence in us all: through Adam. And it also annotates that righteousness also is available for us all through Christ. If sin entered humanity because of disobedience then, then sin to this day enters us because of disobedience as well.

The difference is that in Old Testament times, an animal sacrifice was needed for atonement for that sin, and the people had to confess their sins for the atonement to take place.

Today we no longer need an animal sacrifice for atonement because the Lamb of God was that sacrifice and atonement once and for all. We still need to do what the Old Testament people did, and that's confessing our sin; that part remains.

Therefore, the forgiveness of sin has to come by way of confession; the sacrifice is automatic, the confession isn't. There is no other biblical way for redemption than confession onto repentance. We sin willfully and are not forgiven automatically, and nowhere in the Bible does it state you can get automatic forgiveness, not initially and not during the journey. If it took confession to begin the journey, it will take continual confession after we sin to continue in that journey of life in Christ.

Verse twenty of Romans, chapter five, tells us that under the law, sin was magnified, making the law work against the sinner. "But where sin abounded, grace abounded much more" (Romans 5:20, NKJV). Grace was always there to redeem the sinner. In this case, it was the entire population that went to the priest for atonement yearly. Grace is not a thing of the New Testament; grace was always there because God was always there as a gracious God. Verse twenty-one unlocks the period between sin and redemption, which comes (then and now) by confession. That part remains the same, as stated earlier.

The next verse validates what I'm trying to convey here: "What shall we say then? Shall we continue in sin that grace may abound?" (Romans 6:1, NKJV). These are the questions; now let's have the answer: "Certainly not!" (Romans 6:2, NKJV). You can look up what "certainly" means if you like, but there is no provision for the idea that living under grace is a license to sin. "How shall we who died to sin live any longer in it?" (Romans 6:2, NKJV).

Here's your answer. Romans 6:2b clearly states a sinful lifestyle, not an individual sin. "Living any longer" is speaking of a lifestyle in sin.

Living in sin is a premise directive of a return to sin wholeheartedly. An adoption of sin, if you will. Do we not know that the proverb *only a dog returns to its vomit* is a return to a lifestyle of sin and not an "oops, I've sinned" instance? (See Proverbs 26:11, 2 Peter 2:22). Why have two scriptures to redefine the same edict? We don't!

Imagine an opening statement like this one aimed at you: "I marvel that you are turning away so soon from Him who called you in the grace of Christ, to a different gospel" (Galatians 1:7,

NKJV). Turning away from the *grace* of Christ to another gospel is no small thing. Otherwise, it wouldn't be written in Scripture. And He who called you is God. Maybe the understanding of grace is not clear yet, and that's because that particular grace is a period between sin and judgment, which is exactly what grace is. A grace period, if you will. And turning away from grace denies the element of grace being a sealed deal. Turning away is leaving the grace that some call eternal security for a false sense of security.

Paul was speaking to the Galatian church about this, and if he was, then it meant they were believers and thus brethren. Just as he addressed them in verse eleven. This particular discourse was aimed at the objective teaching of circumcision. Supposedly, some people were making that a requirement for the new faith, or people of the Way (Christianity). Verse seven drops a bomb on them about a group who is preaching a previous doctrine of works, and verse eight drops a nuclear bomb on anyone who thinks they can teach outside the truth of the cross, meaning the way to it and how to stay in it,

> but there are some who trouble you and want to pervert the gospel of Christ. But even if we, or an angel from heaven, preach any other gospel to you than what we have preached to you, let him be accursed.

> Galatians 1:7-8 (NKJV)

He includes an angel of heaven; let that sink in!

If Paul, and assuming Paul wrote Galatians, is conveying the ominous repercussion of being accursed simply by instituting circumcision, how much more severe is the sin of suicide promoted by Once Saved, Always Saved (OSAS) because it's clear that this doctrine teaches one can still go to heaven if they kill themselves?

But in case we weren't clear about the repercussions of false teachings, as OSAS is, read the next verse, verse nine: "As we have said before, so now I say again, if anyone preaches any other gospel to you than what you have received, let him be accursed" Galatians 1:7-8 (NKJV). Let me reiterate the premise one more time, and not for redundancy, but if this language was used to address circumcision, what do you suppose the punishment is for advocating suicide to believers who have fallen to hyper depression or perhaps a broken heart?

Suicide is the demolition of God's temple and the demolition of a building that does not belong to the one taking it down as in their own life, thus destroying a building that was bought at a price by Jesus. If you are a Christian, then you are bought at a price. Look at what 1 Corinthians 6:20 (NKJV) says: "Therefore glorify God in your body and in your spirit, which are God's." I have a question: How is it that suicide glorifies God? It glorifies the god of this world, but not the God of heaven!

"Or do you not know that your body is the temple of the Holy

10

Spirit who is in you, whom you have from God, and you are not your own?" (1 Corinthians 6:19, NKJV).

Deemed a temple or a building, if you will, the body and its concerns of continual sanctification after conversion are centered in ongoing biblical developments of exponential terms of genuine revelation. These are based on a required directive by the Holy Spirit for a personal relationship with the third person of the Godhead.

Terms that are alternative in nature and in guidance for the sole purpose of self-transparency and sanctification (Galatians 6:4) are coupled with conviction to always keep believers (you and me) at bay (in case we wanted to default as the Galatians did [Galatians 6:7]). The flesh does not take a break or a holiday, and neither should our spirit man.

When referring to the body of Christ's maintenance, which is required through continual sanctification for the survival of such a faith, and may I remind you that, that's regardless of if you're speaking of an individual or the church itself overall or in a corporate manner, we are one body, which is both referred to as the body of Christ, His bride.

Upkeep is generally necessary for any new structure that is built with intent for longevity and its service thereof, or else that structure will be brought to ruins before its time and will not serve out its intended purpose overall. It will come to shambles and ruins before you know it if neglected, but for its sustainability to help it remain standing strong throughout life's storms and other natural disasters along the way and for it to remain operational for decades to come or perhaps centuries at the very least, a maintenance program of some sort has to be implemented in its continual upkeeping for its preservation and survival. Perhaps to resolve the builders' long-term goals, prestige and also to minimize cost and loss that can happen through the negligence of the structure, there must be a plan of maintenance in order to customize such desires.

That is true of any formidable structure to always remain operational and in code with all building and governmental guidelines, but much more so of the body of Christ since we're talking about God's temple. Therefore, its upkeep is inevitable, or else?

The temple of the Holy Spirit is no different than a brick-and-mortar temple in theory, if you will (Genesis 3:19). When it comes to maintenance, we must implement a system of upkeep, and of course, we are that temple, and we need to maintain it in order to please God.

We are that building, and building is something of a verb that continues daily, which is called growth, and building a kingdom, whether personal or otherwise, never ends for the believer. Maybe not in a solid structure after the last floor is added to it, but in our lives, it continues. And the temple of the Holy Spirit's sustainability doesn't come without the Spirit's daily presence, which helps us in that continuous upkeep in the day-to-day operations thereof.

Good days and bad days both need the Holy Spirit in them.

The fact is it should be treated with much more reasoning and sensitivity because of the adversity at bay and who it is that inhabits such temples. And not just treat it with basic religious overtones. Like those of the Pharisees who felt they had arrived because of their vast biblical knowledge, and let's not forget their religious achievements. What a mistake such an attitude was on their part! To think that accolades, which are presumptuous feats, are greater than that of a relationship with the Creator of the universe, and sadly, humbleness did not make their top ten list just because they got it over their heads on that false knowledge of elitism, and that's how they missed it by a mile. Not that the Torah is false, but that their application and the transition to the New Testament were not handled right. And to top it off, they felt they were right, though the Lord told them time and time again how far they had drifted from the real Jehovah. And did so to their face. Sadly so, they thought they had salvation on lockdown.

They ended up misplacing fellowship with the one true God with religion, and misplacement came because of self-righteousness. No doubt they knew they were over their heads in almost everything they did (John 11:49-53). And no wonder they missed out on the most anticipated event in world history by choosing religion over a relationship and standing on the wrong side of history at that.

Perhaps without hesitation, in such a devastating disconnect with the One, they claimed to follow and revere, which is today's equivalent of something religious that derives perhaps from a classroom in Christian academia somewhere around the globe. Just as it was the case with the Pharisees then, it could be the same thing today. They believed they were right, and good intentions say nothing about erroneous endeavors. And I say it again: it may be the same now. Like them then, where their crown (achievements) was more important than the cross they bore (their calling), today as well, we are not exempt from the proverbial *bighead* syndrome.

They had the Word of God down to a tee, academically speaking, and we cannot take that away from them, but did they have a solid relationship with the God of the Word?

Presumably, a quest centered on book knowledge and information at best is half the journey we are trying to embark on as the faithful. Not that learning is bad, no, please don't get me wrong, but that learning is just not enough, and we have the Pharisees to prove it!

A PhD in medicine means absolutely nothing if it's never put into practice in helping people with health conditions to help them achieve better health results and help them resolve a standard to better health. Medicine must be practiced outside of book knowledge. We call it medical practice, with emphasis on *practice*.

Thus, biblical revelation does not derive from a book that's inclined to inform you, at best, and not anoint you for the task prescribed, which is outside of the book. And Christianity must also be practiced just like medicine is (1 John 3:10b). One that transforms as it informs is the kind of word needed for personal growth in the Lord, but simultaneously, and since that capability can only come from God, who gives gifts to the gifted. We must then attain all the necessities to achieve it.

It will take more than book knowledge or revelation to know what the perspective calling in us as individuals in Christ. We need them both, and once we have that, we then practice that which we believe. Paul said: "I believed, and therefore I spoke" (2 Corinthians 4:13, NKJV) as he was quoting King David (Psalm 116:10). We must act upon what we believe.

I'm speaking about the kind of revelation that resonates uniformly in a very distinct manner deriving from God's timeless and unequivocal Word. One that rhetorically precedes all that is taught in Christian academia and beyond, and the fact that such a revelation is needed as well as a fair, balanced Christian education, which identifies as secondary to all biblical application and information in its narrative, but with a directive involved for hands-on practice. Also, don't forget that much prayer is needed as well. Outreach is an amazing expression of love by the body of believers, but "in-reach" cannot go denied either.

In any alignment of spirituality, prayer must be implemented for a well-balanced ministry. Prayer is coveted for such ministries as well as fasting and the like. And to make a correlation to a connection for a successful ministry if applied as directed, fasting and prayer can illuminate much of the blur we sometimes come across during trying times, and that by all means, when referring to the anointing of God, which primarily carries a purpose intended for a need of some sort, for someone's life, whether it be local, national, or even a global event, should always be viewed as a commencement for something of magnitude if God is behind it. Not simply a thought, or to suggest it as a wishful thinking approach, but a calling from God Himself—then, and only then, we can achieve true biblical balance for that specific task we were called to do, and its magnitude is at God's jurisdiction. He gives directions, and we do the logistics; that simple!

The revelation of Word knowledge can and will go a long way when exercised as intended, and we march in that sentiment. That's why implementation sometimes comes in the form of a gentle whisper (1 Kings 9:12) but other times as a wrecking ball (1 Samuel 11:7).

Fire from heaven did not come down due to the prophet's knowledge it could be possible. Fire from heaven happened because God's prophet believed and acted on that very belief and because he had to prove, making it intentional, that God was the one true God and not Baal, and the only way to do so was to call fire from heaven (1 Kings 18). The prophet's presence of mind was to accomplish this impossible task while at the same time using the event to bring God glory. The law is not based on faith, says Galatians 3:12; therefore, Elijah applied his faith and not his knowledge of Scripture to discredit idol worshippers because the law did that, but the Spirit, not the law, rained fire from heaven, redefining the premise is futile.

Information is not equated with wisdom in any implication of that apriorism. Proverbs 17:16 (NKJV) says, "Why is there in the hand of a fool the purchase price of wisdom, since he has no heart for it?" And since lack of wisdom can very easily take information and make it seem as if it was misinformation, we must be wise, have the heart for it, therefore, disconnecting from emotions that cloud even our simple minds from acting upon God's command, and follow through on His directive.

I will explain thoroughly what the measures are but let me begin by refreshing your memory of incidents where the unbalance of ministry was indeed evident. Once we understand what goes on in the spirit realm, we can then appreciate what we are attempting to accomplish to embrace a true calling in Christ for the believer(s).

For example, Simon the Sorcerer attempted to buy the gift of the Spirit because of the power behind it. Power is attractive, and as we read in Acts 8:17-20, I ask: What's the difference between something that you can attempt to buy, and I mean from the Spirit's perspective—like trying to get the Spirit's anointing with money—and by enrolling in a Bible course regardless of time enrolled or money spent for the course itself? I see no difference in this parallel. But what I mean by this is that there are a lot of well-informed dummies out there (no pun intended) who mean well, and I'm sure they do mean well, but there are scores of them out there, and they are clueless of who Satan is. And they are sent to teach a book of stories without expressing the power it contains within. The Bible is not a storybook; it's literally the living Word of God. It has the power to transform those it informs.

We are not told of Simon's intentions to obtain apostolic power, but even if he had good intentions of advancing his ministry, the fact of the matter is we don't dictate to God to give us gifts; we can only ask and then wait for them, and if He does or not, we stay the course!

Is this something new? Of course not! When God said, "My people perish for lack of knowledge" (Hosea 4:6, paraphrased), He was being nice. If it was me saying it, I'd picture Fred Sanford delivering that statement better than anyone I know, and I'm sure he would wrap it up with: "You big dummy! There are schools of prophets out there, why?"

That's because one is taught by common knowledge, and one is given directly by God. One is publicly attained, and one is selective. The parable of the talents tells us God knows not to give five talents to a *one-talent* individual. Some say that "God does not call the qualified but qualifies the called," and I completely agree!

The Pharisees are utter proof that human knowledge is still incompetent when compared to the anointing of God or the skill of a doer of the Word. The disciples exemplified that notion by acts (actions), and since none of them were scholars at first, they proved the anointing was primary to biblical knowledge. Especially when clouded by aristocratic greed as the Pharisees and Simon the Sorcerer did.

God told these *well-informed* individuals that they missed the day of His visitation due to the atrocity they created by their frail religion, which was not biblical at all. At some point, they abandoned Scripture and went with self-absorption. Therefore, they had to manufacture a lie, and they did so to escape criticism and perhaps avoid responsibility for their misguided actions (Luke 19:44). And we are speaking of a visitation they were all in anticipation of for centuries. *Visitation* was staring them in the face. Visitation was speaking to them daily, literally, and not in a good way because visitation pointed out to them who they had become, yet they missed it. In other words, the Spirit and the letter go hand and hand for God's intended purpose.

This means that an expectation of such accounts was their motivation to follow the one true God, yet in their informality, they miserably failed at the one-yard line. They punted on first down rather than score. Who does that?

I think it's safe to say that although the Pharisees knew the purpose, they did not know the method, and I mean by a long shot. In a way, it's understandable because Satan was clueless about what God was doing as well; otherwise, he wouldn't be asking Jesus every other day if He was the Son of God while tempting Him in the wilderness, and that was a good thing, my friends, a clueless devil is always two steps behind our amazing Savior.

What I mean by this is that a little light is shed on us from time to time on things we read in the Bible for measures of clarity to help us better understand certain actions that point to tasks exercised by the faithful back then, in the Old Testament times, but also some in particular in today's Christian society. Or better yet, when putting two and two together, we must go beyond the simplicity of the text and acquire revelation of God's intention for expected results in the abundance of the perspective of it so as to solve the needs at hand for the believer and those around us.

Paul had all the book knowledge in the world, but in the end, he was persecuting Christians because of ignorance in such knowledge. What good was that knowledge he possessed if it wasn't biblical? It took the road-to-Damascus experience to set him straight onto Straight Street itself (Acts 9:11) to give him the balance he needed to be effective as an emissary to the Gentile church, as we are told in Scripture. So how should we approach Scripture so as to not fall for the same trap Paul fell for and also thinking that an on/off switch persuaded by money, power, or prestige can help us reach spiritual highs as Simon the Sorcerer did, who also converted to the way, well, he believed it could be done? That's why we must not only read and study Scripture but also pray for the revelation that allows us to see beyond our ability and teaches us to read between the lines to add to our acts or progressive building of biblical character as we mature in the faith. For example, Jesus said this:

You are of your father the devil, and the desires of your father you want to do. *He was a murderer from the beginning* and does not stand in the truth, because there is no truth in him. When he speaks a lie, he speaks from his own resources, for he is a liar and the father of it.

John 8:44 (NKJV), emphasis added

Suppose we were to break this verse down to simplify it and better understand its true meaning, as well as get a full view of what Jesus was unloading here but do so in increments according to the time this was first introduced in, by filtering the account itself and drawing a conclusion to break down its true intention, and search for the revelation embedded within it and also find amplification to its true audience and purpose. For that, we would need a high dose of revelation along with integrated Bible knowledge, but by solely focusing on the actions that Jesus was speaking about, an undeniable *catch twenty-two* of an evident curveball thrown at his adversaries clarifies book knowledge from Spirit knowledge. This was a witness conclusive to why the parables were used by Jesus in the first place, as well as who He aimed them at. Other than the obvious, of course, who, at the moment of utterance in the redundant connectivity of sorts, was like placing a mirror in front of them to show them how much they didn't know of what they thought they knew, if you will.

Chronologically speaking and as eschatologically inclined as possible, there will be two times in history we would have to look at to expand our *revelatory* thought process in the matter. If one was to conclude that His every syllable was connected, *biblically* speaking, that is, to events already penned in other ancient biblical texts, then we must unveil them as collectibles.

Accounts that already took place with many highlights of reasoning that would also lead to historical events and their teachings, when unraveled, will eventually make sense. Ones that only the Holy Spirit can reveal to whom He chooses to are up for grabs here and now.

These are things worth looking into for authenticity and hiding them from whom He would is also His to decide, which He did by signaling to His adversaries through parables that spoke volumes of simplicity, silencing the intellects whenever presented in such a high level of astute ways. As we know, parables were a frequency not practiced by the elite but perfectly understood by the uninformed and the nobodies of the day. Go figure!

But only because He was there, and I mean in both instances, Jesus could speak as if the moment was afresh, and no one can deny Him that position. And that's exactly why they had so much contention toward Him. He spoke as if He was there, and they hated that. (Nails on the chalkboard.)

The second one is when the Spirit is speaking in code to people God has revealed Himself to beforehand. Such as when Paul was told to see Ananias at Judas's house on Straight Street. Though

Paul could no longer see because Paul was blinded at his encounter with Jesus, Jesus told him his healing awaited him there by the hands of Ananias, and that experience pretty much convinced Paul he was persecuting Jesus by his self-righteousness, a result deriving from his vast knowledge of the Law to the point of overdosing from it.

The Bible does say knowledge puffs up. But before Paul set foot into Judas's home on Straight Street, Jesus had already informed Judas as well as Ananias what they had to do once Paul arrived (Acts 9:10), or Saul, if you will.

God reveals Himself to us over time as we mature in Him, and always about accounts that take place in future times to come, and we call such; *prophecy*. But unfortunately, that did not mean the educated bunch known as the Pharisees would get it because they had made up their minds to keep the God of the Bible out of the Bible to protect their own prestige. If they did not agree with the method, it was in part because of the negligence of the relationship and the lack of embracing true faith, and they had no clue to that effect because the pedigree was self-convinced that a stranger was among them. The One who did not fit into their ruling class, or narrative, for that matter, couldn't be the Messiah; "the Messiah could not look like Jesus" pretty much was the premise. At least in their own world of the elite.

These elites who were not part of this eye-opener of intriguing, intricate, and futuristic biblical views were left out to dry to a fault of their own, and they simply absorbed it as they saw fit, which was their misguided error. Otherwise, they would have never crucified their own Messiah. Makes sense, right?

Let's dive into John 8:44 (NKJV) and experience the richness of exploratory biblical revelation that's revolving around intuitive correlation with other scriptures for a resolve that not only will elevate the central thought process of revelatory innuendos but also tie it all together to clarify this claim of veritableness. This also integrates the very thing they failed to see, which was what they missed, though it stared them in the face, unquestionably so, it did!

- "You are of your father the devil," said Jesus!

Now, if you're a Pharisee who has a wide range of knowledge in the Torah, one who breathes the Word pretty much daily, who have phylacteries the size of a boxed truck, and just like that, some new jack comes along, pushes them into a corner, beats them at their own debate, then successfully punks them out in front of their peers. And if that's not enough, after that, they had only two options in their new frail state to choose from: one is to *agree*, take the shellacking they had coming and then a sincere evaluation of self, which could lead to positivity, and if He's right, simply repent. Let's not forget that a forerunner came through right before Jesus did, in John the Baptist, and his message to all Israel was to *repent,* including the elite, or should I say, especially the elite?

In Matthew 23:33 (NKJV), Jesus said to the Pharisees,

"Serpents, brood of vipers! How can you escape the condemnation of hell?" The Pharisees believed they could not lose their salvation either. But Jesus was clear by asking, "How can you escape the condemnation to hell?" He then went on to prophesy they were going to crucify and persecute prophets and wise men just as their ancestors did. Which was the second option, and that's a right-out rebellion, and yes, they chose plan B.

Furthermore, John the Baptist opened up his ministry with these same words as Matthew 3:7 (NKJV) records, "But when he saw many of the Pharisees and Sadducees coming to his baptism, he said to them, 'Brood of vipers! Who warned you to flee from the wrath to come?'" He later said to them to bear fruits worthy of repentance and then added that Someone with a greater baptism— one done by the Holy Spirit—was coming after him. But Jesus did not fit the narrative of the elites and threatened their social standing with something terrible; a possible exposure among the people they ruled was at play, and they ruled people by deception. That was the main problem they faced. Deception only works on people who suffer from a lack of knowledge, not of the Word, but of the revelation of the Word.

The parallel was that Satan was a serpent in the Garden of Eden back in Genesis. Satan lied to Eve and got what he wanted out of her, i.e., rebellion. And the Pharisees also lied through their teeth and eventually got what they wanted (social standing), so crucifying Jesus was to win their case through duplicity, and they knew it was done in informality. Just like David killed Uriah, or had him killed, while the whole time thinking how slick he was, but was he? Not slick enough for Nathan the Prophet and certainly not slick enough for the Lord. The religious leaders did the same by using the Romans to execute Jesus and pretending they were under biblical guidelines the entire time, and the responsibility to do so was the can kicked down the road. He also told them their father *the devil* was a murderer from the beginning, and they ended up murdering Jesus to simulate their father. In other words, Jesus was correct about every insult that landed in their direction by His arsenal of truth bombs.

- "…and the desires of your father you want to do…"

Jesus was telling them about what they were thinking of doing, what their ultimate goal was, and mind you, there was no social media, no fake news, no internet, and no public transportation to persuade anyone speedily to *join in the chant*. Word had to get out by emissaries. These events were centralized in Jerusalem, which was the epicenter of the universe and still is to this very day. And for an entire social, public, political, and religious system of that day to want the same person ousted because He threatened their social standing is undeniably unequivocal. (It kind of reminds you of today's Washington politics with a certain individual in the way, doesn't it?) They all wanted Him dead, and that's why Jesus said they wanted to do what their father desired, and that's to kill Him.

- "He was a murderer from the beginning and does not stand in the truth, because there is no truth in him…"

Jesus told them that Satan was a murderer from the beginning. Jesus was referencing Genesis 4:8, when Cain killed Abel. This was the very first recorded murder in human history, of course, unless Jesus was referring to Eve's bite of the fruit, where death primarily began its macabre work by infecting Eve's DNA and ending human immortality.

Jesus also referred to Satan as a liar, but regardless of where He meant murder began, what we are certain of is that it was started by Satan.

The devil lied to the serpent to get it to do his bidding. How nonchalantly we read that the snake was the most cunning animal on the planet. I'm sure your Bible commentary skipped right over that feat! (Genesis 3:1). Furthermore, deception cannot come from the truth; one can only be deceived if the lie is accepted.

- "When he speaks a lie, he speaks from his own resources, for he is a liar and the father of it…" That's why Jesus began the verse with, "you are of your father the devil": because they were no longer looking at Scripture to be fulfilled, they were simply negating the very reason they were in this prolific realm of a position, to begin with. In other words, they took over religion, and in their duplicity, they dropped the relationship with God, *part of the equation*, and did so for selfish gain. I can only imagine what lie Lucifer told in heaven to persuade one out three angels to abandon their proper abode (Jude 1:6).

How do we know the Pharisees were over their heads? Well, the veil was torn in half from top to bottom, leaving no confusion of who did that tear, kind of like the return of the fingers from the writing on the wall, but in a different fashion (Daniel 5:5). Just think about how, after the crucifixion, the following Sabbath church service went for the high priest?

Jesus was able to see everything they were about to do and did not bother to change their minds. He encouraged them to hurry it up and get it over with, beginning with Judas. And just like God did not knock the apple off Eve's hand, Jesus did not try to stop the Pharisees, nor has He stopped suicide successors…let that sink in!

There is a time when a person is beyond repentance; we saw it in King Saul. We saw it in Judas. We saw it in Cain and a few others along the way.

This happens when someone believes a lie and replaces the truth with it. We call that a reprobate mind. A deception of volunteerism. But for an entire nation to do so is incomprehensible and quite frightening, if you ask me. It's inconceivable to think that unison of evil can run the atmosphere in a global decree, but unless you lived under a rock, you know it is possible because we just experienced the same sentiment in 2020!

Also, the entire religious body, which held the tradition and the law of Moses as their guiding light, sadly abandoned it because their motives had other agendas. All to just end up not only believing the lie but continually manufacturing many lies to get rid of the Messiah they so longed to see one day and embrace at His predicted arrival but in their perception and not God's. Selah!

The Pharisees had the people of Israel on spiritual lockdown when it comes to religion. Let me show you what I mean by that by giving you a word right out of the mouth of our God, Jesus, and He's speaking to a Pharisee who, of course, knew it all: "Are you the teacher of Israel and do not know these things?" (John 3:10, NKJV). This verse says: *you can teach what you are taught but cannot teach what God teaches!*

If God did not teach you that thing Himself, you simply learned that from some sort of biblical education, or in poor words: it is not the same as a revelation from above, and by a long shot, and I'm not discrediting Christian learning, I'm merely pointing out the obvious!

Revelation can only come from God, and one must ask God to receive such revelation, and that takes belief, but we are not to puff up as Paul did as he received his vast revelation, or we will get a thorn in the flesh as Paul did…Here's some revelation on that: Paul's thorn in the flesh was a sin he couldn't overcome; well, until he found himself between a neck harness, his last words to the faithful, his executioner, and a silencing sword that finished his race. And that, my friends, is how he was humbled because this man saw the third heaven and saw it while he lived. And if he had a sin as a thorn in the flesh, or as he put it, "a messenger of Satan"

(2 Corinthians 12:7, NKJV), how did he overcome it?

He repented every single time because none of us are perfect, and confession is the only thing that gets it done (Romans 7:13-25). But he confessed the sin, and so should we because that takes away the ability for Satan to accuse us of sin *because God's grace is sufficient*, we are told.

If we confess our sins, they are forgiven, and that's the end of that. But we are talking about a sin that took place seasonally and not daily. I don't think Paul made it a sport to sin. I've read commentaries that it might have been masturbation, and some believe it was a sickness, but regardless of what it was, he pleaded with Jesus to take it away, and the answer was no, and we know why!

Paul himself was an educated man in regard to the Law, and in the end, Paul, as well as the Pharisees, ended up violating the very law they swore to protect. Paul was reached by Jesus (thank God), but the journey Jesus prophesied for Paul once he converted was that he would suffer greatly for His (Jesus's) sake!

Here's the discourse to Nicodemus revealed:

1. Are you a teacher of Israel? The answer is yes!

2. And do not know these things? The answer is no!

Not brain surgery, right? But that's because knowledge is not the same as the *revelation* of God's word.

Let's allow this same *revelatory* approach to be implemented with what we saw in John 8:44 (NKJV).

- "You are of your father the devil."

What a mean thing to hear from the Son of God, right?

I mean for the religious leaders whom society viewed as God's advocates for the common good of all men being addressed as such, and to *mic drop* in a blunt and audacious way with such destructive overtones was right out disrespectful by the likes of Jesus. These indirect suggestions, to say the least, did not go over their heads every time He addressed them, and they knew He was talking to them in His parables.

Or was Jesus justified?

When Jesus made the statement about the blind leading the blind, He didn't mean they were physically blind, but that their knowledge of *the Law* made them superior to everyone else, and thus, birthed inside of them a type of *elitism* which eventually led to pride, until it finally blinded them permanently, which we know was the same thing that got Lucifer cast out of heaven. Yes, the same heaven you and I are trying to get into. Someone lost their place there because of *pride*, and Jesus was telling the religious leaders that they were treading on the same premise as their father, the devil, as they mimicked almost religiously. He nailed it by familiarizing them and Satan as close to kin.

Jesus was making the statement that the Law blinded them to the point that they missed God's visitation. They were looking so far ahead that they couldn't see two feet in front of them.

In essence, the Law became their God, and doctrine or denominationalism certainly can too!

Pride and arrogance blinded Pharisees completely, so much that they put to death their own Messiah and did so out of sheer hatred because they did not want to be set free from the Romans who gave them a small piece of the pie. So yes, Jesus had every right to tell them that their father was the devil, and, in that complexity, they were out of character when usurping authority that did not belong to them, and that's because Jesus knew that they were the ones to put Him to death (1 Thessalonians 2:14-15) because that's what the devil was going to do being a predictable and a defeated foe.

Not convinced yet? Okay, let's move on to the point we're investigating in John 8:44:

- "And the desires of your father you want to do…" What desires?

We just agreed that society deemed the religious leaders of that day as those who were advocates for the things of God, right?

Were they, though? Because the people were fooled, but God wasn't fooled. Can we pull a fast one over God? And the answer to that is *no*. David thought he had covered his tracks only to find out Nathan had the goods on him after he cheated, lied, and killed. Sounds familiar? (John 10:10).

We must be careful not to try and fool others, or ourselves for that matter. Fooled into thinking we have arrived, we may have book knowledge, and our accolades may shine as bright as the morning star. To even entertain the idea that we have somehow made it is more than enough reason for concern. It was knowledge that motivated Paul to persecute the church because he thought he was right. It was faith that made him change courses. Religion is prejudice against what disagrees with it. Faith is blind to individuality; it must be.

In Galatians 2:1, Paul says that after fourteen years out of Jerusalem, he returned home, and that was fourteen years spent among the Gentiles. Paul had to be among what he was going to influence. This means influence didn't come from knowledge but from fellowship. A pastor who doesn't smell like sheep may very well be a wolf or a hireling. I love to see pastors greet their congregation after service, and I'm sure many do, but no greater example of that, than the Barnett trio (Tommy, Luke, and Matthew). If you are a preacher who is so big that you no longer greet your members, you need a reality check because, without them, you'd be preaching to the mirror, and I suggest you humble yourself because *you aren't all that.*

In Galatians 2:2 (NKJV), Paul opens by saying: "I went up by revelation and communicated to them that gospel which I preached to the Gentiles." We are talking about a different individual here. As Saul, he went around killing and imprisoning believers because of Word knowledge. As Paul, he returned to his roots by revelation, but as a new man. He did not leave behind what had occurred, he trusted what he simply believed and added faith to knowledge, and that's what we should do, or we might become big-headed because fame has a way of confusing the motive for the method!

Let's not forget that the Lord looks at our hearts and not our academic achievements.

It was no different from the Pharisee's angle. Jesus spent quite a lot of time engaging them on how wrong they had it when it comes to *all things God*. Romans 9:30-32 says that the Gentiles received righteousness because of their faith, but Israel, though they tried to pursue righteousness through the Law, did not attain it because it was done outside of faith. And faith is why you and I were able to come to God and be grafted in the vine because habit did not work. Habit is tradition, and tradition is a show and tell when compared to faith. Not too many rabbis can attest to being converted after being sex trafficked, or junkies, if you get my drift. Which makes academics an attainable feat without God, though it is an education about God.

Whether it was about marriage and divorce, stoning a prostitute, sacrifices and traditions, or even tithing for that matter, the

Pharisees found opposition from the Lord on almost all things considered doctrine and did so for a good reason. They had missed the point entirely!

So, what did Jesus mean when He said, "and the desires of your father [the devil] you want to do"? I think that question opens a Pandora's box of sorts. One that's inclined into unveiling who they were in their religious and political standing. As far as the eye can see, they were corrupt, and they were not who they were pretending to be.

- "He was a murderer from the beginning..."

Was Jesus calling them murderers? Yes, He was!

And we can back it up with Scripture by pointing out that for four hundred years, there was no widespread Word from God in the land and no widespread revelation. These are two different things God shut down in their entirety. No prophets, no nothing. At least not until John the Baptist came into the scene to pioneer the coming of the Messiah. In other words, religion continued for centuries without God in it and is no different today for so many religions. Just read Malachi, chapter three, and see how far off Israel had drifted.

But the words of Jesus were written in stone immediately after He uttered them and without objection or opposition because He is God. Like these:

Woe to you! For you build the tombs of the prophets, and your fathers killed them. In fact, you bear witness that you approve of the deeds of your fathers; for they indeed killed them, and you build their tombs. Therefore, the wisdom of God also said, "I will send them prophets and apostles, and some of them they will kill and persecute," that the blood of all the prophets which was shed from the foundation of the world may be required of this generation, from the blood of Abel to the blood of Zechariah who perished between the altar and the temple. Yes, I say to you, it shall be required of this generation.

Luke 11:47-51 (NKJV)

Jesus gave Pharisees a list of all of God's servants whom they put to death because of the ancestral association they had over the centuries, and He even rolled the stone all the way to include Abel, though it was *impossible* for them to have any connection to that murder, other than Satan being present when it occurred, and without a doubt, he was the mastermind of the very first recorded murder in history, and also the Pharisees' daddy according to Jesus.

In essence, they claimed God as their Father because of their religious standing, but Jesus claimed Satan was their father because of their religious actions. Selah!

Are you ready for this? Jesus said their father was the devil and

36

that he was a murderer from the beginning, and that's why salvation was *packaged* (for lack of a better word) in the death of Jesus on the cross.

God knew Satan would kill Jesus eventually because Satan was a murderer from the beginning, and so were they; they who put Jesus to death, even though they used the Romans to carry it out. Jesus called them out to be the ones killing God's prophets. Satan used Cain to kill Abel, and the Pharisees did the same to kill Jesus by using the Romans who executed Jews for a sport.

Saul was the same as they were when it came to the church's persecution, as we see in the book of Acts. Saul of Tarsus understood the same concept that the Pharisees were under; that was well after, when he became Apostle Paul, that his eyes were opened, and it took *blindness* to open his eyes, as the anointing took place right after his radical conversion on the road to Damascus. Paul was then *anointed* to reach out to the Gentile church as his primary calling, or in layman's terms, an advocate for you and me.

But it took the inexplicable, the unexpected, and the impossible to get him to come on board, to reach a man of such a standard who had already figured out a way to God through Scripture alone, or at least he thought he did, and that was observing the Law obsessively in such a way as was the custom of the elite. That was exactly why God decided to call him to ministry: because Paul was an insider to religion, Judaism.

Then he became an insider to the novel Gentile church, and his loyalty never wavered once; it simply shifted from the Law to the faith. In essence, today, the Law represents doctrine.

Now, King Saul was another example of the anointing making a difference in a person's life when gifted with it. But in Saul's case, the anointing ended up being misused terribly by the king.

King Saul sliced up a yoke of oxen as if they were a loaf of bread. This took place after the Holy Spirit's anointing overcame him with strength. The difference between these two men is that Paul never lost the anointing once he converted, but Saul allowed it to slip away through the cracks of sin and disobedience. He was a people pleaser, and that gave way to fear because he trusted what he could see and understand.

First Samuel 11:6 tells us that when the Spirit of God came strongly upon Saul, Saul arose with anger. It doesn't add up, huh? (Anger! The Holy Spirit! Hmm?)

Well, it may very well be an unorthodox reaction when receiving the anointing of God (anger). I believe the verse goes something like, "Be angry and sin not!" This also proves that we cannot limit God or control His purpose, and no matter the circumstances, we must submit to His will and remain in it. In essence, free will exists pretty much only for those who are not in God's will or those who toy around with the notion of going out of God's will for a visit to Self-Ville, or the elusive paradise God doesn't control, if you will. Which many of us are perhaps guilty of, and in judging wrongly in this directive, we must make sure we remove the plank from our eye first!

This same Saul, who was anointed that day in a righteous and godly way, later in life ended up in a witch's house asking her to bring up a dead man from the grave because the living were no longer within his grasp, and Saul did so in violation of Scripture (Luke 16:30-31). In this passage, the rich man wanted someone from the grave to visit his brothers that they might repent, but Father Abraham said no, and since they had Moses and the prophets, his brothers were to look to them for guidance (Isaiah 8:19-22), which renders us lost and confused and leaves us open for a counterfeit anointing. One that is contrary to God's will, God's Word, and God's tolerance, and that, without a doubt and regardless of who you are, with the likes of King Saul, is an evil practice to the core.

Lest we forget, Moses was not the only one who could make snakes appear out of thin air (Exodus 7:12).

We know this because *Saul ended up committing suicide, and there is no repenting from that*, and that's perhaps the biggest lie the OSAS teaching is spewing in our midst. By doing so, this doctrine of demons is compelling people *who need hope, not rope*, to tempt God because that's exactly what suicide is, tempting God (Matthew 4:7).

Suicide is a sin that pleases the flesh just like sex outside of marriage does, except that one can repent from sexual sin and not so from suicide. Paul said that pleasing the flesh would lead to eternal destruction, and killing oneself is murder, and murder pleases the flesh (Galatians 5:19-21) of someone who does not want to live. Pleasing the Spirit, which you can only do by living, leads to eternal life.

The anointing isn't taught; it can't be taught. It can be displayed, at best, but not academically taught.

Elijah passed down the anointing in his life to his predecessor Elisha, but only by the instruction of the Holy Spirit. Even in their case, Elijah was skeptical from his human standpoint on what was to take place in his absence, and since his protégé was asking for a double portion of what his anointing was, that had to make the prophet scratch his head a bit. I'm speaking about when Elisha had asked for twice the anointing Elijah possessed, which he got, by the way!

Sanctification, on the other hand, is a prerequisite to obtaining any type of gift from a holy God, and I mean in the anointing. Nothing worse than being gifted and not having the Gifter [God] behind the gift! Like a gun without bullets, if you will. It's still a gun, yes, but just an irrelevant one. God doesn't take away the gift but does reserve the right to stand behind the gift. (Romans 11:29). Saul is a perfect example of someone gifted and no longer anointed!

THE CONTROVERSY!

We just talked about King Saul and how his lack of sanctification limited his calling, and of course, it wasn't always like that; he was a legitimate godly man once upon a time, but his ability to remain sanctified throughout his tenure was sidetracked somehow, and he fell by the wayside. And this example teaches us this connection can only be broken by sin, which makes an effort to remain sanctified on our part worthwhile, or at least tried as a necessity, but for the anointing of God to flow within us, we must remain in Him. Or we will end up at Endor ourselves talking to demons and witches. And just like the king did and later ended up falling on his sword. Sanctification is a definite must in order to retain our place in Jesus and avoid Saul's resolution in the end, which otherwise would be suicide. Selah!

Sanctification and anointing are in complete agreement when referenced interchangeably in intuitive biblical settings, along with a conjunction in actions together and by utilizing them as they did in both testaments. We can see the need for the supernatural, their circumspect, and the supplemental result; if the truth be told, it's as plain as day for us all to see and mimic (Ephesians 5:1).

We read how God anointed Saul as the first king of Israel as requested by the people. Saul was counted among the prophets at the beginning of his tenure, but after that, the slippery slope of disobedience convinced God that Saul could no longer cut it as the man for the job. Keep thinking God doesn't evaluate our calling, and you'll see how wrong you are.

King Saul couldn't ever make the case that God did not equip him spiritually or otherwise. Saul ended up calling on demons to speak on behalf of God (1 Samuel 28). We can't lose sight of who God is. Especially to the point of not knowing when it's the devil speaking to us and no longer God! Selah.

Biblical training is a basic root to spring up in ministry as we begin our call in the Lord, or better yet, boot camp for the believer, not the battlefield itself. Facing the enemy will require more than knowing the Book: it will require knowing also the God of the Book. And knowing Him personally. Which can give us that peace that surpasses all understanding because we will need it at some point in our lives!

I'm a DJ on Launch Radio.FM, an internet radio station that prides itself by playing positive hit music and more (emphasis on the *more*). It's also an outreach ministry and a platform for every genre of Christian music, especially for up-and-coming artists. In a recent interview with one of the Christian artists on a tour the station was a part of, I asked @BriSmilez what advice she had for up-and-coming young ladies who wanted to follow in her footsteps in the industry. Being that Bri Smilez was the only female on the tour, I took interest and had a one-on-one with this amazing woman, and she said, "You have to allow God to process you first; I feel like a lot of people want to do things for God, but they don't want to be what Scripture has told them to be. There is a *being* that happens before the doing." And I totally agree. We must go through some stuff before we get stuff!

We read in the Gospels that before Jesus sent out the twelve, He trained and equipped them (the "being"), and He also asked them to give up some things, like jobs and, in some cases, family, before they went out in two to do ministry (the "doing"), which is why I agree with Bri. We have to prepare ourselves, and we have to wait for God's timing. When we don't, we become self-made generals, and that's a scary thought because we go out by skipping boot camp, which is basic training, and we may end up running for our lives as we saw the men in the book of Acts (sons of Sceva; Acts 19:14-19) run for their lives as they impersonated the anointing.

In one of her podcasts (*The Eleventh Hour*), Bri Smilez was talking about how she prepared for ten years before beginning the podcast; in other words, she put in the work and waited for the opportunity to launch after her readiness, and that's the part many people want to skip: *the training ground* season. They want to graduate on the first day of class, and that's not how it goes; we must put in the work. And that's because if it didn't cost you anything, why would you appreciate it as you would if you had the scars to prove your position was the product of your journey and in the hope of being part of the move of God.

Imagine getting connected, and in the end, because of King Saul syndrome, a disconnect takes place, and you hear the infamous words: "Jesus I know, and Paul I know, but who are you?" (Acts 19:15, NKJV). It baffles me how Christian academia that teaches eternal security has missed it! It is beyond me!

It may perhaps be intentional in order to preserve an age-old doctrine, or it perhaps may be done so in sheer ignorance. Who knows, really, but what I do know is that it takes a very distinctive biblical directive of exponential and true scriptural identity to remain afloat in today's *ever progressive* body of believers, and the constant moral decay of societal evolution that's in a constant decline is very much evident all around us.

This constitutes for a disconnect of some sort, and sadly, as the times that we live in attest to that effect, the progress seems to be for the other team, one that presumes we are heading right for the cliffs with no end in sight. And in my personal opinion, it's because we have allowed division to creep in in our midst, but for us to stay above the fray and afloat in these challenging times, we need such a resurgence for revival regardless of the task, and that no matter what comes our way, we must continue growing in the anointing we were trusted with, to begin with, and we must embrace living in truth and logic for a constant approach to our direct calling in Christ.

Therefore, let's live like we know God. Let's love like we are loved by God. And let's not make excuses because we can live a sanctified life by clinging to our source (Jesus) daily!

HAVE WE SHUNNED COMMON SENSE?

Sometimes it seems as if common sense has taken a vacation from our midst, and I mean in the church, by the way. And as we allow the world to influence us the most by portals in social media and TV programming (emphasis on programming), especially in these trying times, we can, without exclusion, observe truth and logic being replaced with lies and hate; therefore, common sense is no longer a thing. People can accept anything as the truth. We saw how reporters were standing in front of a burning building during the riots of 2020 and reported it as a peaceful protest. Common sense will tell you arson is the opposite of peaceful. Somehow, we need to find a way to return to our posts as the church if we want revival to take place around us, which means to bring back to life something that died or is about to die (Revelation 3:1-2) lest we end up as the third of the angels who left their proper abode forever.

How could one out of three angels fall for a lie? And fall for a lie while in heaven, mind you! I'm not sure how, but I do know why, and that's because Lucifer thought he could shake heaven and get away with it. Lucifer set the tone as the worship leader; Lucifer was also the "covering cherub"; he had two offices as Judas did. Judas held the purse besides being an apostle (Luke 6:13). If

Lucifer was in charge of the music in heaven, I can see why the music industry and its members, for the most part, are as demonic as it can be.

In my upcoming book *When Science Meets the Bible*, I go into great detail on how Satan and his demons were cast out of heaven during their rebellion eons ago and why the devil decided to challenge God. Both method and premise are significant and biblical, and I will try to make my case by scientifically proving that there was once a war in the heavenlies; after that took place, God's plan went into judgment mode, and the book will be descriptive by things understood and hung on biblical authenticity. At the same time, it will be aligned with the sophisticated scientific discovery of both realms. So, stay tuned, please. But to even fathom the controversy of angelic beings who are not only powerful in nature but also possess an amazing anointing, which is second to none, but do not have enough common sense to the tune of allowing Satan to manipulate a third of them into rebelling against God while in heaven, is beyond me. Although I understand it now because humanity is doing the exact same thing, it's still incomprehensible.

The absence of common sense is the absence of the ability to filter truth. And I refuse to believe that anointed people will spend their time fighting for a position in society based on race, color, or gender. That anointing is somehow questionable.

An anointing that resonates in such a narrative of chronological interactive teachings is exactly what we need as believers in order to frustrate the plans of the enemy and set him up for daily defeat in our lives. I mean, the heavy lifting was taken care of at the cross, and all we have to do is run with it.

Unlike the fallen angels who are now demons and lost their place with God, we need a different approach to being recipients of the anointing, but one that does not challenge the giver of that anointing as the angels did and erred when they rebelled by biting the hand that fed them. We can learn a thing or two from these fallen angels on what not to do.

We are blessed to have teachings that are magnified in this revelatory and most illustrative presentation of truth, which makes much more sense when applied sensibly and expressively as intended. Sheer and unconditional application to the gifts is to be looked at in only one light, and that is to maximize our calling by an attempt to minimize the plan of the enemy simultaneously. Satan possesses people in demonic oppression. We cast demons out and offer deliverance to the afflicted. That's the exchange we read about from the man in the tombs (the demoniac) and from the prostitute with seven spirits, and it's the true sense of the anointing that sets us free just as we saw in Jesus and His disciples as they went around projecting the kingdom of heaven. We are to undo what Satan does and rebuild what he destroys. This is a truth that compliments itself throughout Scripture no matter where you look, which is based on real biblical accounts that still take place today unless you decide there are no more demonic possessions or divine healing, of course. But we know they are as relevant today as they were then. And that they take place time and time again.

Taking our spiritual authority to the next level is exactly what we need in order to grow in the anointing and calling of God for our lives. We can't be intimidated by the enemy ever (Luke 10:19), but if we only focus on the subject of identifying *the faithful* throughout their biblical life's behavior in God's will for them (the twelve and the prophets) and mimic them on how they handled the supernatural when challenged to do so, we then can exemplify the anointing and walk in the same power the apostles and prophets did, which amplifies our course of action in the supernatural. After all, it is the same God who doesn't change, sleep, or slumber and that is giving the gifts to whom He chooses just as He did before.

What man or woman of God can encourage someone to take their own life and dress it as an act of faith?

I got married back in 2001; the marriage got off to a rocky start. It was hard to get by and not expect the end to happen any given day. Emotions and frustration were my companions, and that's what happens when we don't seek God for answers in such sensitive subjects. I recall my wife taking off for a few weeks to Texas to spend time with her grandmother because she was having her issues about the marriage. They were very close, and at this point, I had no opinion because of the situation other than my biblical view of marriage.

I remember we had short conversations when we talked, and it was pretty much revolving around our baby at the time. One night, as I was lying in bed, the bed started shaking violently. I assumed we experienced an earthquake. Later, I found out my experience was no earthquake at all. So, my bed shook for a few minutes, and of course, I got into prayer. I'm not going to lie: I did freak out for a minute, but a scripture came to mind, and I began speaking it out loud. I began saying, "Greater is He that is in me than he that is in the world" (1 John 4:4, paraphrased), over and over, and after a minute or so, the bed stopped shaking.

The very next night, the same thing happened again. I woke up at around three a.m. to another bedroom earthquake, and this time my blankets were pulled to the bottom of the bed in front of my eyes and onto the bare floor. I began rebuking the spirit once again and prayed with such authority to the point that the bed stopped shaking just like the night before, but this time after the shaking ended, I began calling that spirit back and commanded it put my blankets back where they were. And lo and behold, my bed began shaking again, and soon after, my blankets returned to where they were at first, then the bed stopped shaking, and it ended that way. I slept like a baby that night in the comfort of knowing who was in me (the Holy Spirit), and since that day, I realized it was the enemy that was trying to intimidate me to the point of frustration, but unfortunately for him, it didn't work. I've seen too much to ignore who the enemy is and who is within me!

The questions I had were: Why did God allow this to happen? Why was the enemy so cooperative both nights after praying (Luke

10:19)? And I concluded that God allowed me to see this because He wanted me to be aware of what I was up against and that the enemy manifests himself physically for one reason: to use spiritual reverse psychology to try and make us fear him because if we may realize who it is, that's inside of us. Then the power we possess because of that great revelation can be intimidating to the enemy, and we are a threat to his kingdom, and that's why he manifests physically. Kingdom-minded people focus on one thing: kingdom!

Jesus told the disciples not to rejoice because the spirits were subject to them, but that they should rejoice because their names were written in heaven, and because of who it was that was in them (Luke 10:20), which brings up the point that if Jesus was addressing the twelve, then He was saying to all twelve that their names were written in heaven, and that includes Judas, who the OSAS believe wasn't saved to begin with, but this verse tells a different story. Therefore, we have plenty of examples of the supernatural throughout Scripture, enough to last us a lifetime for all our necessities to overcome the tactics of the enemy.

These are also necessary so that we can all see the many faithful's who stayed the course throughout their spiritual journeys. Those who were also under constant pressure at various times in their perspective seasons of trials, who, by putting their own lives in danger, did so, not only to advance the message of God throughout history, and especially when they had to face the adversity of wicked kings and other shrewd leaders as well as mobs who cared absolutely nothing regarding what God had to say about His will.

Kind of like elected politicians do in today's congressional meetings. But also, because they believed God was real!

These men and women who did so without reservations are who we must mimic when in adverse situations so that we can get our point across, just as they did, and that's regardless of society's moral views of today, which are dismal. In retrospect, what they deem moral can't ever pass the smell test in God's presence, just as was the case in Sodom and Gomorrah, where righteous Lot's disagreement about that day's culture in those cities, where sexual immorality did not go unnoticed by God, and neither did the punishment that followed, which will also repeat itself as we see the abominations of those two cities permeate the entire globe begging for a strike from outer space as predicted in the book of Revelation, and as the leftist politicians twiddle their fingers, enduring sleepless nights to try and figure out a way to legalize pedophilia because according to them, we don't have enough licentiousness already, and we must need more—so to unlock hell once and for all by releasing every demon out of the bottomless pit and usher in the long-awaited second coming. Something we as believers should have nothing to do with, or we might miss our visitation, just like religious leaders of that day did! And let's not forget that our silence means agreement with the wicked, as some have already settled for!

Also, the ones who defaulted after having been given a chance to know God intimately (a Judas type), as well as the ones who had enough sense to return to God after a spiritual hiatus of sorts (a King David type), an example to cheapen the work of the cross in that regard. Someone died to accomplish redemption, one we couldn't accomplish ourselves, even if we decided to die for it.

This conducive revelatory foundation is guided and complemented by an array of biblical texts, which are interwoven with rich doctrine pointing to an addition of works through faith, extensively so, and not just merely dismissing them as if grace has no requisites. But most importantly, they're laid out in their true interpretation, just as intended biblically.

And may I add that they are also perfectly understood in their chronological order, which makes it that much more important in its resilience. Therefore, in order to study the subject of salvation much deeper, as well as eternity in its purest form, rather than accepting an erroneous doctrine that carelessly places believers at eternal risks, rather than what the label says, a definite must is to study it as it should be: in the form of *true revelation* deriving from God's perspective with both Word and anointing combined for a clearer introduction of revelatory descent, which is what we must aim for as believers.

The Gospels aren't subjects of objectivity; they are, if you do, or if you don't, *subjects of performance*, and that feat is up to everyone. I don't think anyone knows robbing a bank should be a debate of morals, or abortion, or adultery for that matter. They are sinful in nature, and let me let you in on a little secret: God expects sinners, but not His children, to indulge in such actions. Selah! Not after He brought us out from previous downfalls. And biblical texts forewarn us about this.

Texts that find their purpose and connectivity toward a genuine lifestyle of what a true conversion in Christ is all about and a desire to know Christ more intimately should jump out at us as we study the Word daily, one that implies selflessly who we are, being a part of the flock, and also what a testament to that conversion should be like, in its most genuine display from beginning to end, and also that a biblical view of salvation is fully attained when the end of the road happens to come our way. And trust me, it will, but in its purest form, so that we do not miss the mark as some have already done by embracing sinful lifestyles, thinking their future sins that don't yet exist are forgiven.

That end is what we should strive for when convincing ourselves that this is what we wanted for a lifetime of devotion to God and that at the end of that road, we can all be sure we are ready to meet our Maker as Savior and not as Judge. And just as the faithful of old also did themselves, and as perceived throughout the Old and New Testaments alike, which are lived out by people who displayed exemplary living of *faith in action*. Though far from perfect, they did so in any extreme they found themselves in, which in retrospect begs the initiative that conditions do not make allies for excuses but affirmation instead. There we can find more meaning simply to continue our perspective journey of faith, and just as they did, by their assurance, we have a better promise to our faith walk than they did, though they never saw it. We should find common ground because of the promise, as we see it, since we have a better testimony, being that we read what they prophesied but never experienced it, and that's the manifestation of the Christ that we know. And in a better light through the revelation of His appearing, we can rest assured that what He said He would do will be the case.

Those who once pioneered the way for us all by expressing throughout their lifestyles and the many faithful decisions they made are as examples for us that this faith walk could be done if we stay the course and not give up, as well as by depicting a true devotion and conversion to God, which is fully based on faith alone, where mercy and grace line up as God sees fit, just as it was intended by God for them, and far be it from us to think it otherwise in our midst.

Remember Elijah and the widow of Zarephath, where Elijah the prophet took the last bite of food a starving woman and her dying child were about to consume, as their entire livelihood depended on this one morsel, and he did so primarily for his survival. Imagine doing that today and having to deal with the harshness of Facebook Christianity?

A few years back, I posted somewhat of a mind-boggling and coincidentally determinative post, something along the lines of, "What kind of pastor takes up an offering, allows a woman whom he knows has no money to give into the offering plate, and furthermore, watches her empty out her purse in front of him, knowing she will be broke if he allows her to give it all into the offering plate, even her very last penny?" And boy, did they let this pastor have it.

I left the post up for all day and decided to reveal the pastor by answering every single person's comment a little later in the evening, and all who put in their two cents individually were astonished in the end about who that pastor was, who of course was Christ Himself as I was referring to the time when He took the poor widow's two mites into the offering plate. Maybe we're quick to judge. Maybe we're uninformed, who knows? But this took place, and Jesus allowed it.

Isn't it amazing that a biblical view of an individual sometimes depends entirely on what they are fed from the pulpit? And if the pulpit is feeding them hate, discord, division, error, and/or a dislike for others in the faith, well, you get the picture!

What kind of God are we dealing with today? Has He changed? How is it okay to turn on each other randomly? Do we have to always be right?

He is a God who has revealed Himself in a vast array of *supernatural facets* time and time again. He's done so by various visitations to both men and women alike throughout the ages, as far as we can see in the Old Testament, New Testament, and yes, today as well, all as a sign that we are not alone. It was His promise to us that we will not be left orphans.

God revealed Himself to people of faith like Moses and

Abraham, and we're talking about blind faith at its best as the implication I'm referring to. Take Moses, for example; he was between an ocean and a well-trained Egyptian army of mercenaries, furiously in pursuit of all Israel. In other words: a lose-lose situation for everyone who was a Jew in exile, and he also had to trust God who asked him to leave Egypt, when, I assure you, that was the last thing on his mind because of the stress placed on his person.

Moses had no idea that the Red Sea was about to open up, dictating to the billions of gallons of water to create a wall of protection for the Hebrews, and allow *all* Israel to cross to safety first; then, to think that the same Red Sea would collapse and inundate the enemies of the Jews, simply by Moses lowering his staff, was perhaps a bigger blunder to take in, but it happened, and that's the kind of God we serve. Make no mistake: God is a Finisher!

He did it before, and He can do it again, but one of the saddest feats in our lives as believers is that we forget where He rescued us from in the beginning and what it was that He did to get it done.

Have you not read the book of Revelation and its marvelous cosmic accounts awaiting His enemies?

Even after both Moses and Abraham gave excuses for what they thought was their handicap, little did they know that their Creator had handpicked them both for such a task as leading the masses on His behalf and for His ultimate purpose, presumptuously for us.

Abraham, just like Moses, had to rely on God to provide an alternative option for a dire need that always presented itself at the last minute. *A much-needed sacrifice,* but unfortunately, in Abraham's case, the sacrifice was that of his only child by his wife, Sarah.

He had to place the matter in God's hands and say, when Isaac asked where the sacrifice was, "The Lord will provide" (Genesis 22:8, paraphrased). And yes, the Lord provided, but don't think for a moment that Abraham was not torn inside to proceed to follow God's lead in this very stressful event.

And we read the many other instances in Scripture that are in complete sync with each other on the subject of conversion and sanctification as a basis for growth, one that is done so in an expository rendition of sorts and rather than contradicting other instances for the sake of erroneous doctrinal interpretation, as some would lead you to believe, or by avoiding their true meaning, which is done out of confusion or lack of revelation, and do so by hijacking the severity of biblical truth. In this sentiment, they disagree to canonize genuine scriptural intentions to what faith in God is all about. The same thing we saw the Pharisees do throughout Jesus's ministry is the very thing taking place today, in the same manner, in today's Christian circles!

We sometimes nonchalantly quote Scripture like this one, "He is the same and never changes," yet, we don't believe a single syllable regarding our confession.

We often resort to *men* rather than God to bail us out from pickles we get ourselves into or perhaps are put into by others if that might be the case, and yes, by God as well, who Himself sometimes allows things to come our way, but for a special purpose—to test our faith (Job is a perfect example of that test).

Faith means to trust God and allow Him to make the necessary changes to get us across our Red Sea moments. But with decisions dictated by faith alone, making no apologies to connect our holy living to a holy Lord who works miracles even as you read this very phrase here and now, and this is pretty much the norm for our miracle-working Lord.

The Bible resorts to its Originator for problem-solving, then points us to Him time and time again for the same, and the dire need to always remain in Him simply resonates throughout the ages as we have learned from Scripture in our devotional time. But if we are to continue living a life of spiritual power as intended by our Redeemer, we have to be in right standing with Him, and there is no other way about it. And sin gets in the way every time it's tried!

As a means of our participation in *all things' faith,* we must continue growing no matter what life has in store for us next or where we came from, especially in today's progressive society that wants nothing to do with the God of the Bible or God's church.

Leaving nothing to the imagination whatsoever but in all points bringing insight based on the revelation of the importance that it is to always remain faithful to God, and in all facets of life, and that's regardless of the expectations one might concur faith to be, is what we must do as believers in the faith.

Thus, while professing to be a recipient of Christ's provision for salvation, and thus, pressing in, to both display for others and for the obvious objectivity as a testament to ourselves that our lives now belong to Christ our Lord, we do not need anyone to pump and prime us to achieve it, and that's because we were bought at a price, and we must believe completely and without reservations. We must remain faithful to God as much as it is up to us (1 Peter 1:7).

This revelation finds itself precisely in the sheer doctrinal interpretation of Scripture, or perhaps the misinterpretation thereof, but that depends on which side of the coin you find yourself today in. Of course, none of us know the next step in the Lord until He reveals it to us, and the bigger the decision, the greater the consequence. Paul puts it this way in Galatians 2:2 (NKJV),

And I went up by revelation and communicated to them that gospel which I preach among the Gentiles, but privately to those who were of reputation, lest by any means I might run, or had run, in vain.

Paul gives the example of a dire need to seek God for what to do next and how to do it. He mentions two different groups of people, one is public, and one is private, and the delivery of the Gospel to both groups was different and not metaphorically. The message was the same, of course, but the method wasn't. The means adjust to the needs at hand, but the message is circumspect of them both; therefore, we do not reinvent the wheel: we simply decorate it to attract attention to God.

This is something I refer to as *revelatory science*, which explains hidden messages revealed by the Holy Spirit, and *common sense* is highly essential for its interpretation. The parables were intended as such. Revelatory science is a term I coined for an alternative purpose, especially because of the paradigmatic messaging of God's Word. Hidden codes, catastrophes, and universal distress are events dispersed by way of revelation, not guessing games. Although we are told by the Lord that no one knows the day or the hour of His coming, we were given by Him insight into the season it would take place. Matthew, chapter twenty-four, gives us a description of the events that present themselves as signs in the season of their fruition and the end that will be implemented in its finality. He did that so that we would be ready. We may not know the hour, but rest assured we know the season!

In my opinion, when we are done reading Matthew, chapter twenty-four, we do not turn the page to Matthew, chapter twenty-five, no! When we are done reading Matthew, chapter twenty-four, we turn the page directly to the book of Revelation, chapter seven, and on. But salvation has its place in Scripture as well.

HAVE WE SHUNNED COMMON SENSE?

Although several scriptures point to when salvation is initially obtained in a person's life, or primarily acquired, that is, Romans 10:9 is a perfect example of that start-up stage for a believer who steps into the light, fresh out of darkness for the very first time. A time where an individual takes their first glance at eternity in Christ, or day one of a new life of hope in the loving arms of a Savior. And it is at that point when inner peace finally begins manifesting itself while making a difference in a personal manner, and that's regardless of what's going on around us at that season in life, which is probably somewhat chaotic more than likely, if you know what I mean.

Self-rendering the initial reflection of this genesis to be one of hope always, may very well have its challenges, but when it's all said and done, the decision will never be one of regret. One that begins more than likely in the excitement of what it means to finally be set free from a life of sin and bondage, which can only come by way of confession of past sin(s) and no other way, and who wouldn't be excited about that, right?

I think that's why beginnings are so important, especially in Christ. They magnify an era when we proved to ourselves, we could be challenged and took on that challenge, and whether we flinch or not, we will overcome the obstacles or try our best to encounter them because now we have hope. That goes for our first day at our first job, the first day of college away from home, our first apartment, and the independence that comes with them. Well, you get my point, and faith in Christ should have the first day as well—that day should be the one that highlights our entire reason for being. Do you remember your first day with Christ?

ORIGINS!

I know we all come from different backgrounds, we all come from different walks of life, and some of us had good upbringings, I'm sure. Some of us defaulted from those upbringings, some didn't, but one thing for sure is we all have the same desperate need for a Savior when it comes to eternity, and essentially that's what unites us all as believers in the end. But what is it that divides us?

The common denominator is always the unequivocal need for redemption from a sinful lifestyle, and the priceless faith found in God through Christ Jesus is what we all long for when we are lost, and in that diversity of the undeniable struggles in life's journeys as they come and go are a reality. Therefore, a definite dire need for a Savior and a Keeper is exactly what faith in God is all about for us as believers. But what about when we get in, how do we react to others in the faith, and I mean outside of our circle?

We get why we are here in the first place, and that's to make a difference in a dying, godless, hurting world. When it's all said and done, we need God like a fish needs water. But of course, that's only if one was looking for an answer to that effect, or getting down and dirty, if you will. In my journey, I experienced a radical conversion of sorts. It would be an impossibility for me to deny the tangible existence of who God is. Not only in my life but His existence, period. And I mean that sincerely in every aspect of the *word*, respectfully so, because God is as real to me as He was to Moses and the prophets, per se.

The supernatural is the very essence of who God is, was, and will always be!

I've always said that God will never reveal Himself in a way He knew we wouldn't believe because that would be a waste of time for both parties. But that's just me. When I was a teenager, I had for some time wanted to end my life because of the life I was handed down and what my surroundings dictated my life to be, I guess by default, counting that I grew up in Chicago's Little Village, a gang-infested area on Chicago's South Side, about a block away from Cook County Jail, which was the home to Chicago's worst individuals, per se.

Gang life in Chicago, where I grew up, had taken its toll on me at the tender age of my mid-teens and had also driven me to the point of no return regarding what my reality should be.

Though I was very young, I was tired of my life because I had no goals, no aspirations, no will to live. I began a hardcore gang life at the age of fourteen. Perhaps the norm in Chicago's "La Villita" for a kid my age. Nevertheless, it should not be the norm for a teenager that young anywhere in the world.

This sentiment was a powerful source to embrace, one that was tugging at me daily at that intersection in life, that also deemed me lifeless as I found myself living every minute of it in a sea of despair, surrounded by crime and corruption on every front, no matter where I turned, that was, unfortunately, my norm.

One that constantly reminded me of a *dead-end* life story that didn't end well regardless of the effort put in it. It got so bad that my family began entertaining the thought of actually leaving the neighborhood for good in hopes of a *better* place. We moved to Twenty-Fifth and Marshall Boulevard, just a few blocks away from our old place. Then to Twenty-First and California. But once my dad decided to move to a so-called better neighborhood and finally leave Little Village and Pilsen, which were predominantly Mexican neighborhoods, and are to this day. We moved to a white neighborhood, thinking it would be a safer environment for us all, which was southeast of Twenty-Sixth Street, where I grew up. Twenty-Eighth and Short Street was my next stop in a neighborhood run by the Italian and Irish mafias, and the challenge of a lifetime for me was up next.

Bridgeport was a neighborhood that had become a hotbed for racism a decade after the civil rights movement had ended. It was saturated with the Italian and Irish Mob, and racism was very real and evident in everyday life. And I'm not speaking about the silliness of what Al Sharpton, Jesse Jackson, or Black Lives Matter call racism. I'm talking about a white-looking Mexican boy who was beaten at the bus stop almost daily by white kids because he listened to Donna Summer, Frankie Smith, and Bobby Womack as his preferred playlist. A kid who watched TV shows like *Good*

Times and *The Jefferson's* and as loud as the volume knob would allow to, one who would come home from school just to view writing on the sidewalk in front of his home, with at times, swastikas, "Die Spicks," "Disco Sucks," "Rock Rules," or "White is right," or "N-word lover" written in spray paint right in front of his home, and this happened quite often.

On two different occasions, my house was set on fire by these same racist individuals. Both times were racially motivated, of course. If you saw me, you'd think I'm white if it were not for the baggy pants and disco sounds coming from my ghetto blaster. I had to put the fires out myself every single time they were set.

Although the fire department was only three blocks away, it always took forty-five minutes or more for them to arrive, and when they did, it was to rip out the walls with an ax looking for sparks inside the walls.

By then, I had already carried outside of the burning house my handicapped baby sister, my infant nephew, as well as the rest of my older sister's kids. I'd run in and out of the house with two five-gallon buckets of water multiple times after filling them from the bathtub upstairs.

Finally, on my fifteenth birthday, my dad's frustration came to fruition. No, I didn't get a bike or clothes, no! That day my dad gave me a revolver for my birthday, and he didn't say happy birthday either, but instead, with a raspy voice and choked up, he uttered the words, "Here, I rather you kill them than they kill you, or even worse, our whole family." He said that because of the fires.

His only advice was, "Don't pull it out unless you're going to use it." And that began a new chapter in Chicago Street life for me. I no longer had my Mexican friends that I left behind in Little Village and Pilsen. I had me, a six-shooter, and that's all!

Soon after that, I met other kids who were going through the same chaos where they lived in racially infested Bridgeport. We eventually got together sometime later and joined forces. We later united with one of the most notorious Latin street gangs in the city of Chicago, and there's where my life of crime took a turn for the worst.

As we made a name for ourselves soon after our commencement, we began being sought out by other street gangs who wanted a reckoning in retaliation for actions we previously underwent and all that was related to the constant gang wars taking place in the city of violence. If you don't believe me, just turn on your cable news for a few minutes and find out for yourself. We made the news often, and soon thereof. The FBI took an interest in gang-infested Chicago.

Chicago Police Department was forced to spearhead a gang crime unit that began chronicling gang activities. Ones that in Chicago were always at bay. Especially on summer weekends, and besides that, they also began attracting other curious sources of journalism. That's when a group of Christian writers from different places in the country began following the rise in Chicago's gang crime. These journalists came to Chicago to research Chicago street gangs around that time.

They came to interview some of the most notorious street gangs in the city, and in the process, they ran across our gang, which I helped found in the unforgettable early eighties.

I had been a part of a gang since the tender age of fourteen, and this was a typical age for a boy to join a gang in Chicago, although some kids enter at eleven and twelve years of age, as was the case with me, since I grew up in the Pilsen and Little Village neighborhoods, which are gang-infested in the worst way possible. That's where I had a first glance at street gang life in a serious way, though I belonged to smaller insignificant gangs. Nevertheless, they were gangs.

Before joining the Latin Kings, I was part of a few smaller gangs that formed within a system that allowed such small gangs to congregate until they weren't allowed anymore by the bigger and more powerful gangs.

I was a tiny Two Six, I believe, in fifth or sixth grade while living on Twenty-Third and Millard, but we then moved to Twenty-Fifth and Sacramento, and I joined the Troy Boys, which hung around Twenty-Third and Troy. I met a girl from that neighborhood who I started seeing, and her brothers were Puerto Rican Stones, so because of her, I became a Puerto Rican Stone. At this time, we lived on Twenty-First and California, in neighboring Pilsen.

My older brother was already heavily involved in another gang. But we then moved to Twenty-First and California, where I became a Stone Kent. My next stop was Bridgeport, Twenty-Eighth and Short Street, where my reality awaited!

The journalists had heard about the carnage taking place in the city of Chicago back in their hometowns in rural America and other prestigious cities, a carnage which is still going on today at unimaginable levels, perhaps even worse, and an all-too-common problem that seems to inflame tensions between rival gangs representing the two major groups called People and Folks, which house every Chicago street gang under those two categories. Kind of like Bloods and Crips, if you will.

Although there are dozens of street gangs plaguing the city, they all fall into those two terms, People and Folks. The journalists came to hear from us before going onto other street gangs who were more rooted inside the city's web of crime. The group came to us first because Bridgeport had never been known for street gangs at that level, organized crime maybe, but not street gangs. Not yet!

In essence, we were pioneering something new in an over 80 percent white population type of neighborhood, and there we were, bearing it all in front of complete strangers, all for a few moments of fame.

As we gathered under the dark (overwhelmed with graffiti) freeway viaducts under Interstate 55 and Short Street, on gang-infested Chicago's South Side, we began interviewing in groups at first, and as they took interest, one-on-one interviews evolved from that perspective.

Some of us made it into articles about Chicago street gangs, some of us made it into books about gang violence, or both. I was one of those, but when it was all said and done, I was pretty much spent and no longer cared about anything having to do with gang life itself. I felt useless and overwhelmed by it all!

One of the books I was featured in was *Danger at Your Door*. The author who began interviewing us did so usually during lunch and dinner meetings, but unfortunately, he had to finish his interviews with me in juvenile detention, kind of like my second home of sorts, Hamilton Hall, to be exact.

I will never forget what one of the journalists said about me in an article that circulated in the Dallas, Fort Worth, area soon after the interviews were conducted. I came across this article speaking about the gang I was a member of, but in particular what it said about me, as I read in awe, the following statement resonating with my innermost thoughts, was something that hit home. She wrote, "He would be lucky to see his eighteenth birthday at the rate he's living." This is what someone's first impression of me was, and to be honest, that describes pretty much every other kid involved in a Chicago street gang when he is committed to it a hundred percent like I was!

What she saw the day we met was what drove her to write what she thought the end of the road would be for a kid like me. One with no direction at all, at least for a positive outcome. And since that day, I sincerely believed I wouldn't see my eighteenth birthday either.

I thought about it all the time, and as a matter of fact, I very much welcomed the notion as my shrewd reality. I think I was living to die after that day, literally, and as close friends began to die around me because of drive-by shootings, I would just wonder when my turn was up.

There was so much negativity taking place in my life in a bizarre and stressful way of sorts that I wanted life to end, perhaps to spare others. Though I had just begun my life, it was already lifeless; it seemed pointless to hope for a better way. Was there even a better way?

I felt depleted and very much defeated, as I couldn't see past the demise that gang life's end had in store for me. When I finally turned seventeen, I became a father, and now I wanted to live because I felt I finally had a reason to, and something had changed inside of me. I finally had a reason to go on; I finally loved someone. It came as a shock to me!

Crime didn't take a vacation even though now I wanted to change my ways. Now that I had a responsibility and quite frankly enjoyed it, I wanted to do the right thing for a change. So I got a legit job while attempting to finish high school, which I was unable to finish in the end, due to me punching the principal in the face for accusing me of something I hadn't done, and get this, I hit him in front of the police because he grabbed my jaw and I wasn't having it.

I had no respect for authorities of any kind, but the gang also had its many responsibilities and felt I was married to those responsibilities as well, and I was loyal to the gang, and I loved my brothers and sisters in the gang as well.

My part-time job was to transport new, high-end automobiles from a car dealer in Niles to the shop for upgrades and recalls. The body shop was down the street from the school I attended, so I would walk over after class. I drove around in luxury cars and got paid for it, pretty much a dream job for a kid of my age.

A few months before my eighteenth birthday, I was diagnosed with a serious heart condition that I saw a heart specialist for, and all I could think was, *Great, a guy wants to do the right thing finally, and now this!*

I remember running to answer the phone at a new job I got in a church by my house. I think I was about thirty feet away from the phone's base, but since I was connected to a device that sent a signal to the hospital nearest me, I quickly received a call after that incident took place, telling me that an ambulance was on its way to assist me, and to stay put. I said I felt fine, but the nurse on the phone said that according to the readings of the monitor, I shouldn't be alive; my heart was beating over three times a normal heart should.

Now making it to eighteen was, by all means, a marathon. By the grace of God, I did make it, and well, here I am at fifty-four telling you all about it!

I was miraculously healed from my heart and eye condition later in life, after my conversion. But perhaps I can share that testimony some other time. Mind you, I was in my early twenties by now but still felt lifeless and very much worthless. I sort of wished I would have died at eighteen, but now I had another kid.

I knew suicide was not the answer though I did try it once as I stupidly pulled the trigger of my thirty-eight, snub-nosed, Midnight-special Smith and Wesson revolver, deceived, defeated, and aiming for my temple, except that my gun jammed when I tried. A revolver jammed. And that was the only time I've ever heard of such a thing. My next shot went straight to the streetlight, and guess what? It worked like a charm.

I guess I wasn't crazy enough to try a second time because I was Catholic and believed that would have landed me right into hell, and perhaps in first class. If I could make a case for my religion, that is. It compelled me to deter such acts and thoughts immediately after the first try failed. Though I was a thug, I didn't want to end up in hell. Never mind that I was a gang leader and was involved in all kinds of crime and corruption. But one thing I can't deny is that I wanted it all to end and be done with life altogether. So, I welcomed the notion!

I remember it as if it was yesterday: I was at a woman's home having drinks one weeknight when some of the guys came by; they were alarmed and asked me to come with them because our archenemies were in the neighborhood, and they were looking for some trouble and were also armed to the teeth as usual.

I remember thinking, *Perhaps I can die with honor tonight; I'll run up at the gunmen and be killed as if a hero.* Though I was a coward, internally, I had an ego to protect, and certainly, I didn't want to be the one that didn't want to face tomorrow because of the filth and despair I felt within me to the point of an ill mindset takeover that wanted out no matter the cost, and death was included in the menu, perhaps as the main course.

Nonetheless, the opportunity came to end it all…and there I was, running at three armed men, but my intention was to get fatally shot that night; I wanted to close pretty much the last chapter in a life of despair. And I know what you're thinking, *What about your daughters?* I agree! What about my daughters? I mean, I recall being in the middle of a twenty-two-year sentence, shining like a star as a super dad. I saw my kids often when in prison, thanks to my ex and my family, that is.

I often wrote bedtime stories for them and was the epitome of a good (prison) dad. Well, that was until God asked me a rhetorical question. He said, "Everyone thinks you're a good dad; do you think you're a good dad?" And of course, I said, "Yes!" But after His silence, I got what He was aiming at, and that's what my situation enveloped me in at that point. You see, God was making me understand that pretentious actions do not annul the spill left behind simply because we cleaned it up, or should I say, God cleaned it up! He was telling me, "If you loved your kids, you wouldn't be trying to be super dad behind bars, you would have never taken that gun and shot those people, you should have never beaten those police officers, you should have never robbed that warehouse supplier."

In other words: we do not express love through the pain we cause others just because He did on the cross. We must express love by being present in our kids' lives, and yes, me being a good dad in prison was a good thing, don't get me wrong, but the reality of me loving my children was unrealistic just because barbed wire fencing said so. And said so louder than words.

So when you read a suicide note that tells a wife and children or family and friends, "…but never forget that I love you!" remember that blood makes for the worst kind of ink to write a goodbye letter with. And advocates for suicide that are under the lie of eternal security have lots of blood on their hands for not only accepting such a horrendous act of cowardness but also advocating for it.

Me dying at a young age on the violent streets of Chicago would have never been a mystery. After all, that's how it ended for many of my fellow brothers in the gang, but when you know better, you know better. Selah! We must be careful about what our, individuals', normality becomes, and I mean saved individuals. I truly believed my death on a battlefield on Chicago's South Side was prescribed in honor according to gang life. Bear in mind that reality, when ignored, is a dangerous thing!

A week before I met Jesus as Savior, I was smackdown in the middle of the street and calling out my archenemies as they approached us in the dim streetlights blocked by tree branches, where the only vividness was the pop and explosion of three guns shooting in my direction. All in my hopes of a final confrontation with death.

I had many run-ins with death before this one, and with this same gang in the past as well; being that they hung out a block or two away from us, our warfare was periodic and often intense.

I might have heard no less than thirty bullets raining my way that night, in those very few but short moments of decision that I hoped was the last straw I had to endure in my already lost soul, thinking it was finally over, or better yet, hoping it was. But to my surprise, not one single bullet hit any part of my body that time.

I had been shot at several times before, normality of sorts in

Chicago for a young Hispanic kid from the toughest streets in America. Not to mention that once before, I was placed in a coma for two days by this very same gang as I took it upon myself, by myself, to fight over a dozen of them and on their turf, a death wish, if you will, better yet, sheer stupidity, but it happened.

Stupidity is not subject to gun violence alone, as some would want you to believe. But back to the night in question: my leather jacket was full of holes that night. As I held the jacket in my hand up against a lamp back at my friend's home, I wondered, *how is this even possible?* My pants had bullet holes in them as well, but my body didn't. I've always credited my safety to my mother's constant prayers, as she was the first one to come to Christ in my family, and this Thursday night wasn't any different, which came to light the third straight day I was shot at in that week.

How pivotal is a mother's prayer?

Very!

My mother had three sons and a grandson she raised since a baby, who were heavily involved in the same gang. At times, I think she had no other alternative outside of prayer. I went home that day rather disappointed that I made it home alive.

I had been in a coma for a few days in the past, as I said before. I picked a fight with this same gang and on their turf, one that resulted from...I kid you not, the worst case of sheer stupidity. I went to start a fight without weapons and on their turf just to prove

I wasn't just another street punk.

Yeah, I lost that one. I knew my next appointment with death would perhaps be a success; wrong again!

The very next day after being shot on Thursday night, I was making my way to my older sister's house for dinner that afternoon. The one thing about my family that I love most is that we're a very close family. It's eight of us siblings in total. Nonetheless, as I was driving from the neighborhood to her house, a fourteen-year-old kid, whom I fed cereal to at my mother's house when he was smaller, since he grew up with my nephew, had now joined a different gang that I was unaware of, one that we happened to be at war with from a situation that resulted in a conflict a few nights before, of which I was clueless to. That is until my nephew briefed me about it when I saw him at dinner shortly after this incident took place.

As I was making my way to my sister's house, I drove past the kid I'm speaking of on the street. I was about a block away from my sister's house. I waved at him to say hello, but when he saw me, he reached for his midsection and pulled out a gun; he then aimed it at the car and began shooting at me. Of course, I was surprised! Never would I have expected this!

My reaction was to duck down and drive away immediately, which I did, but not before he unloaded three rounds in my way. One grazed my head as I sped away from the scene with my head below the door panel, and just like that, I continued to my sister's house for dinner as if nothing had ever happened.

This is pretty much the norm on the wild streets of Chicago for the average gangbanger raised in a life of crime. Any given night can be your last.

We didn't call 911 back then; we were 911!

My nephew, who was also in the same gang I was, quickly briefed me about the new gang war between the shooter's gang and ours, and I left right away after dinner, no longer confused about this situation, but I did feel something was not right with so much happening to me and so fast in just a few short days. The very next night (Saturday), as I was arriving at a club where I was a DJ, I was holding a crate of vinyl records in one hand as I was walking toward the entrance of the club, holding a woman's hand with my other hand who was at the time my girlfriend. A friend and his girl-friend were walking in front of us as we walked from the parking lot to the club's entrance.

We were almost at the door when we suddenly heard the tires of a car screeching to a halt as the car hit the brakes in front of the building. The driver came out and stood by his door, and he began unleashing several shots in our way after identifying his gang af-filiation and right in the middle of traffic on busy Roosevelt Road. I could hear a good pop coming from his gun, which had to be a .44, .45, or .357 Magnum. It was very loud, that's for sure. And because it was me as the target, the driver did the shooting, when it's usually the passenger who is trigger-happy during most drive-by shootings.

As the bouncer opened the club's front door, I quickly pushed the girls inside the place first, and they reached out and grabbed my friend as well, but once the shooting started again, they shut the door to the club for safety, and I stayed outside. We're talking about a few seconds lapsing as this took place.

At a moment's notice, I dropped to the ground as the bullets kept coming my way. I remember falling to the ground and watching the bricks' particles fall past me in slow motion as I lay on the ground; they slowly fell off the wall as a result of the bullets striking the bricks. Hundreds of tiny crystals were slowly falling past my eyes, but besides experiencing seeing the bricks' crystallized particles fall slowly in front of me, I could also smell the gunpowder from the bullet casings falling around me.

The shooter was close to thirty feet away, and the next sound I heard was the gunman say, "I shot him, let's go." And they burned rubber and drove away finally.

The door to the club opened once the coast was clear after the rivals had left, and the club's security came out, stood me up, and brought me inside. I honestly thought I was shot. But after they checked me out, they laughed and said, "You're all good, go play some music, fool." And I did just that, but I felt in shock, and as the night progressed, I felt as if the end of the road was finally near.

I mean, I was shot at three consecutive days, and that was a first for me. We're talking about over forty bullets heading my way in less than seventy-two hours. Hard to ignore, right? That night I wanted to just go home right after the club. We normally would go to another bar, ask the keeper how much he made a night, then match it and have him lock the doors, making it our place for the next day or two, where only our gang can come in and out.

Not that night, though, that night I told the guys to take me home, they tried to get a very pretty girl to change my mind, but *my mind had been somewhere else for a while*. They eventually gave up and took me home. I walked into my apartment, which was in my mom's basement; she had asked me to move in after posting bail at Cook County Jail a month earlier. I was pretty much broke after selling everything I had to make bail, and I had no other choice on the matter.

Before that, I had been held without bond for four months while in county jail as I was awaiting a hearing. I happened to run three buildings for the gang on the inside while inside the county jail; nothing changes, streetwise. It's just business as usual.

We held our meetings in the church because everyone gets to go to church as a right, and we came together to do logistics for everything imaginable a gang does inside a jail.

I remember sending some of the members in the gang to sit in the front seats of the chow hall, where the church was usually held, so that the preacher could pick on them, being that they were way, way up in the front. I gave them the choice of that or to receive a violation, which would be at least three minutes (punches) to the chest or church, front row, when they screwed up. Their choice.

Well, this particular night, the preacher went out of his way to address yours truly!

He said, looking right at me, "I know who you are, even though I don't know your name. I know you are here to hold your gang meetings, but God wants you to know that He loves you, and if you don't believe me, try praying to Him tonight, and you'll see that you are here for a reason other than the obvious. Jesus loves you regardless of what you've done." My thoughts were, *Obviously, I'm here for a reason.* I was fighting five Class X felony cases. *How is that for a reason?* I thought!

I was so enraged with him at that point that I wanted to ask one of my guys in the front to strike him for disrespecting me like that in front of the gang. But my words wouldn't come out; I was muzzled.

I went to my cell that night infuriated, riot-type infuriated. But I couldn't stop thinking about what the preacher had said that night back at the chow hall regarding prayer and God. After all, I had a lot of baggage needing my attention, resulting from a repertoire in street violence and an inventory of what was at hand in the now, which was a cause for concern. I think it was a good idea in any light to try praying to God.

I thought to myself, *Okay, God, if You are real, then allow me to make bail in court tomorrow*. I had court for one of the cases I was fighting the very next day. After church service, or better yet, the gang meeting, I felt stupid as I perceived it then (the thought of praying), but to even entertain the idiotic suggestion of that preacher back at the makeshift church, to pray, was nothing short of pathetic, but somehow, I did inquire of God in my own way because I was at my wit's end. And I needed an icebreaker.

The next day as they came to get us for the court line at five in the morning, the first thing on my mind was, again, the fact that the preacher said God was trying to reach me. Though it didn't make much sense to me, I did entertain the notion, and as I heard the command, "Court line walking," I sailed for the underground tunnel system to start my day.

Well, by six in the morning, I was higher than the sky from smoking weed in the tunnels under Cook County Jail. You could get high just by being there. Everyone gets along in the tunnels because it's like a big party with all the fellas who are going to court that morning from the entire facility. It's when you learn who is in and who is out and who is in control and what steps to take next. Court was like the United Nations forum to us since every division in the county jail was represented. We consumed the entire morning, imagine that!

When my name was called on the docket, I was sitting on the dirty floor in the bullpen of my assigned courtroom. I stood up and went in in front of the judge, and as the prosecutor read my long rap sheet, with my lawyers by my side asking for the possibility to make bail, which had been denied three times before because one of the victims was in critical condition and could still die, I glanced behind me: my family was watching the court proceedings through the thick, dirty glass windows as they listened on the overhead speaker to what was taking place in the dim courtroom. They were hoping for the best for me, I'm sure. My family was always supportive regardless of what I put them through. And this time was no different.

So much was going through my mind at that moment, and that's besides me being fried, when suddenly I heard the words as if from far, far away, though I was standing right in front of the judge, "Bond is set at one hundred and eighty thousand dollars." Though I was high, I remembered the words of that preacher the night before, and that was to ask God to reveal Himself to me. And this I couldn't shake off.

I thought for a moment, *could this be God?*

But once I got back to my cell, I muttered, "Nah, that was a fluke; God is not real. Why would He help me?" I credited the success of that day to my three lawyers.

What now? I thought.

For starters, I didn't have eighteen thousand dollars lying around to post bail. I figured I'd put God's back against the wall one more time, and I thought, *well, me getting a bond was my lawyers' persistence or the judge's annoyance of seeing me there, time and time again. So, if You want to prove You're real, then bond me out!* I said this to God, as I supposed, somewhat in of a prayer.

It was a Thursday night and commissary day for my unit. I was getting ready to buy some groceries shortly after coming back from court; I had the munchies like nobody's business! And then, after that, I would call my family to thank them for the lawyers and for coming to court once again in my support.

When I returned to the unit, I was baffled that no one was using the phones, which is a miracle, so I decided to call my mom and express my gratitude, yet again!

One of my sisters answered the phone. She sounded very excited, and I asked why. She said, "Al, I need five hundred dollars to get you out; I'm waiting for a phone call. Try and call me later, okay?" I replied, "Maggie, Sister my bond is eighteen thousand to walk, not five hundred!" She said, "I already have the rest!" I dropped the phone and heard a faraway voice coming from the swinging phone speaker, "Al, Al, are you there, Al?" Then she hung up, and I said to myself, "God is real!" I was stunned!

A few hours later, I heard my name called. The sheriff walked in and said, "Garcia! You're going home. Pack it up, sir!"

From that moment on, I honestly couldn't stop thinking about God's existence. I kept thinking about my few talks with God (a whole two of them), but as I was changing from my Department of Corrections' clothes to civilian ones, I called my sister to make sure this was real, but I couldn't get through, and when I did, I was told she was on her way to pick me up. I thought to myself, *maybe this isn't real*, but as I was on the last steps of release from the facility, I thought about all the months I was held without bail, which was close to a year, and the possibility of actually catching another case while in there was always in the back of my mind. All kinds of negative things were going through my mind.

I believe it's the enemy's way of rebooting itself after sensing he's losing one of his most devoted wicked children. Confusion and doubt are the norms once a transition onto Christ takes place. I walked out of the county jail at last, and yes, this was real. I received a bus token and a dime to get home. I received my personal property, and I walked out of the living hell called Cook County Jail.

I walked across the street to a Popeyes Chicken restaurant where the California Avenue (South) bus stop is, which is on Twenty-Sixth Street and California Avenue. Literally down the street from where I grew up as a kid, and as I was walking to cross Twenty-Sixth Street, I noticed a younger kid that was released after I was. He was walking behind me, and I saw him acting like a fool, acting as if he was all that and a bag of chips; he was throwing up gang signs to passing motorists.

Now, that side of the county jail is the dividing line between my ex-gang and their archenemies. That was our side and my safe zone, if you will. The gang I belonged to is one of the most notorious street gangs of Chicago, and their archenemies a close second, who usually patrol that area on their side as well to catch inmates being released in hopes of finding them on the wrong side of the street. It's obvious that the released ones are unarmed, being that they are fresh out of county jail, but not the gang's patrolmen, not them; they are armed to the teeth.

I saw a white pickup truck pull up in front of Popeyes Chicken, where the bus stop is. There were two guys from my gang in the vehicle. I could tell by the colors they were wearing, and normally when released from jail, I usually went to clown around and brag a little about my recent jail stay in the neighborhood, which is where the county jail is.

Since I grew up half a block away from Cook County Jail and knew the entire block, it made me feel at home after being released in prior times. But this time, I wanted nothing to do with it, and the weird part was that I couldn't understand why. I could have used some of the amenities the gang offers, if you know what I mean.

As the men in the pickup pulled up slowly in front of me, they stopped, looked directly at me, and made eye contact. I saw a sawed-off double-barrel shotgun staring right at me, at about five feet away, at that. And as they slowly drove by, the gunman said, "What you be about?" Or, what gang are you in? I just looked at him and thought about saying my affiliation or snatching the gun away from him; one of the two thoughts was ready for release, but instead, I smiled.

Now the kid next to me, who was acting like he owned the street, literally urinated in his pants when they approached him next because he belonged across the street at the enemy's camp. The passenger opened his door as if he was going to jump out in front of us.

As a sheriff's squad car pulled up on Twenty-Sixth Street going east on our side of the street, the guy got back in the truck and slowly drove away; the two men made a right turn and went back onto Twenty-Sixth Street, going west, quickly driving past the squad car as if nothing had happened, speeding away nonchalantly while laughing.

Their visit was obvious; I knew they were patrolling the neighborhood. I'm talking about the gangbangers, not the cops. So, I told the kid to go inside Popeyes and I would get him when the bus came. I said "kid" because he was seventeen, and I was twenty-seven, so I was way older than him. The pickup came back around again as expected, which is typical, but for whatever reason, the sheriff stood at the corner with their lights on; maybe they sensed something. The men in the pickup drove past me and only smiled.

Finally, the bus came; I knocked on the window at Popeyes.

The kid came out, and I lectured him on his behavior (I know, right), and as I was about to board the bus, my sister honked the horn from across the street. She was trying to get my attention so that I did not hop on the bus, and when I finally saw her, I walked up to her car and drove away.

She told me how my mom's church was praying for me and that my mom made food to receive me back from jail. I was grateful, of course, but I couldn't shake off what was taking place. I could never leave the gang because my gang's only way out was *death,* and we made that known at the beginning and very clear during.

My thoughts were, *God has a funny way of showing you that He can get you out of jail and then allowing someone to take a shot at you as you're a free man, at last.* I think that meant "I have My eye on you, be careful" kind of thing.

I was out on bond for a few months, and the day I was shot at in front of the club, which was a Saturday night, I went home in despair. I was confused, I was empty, and quite frankly, I was dead inside. It was still early in the wee hours of the morning, and as I walked into my apartment, I heard my mom's footsteps from the hardwood floors. I made myself a drink, and as I was about to take a sip, I heard her talking to someone.

I was curious to see who it was and why they were here so early. I figured it was one of the annoying church friends she had.

So, I decided to go upstairs and tell whoever it was, "Off!" as well as my mom, and to pick a better time to chitchat. I began walking up the stairs, and as I took three steps in, I felt a hand stop me from going up. I fell backward, but the hand stopped me from falling; I am not sure how else to explain it, but the hand was pushing me back and at the same time holding me and keeping me from falling back.

After a few seconds went by, I said, "Okay God, You win, I'll get right." And the hand, which I never saw, simply disappeared, or the feeling of it being there. I walked in and found my mom praying by the sofa as the sunlight was beginning to break through that beautiful early May morning. She saw me and said that the Lord had woken her up since three a.m. to pray for me. Then she said that the Lord had been waking her up at three a.m. since Thursday. Lo and behold, I got saved later that day, but when I had my day in court, I pleaded guilty to everything I was facing because I had accepted the Lord as Savior in the few months I was a free man, and I wanted to start fresh more than anything. I was guilty as charged, and I needed to take responsibility for my crimes as the conviction set in, and as I remembered the hand by the basement stairs, I felt God wanted it that way.

That's why I'm a firm believer of when salvation begins because there are those unexplainable moments when nobody can do it but God. Or when the door opens for redemption for every single one of us who accepts Jesus as Lord and Savior, regardless of what we are going through now. And I'm sure it can be worse than what happened to me, but no matter what wrong anyone can do, there is a God of mercy and grace that wants to erase our wrongs and wants to set us up for a better way of thinking, which will lead to a better way of living, or as it says in John 10:10 (NKJV), "I have come that they may have life, and that they may have it more abundantly."

TRACING GOD THROUGH LIFE'S EVENTS!

There's always a moment when you know you can trace life's events back to God, and that's what I call a Romans 10:9 moment. Not only can we understand the initial premise of meeting God for the very first time, and that's regardless of where we find ourselves at that *magical* moment as it will sometimes feel utopian, but also when that salvation is primarily redeemed in the fullness of its culmination, and that would be, in my view, a 2 Timothy 4:7 moment. Unfortunately, that's where, in my opinion, people err the most regarding the subject at hand.

For some reason, people believe that salvation is a sealed deal by initially accepting Christ as Lord and Savior and that's it; however, this new life of faith in Christ is just the beginning of an indifferent personal journey that pretty much will be centered as a one-day-at-a-time endeavor, one that's set apart for a special purpose in Christ Jesus, and the purpose is chosen by Christ Himself. And for that, we can look at Hebrews 9:28, where the answer to that effect hangs quite circumspectly and eternally balanced, so as to express what the reality in Jesus is all about and does so quite eloquently and in plain view for all of us to see. This also helps us, as believers, to understand what the end of the road looks like for our faith journey in Christ Jesus.

Not only that, but also where it resides in its completion, or its culmination if you will—as in the day we finally get to meet our Maker (Psalm 116:15). This should be the thing we ought to desire the most as God's children, and after we depart from planet Earth and into His loving presence, and just as the promised, long-awaited embrace from our Lord nears at that moment, that is exactly where we find the end of the entire matter, *salvation*! In other words, when we die!

Just as Paul himself puts it in 2 Timothy 4:6 regarding *his* departure from the rut of living under this world's broken system, one with collapsed moral values that utterly and abundantly surround us on all fronts.

Ones that we can only see now because we were changed by God's love and his long-awaited translation into eternity's final resolution, meaning Paul's description of his departure. Just as promised by our Redeemer—by ignoring the process because of the destination ahead, which trumps all else. But since we know our expected end is an eternity in Him, a redirection from our sure way to hell, I'm sure we all know that was our destination if it were not for God's grace and mercy that reached us in time, and now, thanks be to God, a transfer to heaven is awaiting us as we *continue* in Him, but only thanks to God's grace and mercy for us, and no other explanation for our redemption is obtainable or possible.

Somehow, for whatever reason, what takes place in between acceptance and redemption in a believer's life's journey has gone ignored. A journey with its many ups and downs and downs and ups, which guarantees only one thing for sure: a struggle with the *flesh* for a lifetime!

We can potentially become our own worst enemy if not careful, especially if we are called to *greatness* (leadership and ministry). It's no secret God gifts us all differently (Luke 19:11-27) and for a good reason.

The times we are living in are what we call *trying times*, which are supposed to build character within us as we walk in our experiences through faith. The first-century church is no different than the last-century church because Jesus will be bodily present in both for a formidable transformation in a believer's challenging life of faith and not the other way around, a transformation of one in decline and defeat, leading us away from God or ending up in some sort of depression, resulting in a lukewarm and stagnant state of weakened faith. Or worse yet, *apostasy*! Or even suicide!

As in the case of Joshua Harris of the Christian faith. A renowned name in the '80s, who after twenty-five years of pastoring a church that grew to over twenty thousand members, somehow decided he no longer wanted to be a Christian. Imagine that? Giving up decades of ministry, marriage, and only God knows what else he gave up just to end up apologizing for the sin he embraced, which he once spoke against, and that is exactly what apostasy is: when Satan convinces you that God is okay with sin. Or it could be worse—depression's goal is suicide. We cannot put anything past the devil; he is a deceiver and is quite good at it.

A *default*, like that of Harris, can be blamed partly on the lack of sound doctrine from anyone avoiding the reality of the struggle that it is to live a sanctified life in Christ. And I always mean as prescribed by God throughout Scripture.

The notion is that by adhering or conforming to an unchecked walk of sorts, one without checks and balances can easily become a sure possibility of a fallaway over time, in other words, a recipe for spiritual regression. One that possibly denies the reality of a struggle with the flesh, but surrendering rather, and how it also dismisses what a sanctified life in God truly is and is doing so by applying actions contrary to Scripture.

Struggle with sin ends when we overcome it or when it overcomes us!

One leads to victory, and the other leads to bondage, and bondage is no longer a struggle with sin; bondage is embracing a sinful lifestyle one we must repent from, especially in Christianity because when it comes to leadership in the body of Christ, most of us are good at hiding it for obvious reasons. As was the case with Joshua Harris and the like…because it is a struggle nonetheless, and when we advocate for sinful lifestyles, knowing the truth as biblically interpreted is when, in my opinion, that apostasy is as tangible as it can be (Romans 7). And nothing short of that is a reality, one we must face with God at our corner, or else?

Not to mention the self-denial that goes on into a lifestyle of sacrifice unto God (among other things), which makes the journey of a life set apart unto the Lord a voluntary commission, and in its primary premise a challenge nonetheless (Psalm 110:3), but at the same time, a worthwhile long-life event to undertake regardless of the many challenges ahead. And all this while being constantly conscious of its demands. Regardless of persecutions or foreseen unrest, which are prescribed to test us, quite predictable and in plain sight of Scripture. As if the turmoil keeps us on our knees a little bit longer than what we might want to admit; if the truth be told, storms validate strength within us. We can all be Gideon at some point in our walks.

Yet, the biggest challenge for any individual accepting the invitation of keeping oneself set apart till the end of such things becomes vivid is exactly what searching for holiness and the desire to please God *always* is all about. That way, you don't have to guess whether you're saved or not. Not the nonchalant and evasive lifestyle that suggests that no matter what you do in life after conversion, you are eternally secure because of OSAS's empty promises and their fallacy of instructions that continually affect their institutions and are adopted in sheer ignorance. Just Google what holiness means, and that ought to clarify your intuition, I hope.

I submit to you that all unconfessed sin is sin that is retained, regardless of what anyone may falsely claim; that, my friend, is the rendition exponentially spoken of by practically every biblical writing regarding the true faith and its basic teachings.

Unconfessed sin in a believer's life allows for a type of growth in the kingdom of darkness that gradually begins to tug at us mischievously, and its recipe for regression is evident over the horizon. And whoever your demon is that encamps around you at this point—of course, assigned by the enemy of our soul as a personal tormentor—will always know exactly how you like it, and you know it's true because no one is tempted to do things they once hated or didn't enjoy (James 1:14).

If the angel of the Lord encamps around those who fear God, then the demon of Satan encamps among those who don't fear God, and I think that's a fair analogy, don't you think?

In other words: Satan builds on the stronghold he lays out for us when we live in rebellion in contrast to what the Word of God states and does so by simply accusing us of default. We will all experience the wilderness at some point in our lives, and that's when temptation becomes a reality. If Jesus had to, so will we, and we can triumph as well because He did. Things that the Bible refers to as snares are nothing but land mines, and if it was good enough for the Lord to go through such trials and temptations, then it's good enough for us as well.

Just like the angel of the Lord encamps around those who fear God, the fallen angel of the lord of the flies also encamps around those who don't fear God as stated above, and as a decision to indulge in licentious lifestyles arrives, and if our decisions tend to run in that direction, then don't be fooled, Satan's demons are present to indulge along with anyone attempting such resolutions.

Sin is rebellion against God, no matter how you slice it. Sin is making an ally of God's enemy (Satan). Sin is missing the mark, but a sinful lifestyle, that's another story. A sinful lifestyle after conversion is sin gradually manifesting toward its goal of self-deception and apostasy.

Sin is a realm unknown to God. God has never sinned, so He doesn't know what that realm is like, nor will He ever be in it. Since we were once in that realm, we are now known by demons in that realm, and when we come to know Jesus as Savior, we then leave that realm of sin and are now sitting in heavenly places or, better yet, a different realm where God is always present and not Satan. This takes place by confession unto salvation. Repentance commands this realm to release us, and we are not to go back under any circumstances because there is a disconnect to Christ when we are in sin!

Christ and sin do not coexist in both realms—it's impossible, so when we leave the kingdom of darkness, we do so by confessing Christ as Lord. That's why it is important to confess our sins as believers so that we are not sucked back into the realm of sin: not your body, but your spirit, which was cleansed from filth.

We know God cannot look at sin because He called Adam out of the realm of sin and could not see him until Adam spoke. Adam did not confess his sin but rather blamed the woman; she then blamed the devil. God put them out of the Garden (another realm we cannot enter until the end) and read them their rights; therefore, curses fell upon them. This was before the Law, but we know Jesus said the Father forsook Him as He took on our sins. As we very well know, Jesus went to hell for three days thereafter. Confession releases us from the realm of sin, and when we refuse to confess our sins, we may very well default from the faith by adding more sins to that sin that got us away from God, and that can eventually lead to a sinful lifestyle once again as if we never knew Him.

The time you remain in that sin after conversion, and the longer you refuse to confess it, is the same as the accumulation of interest in a loan you refuse to pay, or can't pay, per se, eventually resulting in a return to a lifestyle of sin, or perhaps getting *lost* all over again.

You will be judged for your sin if it's gone unconfessed, and how much interest and other fees you suppose you've accumulated over time because *the wages of sin is death,* so we are told? And to those who believe your past, present, and future sins are forgiven, let me be the first to tell you that unconfessed sins are retained sins and are a past tense, since if something hasn't happened, you can't be charged as if it did happen, so future sin's forgiveness is as ridiculous as being a rock star on a cross-country drive with a car full of children with your wife riding shotgun. I believe we call that *daydreaming*!

David asked God to forgive him of sins he didn't remember (Psalm 19:12), but he still tried to ask for forgiveness of past sins. Present sins are what we deal with today, and if we sin, we will know it, and we also know we must confess them to gain forgiveness, which is access to God. Future sins simply do not exist. Why do I even have to express that? You can say that someone is your future wife or husband after a proposal is made and accepted, but to claim a future spouse without the prerequisites is insane, so is claiming redemption for something as unrealistic as what tomorrow holds because obituaries today will end that discussion. Otherwise, you could be charged with murder if someone accused you of murder in the future. If it hasn't happened, it doesn't exist.

But let's get back to payment. Not to mention court costs, which will eventually repossess something you once enjoyed, whether it was a house, an automobile, a boat, you name it, but rest assured, you will lose something to your creditors. The Bible says that the borrower is a slave to the one who lends. In this case, it's your salvation. Remember that only Christ can afford to pay for the sins of the world; we can't. Our part is to confess those sins and try our best not to return to them. When Jesus told the woman caught in adultery to go and sin no more, He wasn't telling her not to sin ever again. When Jesus told her, "Go and sin no more" (John 8:11, NKJV), He was being specific regarding the sin she was about to

101

be stoned for. In other words, He meant not to prostitute herself anymore.

How much more of a loss will the most expensive item on the shelf of humanity be if we reject it after having it for a while (*salvation*) then simply discard it as a common thing?

King David forgot to confess his sin with Bathsheba or perhaps refused to. He then accumulated quite an extraordinary amount of interest and fees he couldn't afford to pay because there are certain things a king's money can't buy, and forgiveness of sin is one of them.

Though a king he was, and a filthy rich one at that, when King David crossed a line he should have never crossed, he was called on it, and when he had to pay for something his money couldn't afford, he felt the impact of his wrongdoing as he saw this thing get on his children.

David's worst mistake wasn't adultery; it was not confessing his sin because it birthed several atrocities in the aftermath of the judgment that followed. Sin adds to sin when unconfessed, and eventually, in David's case, it set up shop in his home for the destruction that follows sin's transgressions. And that's the premise sin brings into our lives when we decide to play dumb and not think God has a say on how He will deal with such sins once grace takes the day off. If you like to hide under the bubble of grace, you better study the life of David because it appears to me that God burst that bubble in an inexplicable way!

Remember that 1 John 1:9 (NKJV) tells us that "If we confess our sins, He is […] just to forgive us our sins," and may I suggest we focus on the word *just,* which means that even though God forgives, He has to judge our sin, and in David's case, He chose to bring justice in horrendous ways the king undertook, and I believe it was because David stood so close with God when the sins took place, and one sin led to another. God simply used a prophet to make things clear for God's kingdom and reprimand David for his wrongdoing. Look: "Then David said to Nathan, 'I have sinned against the LORD.' Nathan replied, 'The LORD has taken away your sin. You are not going to die'" (2 Samuel 12:13, NIV).

God dealt with the *man after God's own heart*—a king's kind of sin—in an unprecedented way, but only after David confessed his guilt, and not a moment sooner.

That's exactly how He will deal with the average believer. After all, God is not a respecter of persons. At least that's what we are told in Acts 10:34. And that judgment came after David's confession, or better yet, acknowledgment of his deviations from chasing after a woman and not after God, as in the usual relentless pursuit of God as before, but replacing Him with Bathsheba for that season, was a huge mistake, or better yet, the sin of adultery, which is what brought David's kingdom down to the ground. But notice that adultery was a concept born out of being out of place, or as we like to say it, in the wrong place at the wrong time. But the act of adultery wasn't a secret, David sent for Bathsheba, and she wasn't a rape victim either.

The very thing that invited rape, incest, treason, daylight orgies in a crowded gate before the city's entrance, as well as murder into David's own home, and by his children, was the product of a season in an unchecked sinful lifestyle that went unconfessed for a period of time. It can lead to scores of derogatory events, which go from bad to worse before you know it if adopted, and we have David's accounts to prove God is not asleep at the wheel simply because we are not struck by lightning when we are in sin.

That's what sin is (deception), and that's what sin does (deceive); it's what sin does when ignored. It simply graduates to different unimaginable ways of destruction in what God is building in us.

All sin must be judged by God for God to be God (Jude 1:15) and to keep order in His most precious creation called humanity, which makes us subjects of His grace, mercy (Jude 1:21), but also judgment. God must intervene on our behalf as He did with David, or we may end up lost forever if He doesn't. I think we all need a Nathan in our lives from time to time, don't you agree?

I believe the book of Revelation has quite a lot to say in that regard (judgment). Therefore, all sin is subject to judgment. Mercy and grace can only be implemented by God. The umbrella of grace is simply an extension to get right, but that bubble will burst when

God says, "Enough is enough" (see Romans 9:15), and at His discretion is His entirely right to define, of course. Without a doubt, only after our admission to such sinful transgressions is when we can find ourselves making a case for redemption, and that's the birth of the life story of psalm fifty-one.

Therefore, all sin will be judged, and that's according to the first letter of the beloved apostle John. It will go down this way; make no mistake about it. He lays it out perfectly and in its fullness of context. If we don't confess that sin, as we saw in David's case, the separation between God and us is surreal, and we then, without a doubt, *will* retain that sin as long as we keep it inside and alive in us. Nowhere in the Bible is there a reference to automatic forgiveness of sins. Again, thinking a future sin is forgiven without yet taking place is at least preposterous or perhaps insane. Plain and simple!

David was released from personal punishment because that's what God decided in that setting, but judgment did not go ignored. David's family, as well as all of Israel, suffered the consequences of the unfortunate demise of one man's mistake. And that's proof that our destinies are tied together with the people around us. His children became evil, and the nation lost battle after battle because of one man's sins (Ecclesiastes 9:18).

My dear friend and pastor, John F. Hannah, always says, "One man's obedience is connected to so many other people's destinies." Isn't that the truth?

Some people do believe that someone (or Christians) involved in the act of any type of sexual immorality (adultery, fornication, or homosexuality), at the time the *rapture* takes place, will be raptured because they cannot lose their salvation, and according to them, they are safe; imagine that?

And of course, this kind of behavior will be prevalent in the last-day church because it's taking place even now. The distraction of the so-called prosperity gospel is in effect because of ongoing sexual behavior in the church, and you can quote me on that. It's easy to demonize others when you are trying to redirect attention away from yourself. Such behavior was not subject to kings and palaces, and if someone was involved in such an act at the same time that the rapture took place, suggesting Jesus will wait on them to finish their dirty deed is insane, no, Jesus is not going to be waiting outside some motel room's door waiting for some "believer" to be done with their sexual sin just so that He can proceed with the rapture at their convenience. Otherwise, the rapture will never take place! And yes, there's also the idea that some church somewhere in the globe will be in worship service during the rapture's eve... hopefully (for our sakes), the latter is our destiny's end.

Imagine being raptured during worship service? (Smiley face.)

There are so many benefits to a life devoted to Christ Jesus, and of course, salvation is the main one. But the overwhelming peace that comes with such an assurance that He is with us at all times is priceless, and of course, it makes for why we as believers decide to take on the world and its uncertainties, a reason to believe in the unseen, but only with His help, and that's because we've learned to trust Him as we walk closely with Him daily as a testament of our faith in the reliance of the Holy Spirit's lead.

A thoughtful assurance on the guidance of God's Holy Spirit's work is a present and is present in our lives as we seek Him the more in our daily endeavors. One that is to be utilized in our everyday walk as much as it is up to us as a stabilizer for our faith, and the decisions we choose to make thereafter promote our confession as genuine because His leadership and patience toward us is the thing that causes us to engage in a continuous motivation of right living in Him. This resonates as part of His perfect will for us as it testifies of our love for Him by our actions and also the need to *remain* connected to the Source for our very own benefit. Especially for those around us who depend on our obedience to God for their good, our friends and loved ones included, which is the caveat of a resolution to faith itself and its many perks (Psalm 103:2). Who wants to be in heaven without their loved ones, right? That's because He is a rewarder of them that diligently seek Him (Acts 16:31), just as is stated in Hebrews 11:6. Making an intimate relationship with Jesus in our daily lives our aim is a reason for each season of our days in Him, and how rewarding it is just knowing Him. Even without the add-ons, it is the very thing our souls were longing for all our lives, and more so now that we can introduce our friends and families to Him as we know Him personally.

But we find the obscurity on the other side of that coin (rebellion in a believer's life), a place in time where one may jeopardize such a decision to continue to follow Christ fully and faithfully, just as is prescribed by God's Word, daily.

Just as it was designed and foretold by God in His master plan for every individual who accepts it by a conscious confession unto salvation, and the downside of that, a default due to the embrace of a sinful lifestyle somewhere along the way, and nothing "light-weight," might I add, will pull someone completely away from the Lord's presence (Hebrews 6:6) as it happens to so many believers nowadays. That's what we call playing with fire, hellfire!

I'm speaking of events happening sometime after conversion to believing in Jesus. People, unfortunately, return to a previous sinful lifestyle they once embraced, which is exactly the result of an unchecked lifestyle that resorts to eternal security for validation or shelter in one way or another for its expressive error, sin, or a gray area going pitch-black if it were the case, and this, without expect-ing repercussions because of the illusive injunction eternal security promotes as its norm (Hebrews 12:6). This is erroneous in itself and by default, but to suggest that sinful lifestyles after conversion are nothing short of the basic norm for a believer is quite absurd, disingenuous, dangerous, and false, as well as is in complete dis-agreement according to the Word of God just as written in the first letter of John 1:6-10.

Besides that, God's Word has quite a lot to say about salvation and sanctification in that regard, and the many more scriptures leaning to that effect speak volumes to these facts as well, and as we see them throughout the entire Bible, and if you could see what I see, you'd understand why it was necessary to pen such findings, and as you prayerfully continue reading this book, I hope you come to the same conclusion as I have in regard to eternal security, and of course, its error.

Believing you cannot lose your salvation when never paying attention to other Bible discourses that deny such doctrines is a disservice to yourself and those around you, in my humble opinion (Jude 1:6).

Just look at verse eight of the first letter of John, chapter one:

"*If we* claim to be without sin, *we* deceive ourselves and the truth is not in us" (1 John 1:8, NIV; emphasis added).

Call me crazy, but this is the beloved apostle speaking here, and he has included himself in this category of potential self-deception by saying "we" twice in the same sentence. I think he wanted us to pay close attention to this warning, don't you agree?

What about verse six?

"*If we* claim to have fellowship with Him and yet walk in darkness, *we* lie and do not live out the truth" (1 John 1:6, NIV; emphasis added).

There is no confusion about what living in darkness is all

about. And it is *sin*. Again, John says, "if we," so as to insert himself in the conversation! This is nothing short of a *mic-drop* verse. John makes it clear that if your confession and your walk do not match, you are living a lie. We call that *practice what you preach,* I believe!

Verse seven says that *if* we walk in the light, the blood of Jesus purifies us from all sin. But wait a minute here...why would we need His blood to purify us if we are walking in the light? Isn't walking in the light and having fellowship with Him an observation that we are not living in sin? Isn't walking in the light the epitome of a sinless (less sinful) lifestyle?

Why then would we need to be cleansed if we are in the light and clean from offenses (sins) as clearly stated in the verse? I'm not implying that we should articulate controversy to such directives, but we may expound on what the beloved apostle was conveying to us. This is a pivot moment to embrace. All his letters are in circumspect aligned to this directive and not as an alternative to the opposition as if we had a choice in the activation thereof. Especially this one.

In 1 John 5:16, John writes us a profound and articulate paragraph about two different types of sin: one that leads to *death* and one that doesn't. Look as he recreates a different approach to categorizing sin, as in "not all sin is the same!"

If you see any brother or sister commit a sin that does not

lead to death, you should pray and God will give them life. I refer to those whose sin does not lead to death. There is a sin that leads to death. I am not saying that you should pray about that.

1 John 5:16 (NIV)

What was John getting across here?

If we were to take John literally here, we would conclude that suicide is a sin that undoubtedly leads to death; in fact, it's a guarantee that's its projected outcome. And he suggests not praying about that. How far from God must one be to want to end one's life, and I'm not saying that life isn't tough because it is. We aren't told about the countless suicides in the LGBT community because that would mean something is wrong there, and they don't want any negativity coming out of their members, but the numbers are high, and how sad is that? But we are talking about believers here, and as believers, we know better, we all know God did not knock the apple out of Eve's hand, and God will not intervene when someone decides to pull the trigger and end their life. Unless, of course, someone is interceding for them as the verse above suggests because the only prayer that moves God to act against the obvious, and the only prayer that changes things is a prayer uttered by someone connected to Jesus.

Furthermore, John calls them a brother and a sister, and that terminology is only used to describe *born-again Christians.*

Suicide is in no way, shape, or form entertained, accepted, or promoted by God anywhere in the Bible! There is nothing more heartbreaking than when a person commits suicide!

When Jesus was tempted to commit suicide (He was) by jumping from the temple's pinnacle following the wilderness temptation experience, He simply said no! And added, "You shall not tempt the Lord your God" (Matthew 4:7, NKJV), which is what suicide is: tempting God! And a bad idea in any light! Not only was Jesus being tempted, so was the Father as Jesus quoted the commandment.

Why is it not a good idea to tempt God? Well, because He will not send an angel to prevent the "lest you dash your foot against the stone" prerequisite (Matthew 4:6, paraphrased).

The COVID 19-related overwhelming suicides in the timeline of the recent lockdowns mostly happened because of isolation that led to depression in so many people, which was mainly driven by the falsehood of what was being promoted by the media as a whole, and their fearmongering reports are to blame, and as people of God, we should know better than that because "Weeping may endure for a night, but joy comes in the morning" (Psalm 30:5, NKJV). We have hope, and that should be all the motivation God's children need in order to see tomorrow if the Lord wills it and not if we will it.

To suggest that someone can take their own life and play God is to suggest the unthinkable. I know that to get to that chapter in life is not easy, but regardless of the vehicle that drove someone to that conclusion, hope is always a means to redirect traffic to a better ending. We must exit that vehicle and ride with Jesus and ask Him to take the wheel.

It amazes me how men who have PhDs in divinity and run big Christian institutions can somehow promote, *whether* directly or indirectly, such a *possible* hellhound sin as suicide is. And do so continually and without conviction since they write about it and promote it daily during their broadcasts and preaching's from their pulpits. As you will see later, there are men who have such a reprobate approach to this terrible life-ending sin that suicide is, as well as other obscure doctrines along the same lines, which have gone unchecked for far too long, at least in my humble opinion.

Take a look at what Peter says in his second letter of chapter two and verse twenty as it's laid out for us all to feast on in a spiritual theater of uncompromised efforts:

> If they have *escaped* the corruption of the world *by knowing* our Lord and Savior Jesus Christ *and are again* entangled in it *and are overcome*, they *are worse off* at the end than they were in the beginning.
>
> 2 Peter 2:20 (NIV), emphasis added

This is not someone who wasn't saved unless we want to lie to

113

ourselves and pretend otherwise, and if that's the case, then let's accept Scripture for what it is.

Denying that this verse is speaking about someone losing their salvation because they've decided to embrace a sinful lifestyle or perhaps ended their life due to its fruition, one that could have resulted from some form of depression, is denying that sin is the ugly thing that ruins a relationship between a holy God and us, which stares us in the face whenever it is present!

The suicide rate during the pandemic skyrocketed, and God did not step in and stop it, which means we have control of our lives when we do not give Him control over our lives, and suicide is always done by a person out of control or with *too much control* of their own life and not enough God.

Peter doesn't beat around the bush when he expresses exactly what God wants him to convey in regard to someone walking away from God in a voluntary fashion. He clearly says that if you (keyword, "escape") *escape* the corruption of the world by accepting Christ as Savior, it constitutes a genuine conversion and not at all what the watered-down version of the "once saved, always saved" unhinged rhetoric attempts to convey in their views on salvation, which suggests that they were never saved because that's what they were taught in church or Bible school, and shame on those preachers who teach such error.

Don't forget that unless you repent, their blood is in your

hands; you, preachers, are accountable for every suicide advocated by your teachings!

Just like they say of Judas, an apostle, mind you (Luke 6:13; Matthew 10:2), one who was never saved according to their ill-advised revelation of the Word, and it is so in almost all doctrine perceived by this indoctrination. Including salvation, which is the most important one of them all!

Peter says that "they are again entangled in…" Entangled in what, Peter? Entangled in the world and its many sinful pleasures, or better yet, a sinful lifestyle of sorts. Furthermore, Peter says, "and are overcome…" In other words, they abandoned Christ altogether and can't break free from the bonds of that sin and its lifestyle.

Suicide is always a premeditated sin. One you cannot repent from unless you come back from the dead, and it is also possible because it's sometimes tried several times over until suicide is successful. John puts it this way:

> Watch out that you do not *lose* what *we* have worked for, but that you may be rewarded fully [meaning salvation]. Anyone who runs ahead and *does not continue* in the teaching of Christ *does not have God* [continuation is required to remain saved]; whoever *continues* in the teaching has both the Father and the Son. [And whoever

doesn't continue doesn't have them!]

2 John 1:8-9 (NIV), emphasis and brackets added

We have an obvious observation on the part of Peter as a result of harmonious edicts between his and John's writings. Ones that are stating someone's departure from the faith are a reality. "They have left the straight way and wandered off to follow the way of…" (fill in the blank, please) (2 Peter 2:15, NIV). Anyone can walk away from God for any given reason (2 Peter 2:18-22).

These verses alone can destroy the OSAS doctrine, and undoubtedly, so they do.

John and the rest of the New Testament church are in perfect sync with the same positive message of holiness that we must adhere to in order to retain our connection with the Lord Jesus, and at all times, not only when it's convenient. We are warned not to entertain the progressive and watered-down OSAS false gospel that living like hell will get us into heaven someday.

The "it is finished" statement Jesus uttered before He took His last breath when on the cross as a human was a statement we can make when we're about to take our last breath as well, after we finish our assignment, just like He did, and not a moment sooner. This is not a catchphrase, this was the Lord's reality, and it should be ours as well. He finished what He was sent to do, and so should we.

We must research the entire Bible to validate such audible attributes that point to vast decisive, loud-and-clear warnings regarding the topic of eternal security and salvation as a whole.

When a believer is walking closely with God, sanctification and spiritual growth should be what progressively takes place in his or her daily life, and that life's increasing quality is one without resentment as we progress to live out our faith, which is the expected behavior of a life change in anyone who is now led by God's Holy Spirit. That's exactly what's supposed to take place in the behavior of individuals who profess Christ as Savior and do so as an outward and ongoing expression of their confession because we all know that faith without works is dead. This expression transitions into the manifestation of such an embrace and lifestyle that is a life in Christ Jesus, and a life-long commitment to faith with its many challenges and the promise from us to Him that we will do our best to overcome these challenges thanks to Him as we encounter such objectives during our journey.

The Bible tells us that we are supposed to go *from glory to glory* as believers. An encouraging feat for us all to embrace and the *in-between* part of a life that we live as God's people should progressively get better as we mature in the faith, and its uncertainties, which are somewhat of a gray area, to say the least, have now a light of hope in them as mentioned throughout the Word.

I think challenges are the same pretty much for us all, though different in magnitude. At least at some point in our walks, we will have a chance to test our faith, but the fact that challenges pivot decisions to cause growth in the faith walk of those of us that, after such acceptance and conversion to the Lord, somehow become a personal testimony to His existence within us is when these trials become a game changer for monumental self-growth.

Especially, how trials help us find common ground even though we may find life's challenges as colossal obstacles at times, and when we somehow become overwhelmed by the same tidal resolutions we face in between, the demur is when our faith has to kick into high gear, and we have tools like fasting and prayer, which help us become more relevant to ourselves as tools for relative comprehension, as an escape from reality.

As overwhelming as trials can be when breathing down our necks, it's then when we get to live in the guidelines of Romans 4:17.

I believe that there's no better time to seek God during our journey as believers than when we're at wit's end, and right when our backs are against the wall is a perfect time to remember Moses and the Red Sea remonstrance. We search for answers in monotonous sustainability to counteract the chaos that befalls us all at times, and they are almost a sure thing if we maintain the relevance in the scope of an intentional focus on the supernatural. Knowing that no matter what we face, we will be okay because we are living a lifestyle that God agrees with and is well pleased with, then, our decisions are filtered by faith itself due to our love for Him, and as our behavior is solely dependent of His provision for clarity. We all know where we came from. We know where He rescued us from. And we know that He will never leave us or forsake us, and we shouldn't do so with Him!

These hurdles that have our backs against the wall at times feel as if a perpetual stay as they tend to overwhelm us with their lingering counteractive solutions, but we must understand that these are sent our way for a perfectly good reason, if we are not bringing them on ourselves, that is. When Jesus told the disciples to meet Him at the other side of the lake, it was because they were going to make it to the other side of the lake. He didn't mention there would be a tumultuous storm. It's a known fact that trials provoke some of us to pray harder in search of answers we cannot attain otherwise, and yes, some of us do welcome the challenge of walking on water!

Salvation is much more complex than what some people think it to be. Otherwise, the writers of the New Testament wouldn't have gone out of their way to enlighten us with different stages to our common salvation. They referred to us as babies when we first came to know Jesus.

"Like newborn babies, crave pure spiritual milk, so that by it you may *grow* up in your salvation" (1 Peter 2:2, NIV; emphasis added).

I think that the understanding of what salvation is often downplayed by erroneous biblical views that are handed down over the centuries through progressive Christian academia, but for the most part, they are preached from the pulpit almost daily. One being the OSAS doctrine. The verse says *babes* are supposed to grow in their salvation. That growth takes our entire life, and there is no other explanation because babies will be, at some point after that, toddlers in the faith, then children, and adolescents, and finally seasoned believers. None of us can ever claim we have arrived!

Being saved is an ongoing process that takes an *entire* lifetime to achieve. And it doesn't happen overnight. If I can put it in my own words, I'd probably say: once saved—better stay saved!

GROWTH IS PROGRESSIVE!

There is absolutely no room for growth if one has a mentality that no matter what they do, they can't ever lose their salvation. Now, yes, God can forgive sin, but there is a pattern we must follow in case we do sin, and *sin* we will. There is a code we must adhere to or a combination that unlocks our freeform as believers if we fall, and that code is called *confession.* And generally speaking, sin in its progression shows up in stages of self-deception. For example, comfort, necessity, feelings, emotions, and the like, or in layman's words, meeting a legitimate need pretty much in some illegitimate way. These are situations that raise or should raise awareness that something is about to go south. Therefore, patterns begin to form.

That pattern goes a little something like this:

• Sin (in a believer's life)

It takes place the moment we decide to rebel against God and follow through with such rebellion. Sin, however, has to have a certain amount of *conviction* as a follow-up for us to regain that lost relationship back with God. It may feel physically good, but spiritually speaking, it has to disgust us to the core because it's wrong so that conviction can set in and lead us back to God. We know that godly sorrow leads to repentance (2 Corinthians 7:10). In essence, we cannot ignore the elephant in the room.

- Conviction

It takes place the moment we realize we've primarily done wrong to God, and of course, others as well. Though we sinned, we didn't enjoy it because the self-awareness of Christ in us compels us to retrieve, which is the Holy Spirit grieving within us. It causes an inward desire to want to be right with God and persuades us to *confess* that sin, whether to someone or just God. Confession has to take place in order to head toward step two.

- Confession

It takes place the moment we verbally express genuine remorse for the trespass that separated us from our Savior. We then long and desire a right standing with God once again. We do this as a uniform standard that begs for the need for *repentance*. It has to be verbal, and if confessed to another believer, even better. A Christian who is living in sin has a spirit of oppression inside and needs deliverance, or that spirit of oppression will triumph or can graduate into a spirit of possession, and possession is the best indicator a believer has lost their salvation (Luke 22:3) and has embraced a sinful lifestyle. Of course, the silver dollar answer to the million-dollar question from OSAS would be, "They were never saved." Although godly sorrow leads to repentance (1 Corinthians

7:9), godly sorrow can be suppressed by shame and condemnation, especially if we are torn in between sin and repentance.

Paul is speaking to the Corinthian church in this letter, and they were of the Way, which means they were saved. Yet, Paul wrote, "For godly sorrow produces repentance leading to salvation…" (2 Corinthians 7:10). He told that to believers, and not only Paul did that, John as well wrote seven letters to the churches, pleading with them to repent or else, as we see in the book of Revelation. Selah!

- Repentance

It takes place as we return to God and as we feel broken by that particular sin that set us back. As we turn from it, we then tend to turn to God and away from that sin to complete the cycle of repentance. We practically do a 180, and the challenge to turn to God in that shame is a change of heart to a full circle that gives us access to God once again in the exchange so that we may begin restoration at once. It's pivotal, and it's also gauged by our quest for restitution, which redirects to *conversion* or reconciliation if already a believer. There are countless instances when God makes a plea of "return to Me, and I will return to you" in the Bible to His children.

- Conversion

It takes place every time we repent, besides the initial prayer of salvation. This is due to sin's powerful induction of separation from our Savior because sin in our lives means we failed. We don't get saved repeatedly when we repent; we do *stay saved* when we repent. Our conversion is from the sin we committed to the forgiveness He provides. Conversion means an exchange. Our sin for His forgiveness is that exchange. Without confession, there is no remission of sin because it lacks the sacrifice provided.

> Therefore, dear friends, since you have been *forewarned,* be on your guard so that you may not be *carried away* by the error of the lawless *and fall from your secure position.*
>
> 2 Peter 3:17 (NKJV), emphasis added

And since 1 John 3:4 states that all sin is lawless, then Peter is certainly speaking to believers as well. I don't think he meant demotion from pastor to deacon as a secure position. Our sin remains active if unconfessed, and believers who had a secure position somehow lost it (1 Corinthians 9:27), and if we're going to stay within the text itself, we then have to honor it to its fullest. Otherwise, he wouldn't have said it, and diversely, Paul would not have said he could disqualify himself after preaching to others. It is sin that disqualifies, and not just sin, but embraced sin!

Now, how can someone fall from a secure position?

Lawlessness, which is sin, can cause someone who thought he or she had eternal security to fall, and as the verse says, we have been *forewarned* and must *be on our guard*, which begs the reasoning why Jesus said He would come as a thief in the night. He said that so that we may be watchful, as He Himself put it, "Watch and pray…" (Matthew 26:41a). As well as 2 Peter 3:10a (NIV) that reads, "But the day of the Lord will come like a thief…" As you can see, nothing here suggests that salvation is secured on our part and that we can raise our feet and just kick it without a care in the world.

And just as Jesus asked all ten virgins to come to the wedding, what happens when only half of them decide to focus on the invitation and not the actual banquet itself, which is the caveat?

They missed the wedding because they thought being invited would suffice, and they missed it due to a lack of preparation. Oil represents the anointing of the Holy Spirit in Scripture. This story should resonate with us all because it's invitational and, at the same time, instructive. It's important to acquire spiritual gifts along the way in our faith walk or develop them if we have them because we will need them at some point. The five foolish virgins taught us all that valuable lesson in Matthew, chapter twenty-five.

The chapter begins by saying, "At that time the kingdom of heaven will be like ten virgins who took their lamps and went out to meet the bridegroom" (Matthew 25:1, NIV). There are some key resolutions in this introduction alone, and this strikes me as being invited is enough, and that makes one think a little deeper about the seriousness of conversion to our Lord. "At that time" is referring to the end times, so that's exactly what will take place in front of us, right before His return.

"At that time…" is speaking of either anyone's conversion or the end times because this dialogue resonates with the previous chapter, which is eschatological in its premise. It's a bridge to connect the two.

Therefore, the setting of time is induced within Jesus's exponential assertion to categorize the invitational part, and along with the instructional part that is to reside in society after such initiation in its entire observation. The highway of information is to prepare for the wedding and not "hey, look at me; I was invited to the wedding" attitude!

Furthermore, all ten virgins were invited to meet the bridegroom, and there's where we find the invitational part, that's salvation in its purest form. Did Jesus know that five virgins were foolish? Well, did He not *gift* three individuals, and the one whom He knew would bury his talent received only one talent and not five?

I think we sometimes tend to forget that He left us a verse to see in John 3:16 to help us understand that all ten had a wedding invitation and that half of them would default due to unpreparedness, in other words: lack of zeal, but the invitation in John 3:16 is inclined to represent an opportunity of salvation to all. We are speaking of splitting hairs, or things in half, if you will. We see that two will be at the mill, one taken and the other left behind, two in the field, one taken, one left behind, which mirrors John 3:16 and is a parallel that half the church is saved, at best.

All ten virgins had lamps, all ten had oil in their lamps, which means they accepted the invitation because they all went, but only five took *extra* oil with them, which was the game changer in the end, only five prepared ("but the wise took oil in their vessels with their lamps" [Matthew 25:4, NKJV]), and five didn't. The five wise virgins took extra oil, and that's going the extra mile to make it to their destination; it will pay off in the end, as you will see.

Try going for a ride without gassing up and see just how far you'll get. In Matthew 25:5, we read that the bridegroom was delayed, and that was said to reinvent the virtue of *waiting*; think about it, the extra oil came in handy at that point, and that simple decision as that pivot moment arrived literally made all the difference in the world. In my opinion, the virtue of patience is exemplified here as a great value.

We know to wait on the Lord, do we not? But once He did show up (the bridegroom), only five virgins were ready to meet Him (half the church).

That part is either the end of a Christian's life or very well may be the end of the age. And, of course, it's probably both. God's part may be secure, but not ours. Though He will never leave us or forsake us, that says nothing about us leaving Him and forsaking Him, which is always the case.

Not having oil is not having an intimate relationship with the Holy Spirit. Outside of that, it's called *going through the motions at best*, and if you are a believer and you don't have a personal relationship with the third Person in the Godhead, then as the parable of the virgins says, you will not get in.

This parable says *Jesus is the invitation to the banquet, but the Holy Spirit is the ticket in.*

Before you arrive at the airport, you download your boarding pass back at home, which gives you access to that flight, which means your ticket is paid for, your receipt is proof. Whether it was you that paid it *or someone else* is irrelevant; at the security gate, you will be asked to present proof of *ID* (proof that you are a Christian). There's a book in heaven with all the names of the people that are getting in, and just like the plane, your boarding pass may very well be legit, and as paid for as it may be, it's still not enough to get you to board your flight. The ID is the oil; you have to show proof that you actually have the Holy Spirit in you at the time you're planning to board the flight to eternity. Otherwise, the words Jesus used when the five foolish virgins tried getting in was, "Truly I tell you, I don't know you" (Matthew 25:12, NIV). And you don't want part of that foolishness because all ten were invited, which means He did know them at some point! That's why it's impossible to think someone who kills themselves did not lose their salvation!

Call me crazy, but committing suicide would be the total opposite of a godly and holy life. Again, that's a gray area going pitch-black for any believer who ends up at such an intersection because they allowed depression, which derived from whatever dismal agent of irrelevancy, to successfully bring them down to the end of the road, and thus allowed themselves to fall distant from their life source by making the issue their god (suicide)!

That concept denies this gray area of trials and tribulations where our faith is tested indefinitely to cause spiritual growth in us, which is what should take place when this happens, just as we see in 1 Peter 4:12. These trials test us only to make us better at life in Jesus.

It's in that gray area that we must find common ground and attempt to be honest with ourselves about who we are in Christ.

We then can finally manage to launch into a continuous seeking of God and His direction from any form of trials we may be experiencing at that particular moment, and if we are successful thanks to His guidance, we are successful because of Him. The truth is we don't have it all together, none of us do; thus, we need His guidance daily, and we have our past lives to remind us what it is like to do life without Christ. A scary thought to embrace, but a real one!

We may not be able to decode the entire Bible and understand the mind of the Lord altogether, but without a doubt, we must at least get the topic of salvation right, lest we forget that eternity is at stake, and *suicide* is one of the reasons I decided to write this book among other reasons because this is a very serious issue in the church, and that issue has to be dealt with in the body, and be met with truth and sound doctrine.

It was inevitable for me to continue to allow the error that keeps inviting many a Christian to take a plunge not intend-ed for them as Scripture clearly states, "Therefore choose life" (Deuteronomy 30:19, NKJV). Also, 1 John 2:3 says that if we are His, we must keep His commandments, and "you should not kill" is one of those commandments. Therefore, since suicide is murder, and premeditated murder at that, as Christians, we are not to take part in it, per the commandment and as an action of our love for Him!

What's the difference between an abortionist who takes an unborn child's life, which we as believers deem as murder, and a pastor who advocates to his sheep that it's alright to kill themselves because they can't ever lose their salvation? I think none!

I find the pastor's advice more disgusting because they should know better, and on the positive side for the baby (if you will), that aborted baby does end up in heaven. Whereas the believer who commits suicide doesn't, and their blood will be in that pastor's hands.

The abortionist can care less what God thinks, but that pastor advocates for God, or should!

It's not at all hard to manipulate biblical interpretation erroneously when it comes to the Bible; after all, we do have scores of false religions that find their genesis built in error no matter where you look. Perhaps way back since the human race came into effect. But all of that is nailed to the cross in Acts 17:30.

Over the centuries, societies have learned to cope with whatever forms of wisdom they had to work with regarding the many religious beliefs of their day, just as it is today in our common circles. Which, by the way, tend to exclusively take the Holy Bible out of context to create a way of life that God never intended for them to observe, to begin with.

A narrative that suggests we can manipulate religious beliefs to fit our very own lifestyles, as well as other agendas in criteria for a feel-good gospel that is right out ridiculous and ineffective for sanctification, and that's regardless of what those practices may be, especially if immoral when it should be the other way around, and the core values of our, as believers, livelihood should be mandated by biblical principles as prescribed by the Lord in His many examples in the Word.

In fact, *there is nothing new under the sun:* being that it's contrary to God's will and purpose to think that we can manipulate God, or try to do so, simply because we do it to everyone else we know, and normally do as it seems fitting to our agenda and to whatever other watered-down religious beliefs we might embrace as canonical overtones. This, of course, is according to Scripture and in its interpretation thereof, better yet, its *misinterpretation.*

This gives us the notion that out of all the claims made (in suspicion), they lack support for their validity, also putting into question which one is the one we should embrace as the true religion and which one we ought to shun as deceptive because of its false rhetorical language in regard to biblical obscurity and sound doctrine that is nowhere to be found when the fruits of the Spirit come into play. But in the end, which one do we choose as legit?

A perfect example of a *misguided religious* feat is, without a doubt, the various cults that exist in today's new-age society and that have existed perhaps throughout modern history; only God knows how far back they go. Also, they have sprouted from such doctrinal errors over the centuries and are purely agenda driven in nature, perhaps from ignorance or maybe even a well-thought-out plan of implementation from the enemy of our souls (Satan) himself.

Who knows really, but the bottom line is this: these cults, as well as other pagan religions, find themselves in the same boat in regard to unbiblical continuity, and of course, they all make the claim that their values come right out of the pages of the Bible, but are they right in their views of interpreting such scriptures according to their progressive agenda, and also their many passive tolerant ways, which parallel with their livelihood as the norm and in error thereof? They have embraced such findings as canon, but are we to embrace such beliefs along with them?

And the answer to that is no!

Be holy, for I am holy is not a catchphrase to be entertained as something up for interpretation; it's a command from a holy God to His people, not a shenanigan of a cliché. God did not send His one and only Son to die on the cross of Calvary for a group of people. He made a way for all people to have a chance at eternal life. But He left it up to every individual to accept or reject that invitation.

Therefore, its implementation in such an opportunity is a personal one, and it's supposed to be one of a lifelong commitment—not a seasonal feat of sorts.

The problem is that since it's not an ongoing commitment *for some* and a one-stop shop after conversion for others, it makes it easy to live in sin if salvation is a cinch once you accept Jesus as Savior primarily, as some would lead you to believe to be the case.

The notion is that it's okay that conversion is not to be followed by sanctification daily, or at least tried, but when it's not, it means there's a disconnect!

It makes the method by which all of us should last during the span of such conversion, for all who confess Christ as Savior, somewhat irrelevant. We must contain such actions, and sanctification must remain until its culmination, meaning, *the day we die.* And that does not include us playing God and taking our own life!

That way, that day is not cheapened by such erroneous beliefs, and so the value of salvation will never deflect from the price that was paid on Calvary's cross. Salvation must always be treasured, which is when we are saved according to Scripture (the end of our lives), or of course, if the rapture took place while we live, as it will be the case for many believers on that day.

Nevertheless, when we are saved is expressed without a doubt and in plain view of Scripture, just as Peter puts it in such a resonating way back in the first letter bearing his name,

> This very inheritance is kept in heaven for you, who through faith are shielded by God's power until the coming of the salvation that is ready to be revealed in the last time. [...] For you are receiving the end result of your faith, the salvation of your souls.

> 1 Peter 1:4b-5, 9 (NIV)

One may argue that the first part of verse four as an intricate chance of automatic reasoning to salvation to make a case for the OSAS error (4a [NIV], "and into an inheritance that can never perish, spoil or fade"), but it's the end of the verse that tells us where the keeping takes place. And it says it this way; *this inheritance is kept in heaven for you. Keyword: heaven!* Not earth! Verse five validates this claim that it is through faith that God shields *that* salvation of the believer; Peter keeps speaking about the action of faith. It's *kept through faith.* Faith in what? Faith in God! And adopting a sinful lifestyle after conversion is the opposite of faith in God for any believer who chooses to do so. Faith is a bubble we must always have over us. And when in sin, we no longer have the reality of being faithful to God. Unless you can show me anyone in the Bible living in sin and being right with God simultaneously…I'll be sticking to my guns here.

In essence, it's our faith that keeps us connected to Jesus. The Bible says that even when we are faithless, He remains faithful because He cannot deny Himself. That says who He is, and in no way, shape, or form, it is telling us that we are okay if we are faithless simply because He is faithful. What that verse is telling us is that He remains faithful, and we don't. Faithless is someone who walks away from the faith because when they do, He remains faithful because He cannot deny Himself, so what this is saying is someone denied Him. And we're talking about someone who knew Him as Savior!

That's what being faithful means. Regardless of the circumstances around us, we have made our pledge to Him, period, and we've made up our minds to follow Him always, and that pledge is to follow Him nonstop all of our days. As redundant as this sounds, it is the truth!

Remember that if He is faithful even when we are faithless because He cannot deny Himself (2 Timothy 2:13), it is an attribute to Himself and not us.

We hear the cliché, for lack of a better word, though biblical in nature, that we are saved by grace through faith but never really break down what that means. God's grace is, as Paul puts it, "My grace is sufficient for you" (2 Corinthians 12:9, NIV). This is a word of much depth, one we must dissect. Grace is several different things in the Bible, and that's how sometimes it creates confusion when it isn't addressed as it should be for its intended purpose.

At this level, Jesus is conveying to Paul that in our weaknesses, He remains strong or that He can carry us through something we can't get through on our own. If left alone, we would be lost.

His power never imposes itself in our daily lives; we must volunteer ourselves to Him (Psalm 110:3). So, unless it is through prayer, and to our benefit for that matter, what we call intercession is always predicated upon a need, or miracles if you will.

Whatever the weakness is that may be oppressing us now, He remains strong, period! Our situation does not stress Him one bit; otherwise, free will would not exist. If God mingled in our very lives without an invitation from us, then following Him would be just like going to work…because we must!

Intervention only comes by invitation; never forget that. As believers, we voluntarily yield to God's will, or should, and thus, deny our very own free will.

That's just how it is or should be. That's why Jesus said, with

His back against the wall, "Nevertheless, not My will, but Yours will be done" (Luke 22:42, NKJV), before He was betrayed by Judas as He prepared Himself to die for our sins, and Judas is anyone who betrays the Lord after knowing Him.

I think Jesus made it quite clear when He said that we must deny ourselves to follow Him (Matthew 16:24-25). Just as Hebrews 5:9 (NIV) states, "He became the source of eternal salvation *for all who obey* Him" (emphasis added). And here, the keyword is *obeying,* and *obey* is a present tense verb, an ongoing performance of faithfulness to the believer who chooses God's will over their own free will, and this to their own hurt, *supposedly* for life.

One that immediately takes place after conversion through a learning process of stumbling over one's own two feet as we are desperately trying to learn to walk this Christian walk. A life in Christ isn't easy, perhaps for a season it may be, and enjoy it if so, but also one that we must mature in because no one can remain a baby forever. In due time, growth must be evident in our walks. We cannot continue to drink milk, especially if we have been walking with God for a decade or two. Just saying!

A time of devotion and faithfulness where sin no longer has a hold on an individual who feels strongly about their commitment to Christ is what should be the norm for seasoned believers, and if for some reason *one* may fall, the immediate reaction should be to repent through confession, promptly so. Our reflection in such a fall should result in repentance every single time. We should never go more than four seconds without repenting, and then, well…correct what's broken, or we should always be invested and interested in all its efforts to remain connected to our God, and repentance is reconnection when we miss it. Then restitution should follow repentance in some form, as a fruit of true repentance if genuine, and that's regardless of whether restitution is possible or not. The effort must take precedence.

A faithful walk with the Lord is an ongoing journey of sacrifice for the remainder of one's faith; a walk of intimacy with the Holy Spirit (an encounter with the Holy Spirit) is based on relationship, which is what, in my view, is missing from today's church for the most part. Remember that He will be preparing for Himself a spotless, blameless, and wrinkle-free church before He returns.

Otherwise, without Him, we can open ourselves to stagnation and a source of other stumbling blocks that can lead to a believer getting cold feet or even a disconnect from God altogether. Hebrews 2:1 (NIV) puts it this way: "We must pay the most careful attention, therefore, to what we have heard, so that we do not drift away." The problem we face today, unfortunately, is that so many have already drifted away (not my opinion, but according to Scripture) by embracing eternal security as canon, then walked back into sin, including suicide, due to a lie. They are paying close attention to a demonic doctrine and not to the One who redeemed them.

GROWTH IS PROGRESSIVE!

In essence, OSAS has become their god! I say this because the entire Bible is subject to this erroneous doctrine once embraced, and afterward when the error occurs, every other view of biblical continuity veer in that direction, and once this eternal security doctrine is adopted, a domino effect can be expected of other biblical views as well.

We saw the Pharisees do the same thing when they did not approve of the Messiah God sent them. They thought they knew better than God and simply had Him killed. Their tidal religious perspective became their god!

Just as Hebrews 5:9 does not say, "for all who *obeyed*," but "all who *obey*," it is not as if once you accept Jesus as Savior, you've done all the obeying required for the ongoing faith journey as a prospect. This is the caveat of OSAS; it's all in the name. In the same manner, Hebrews 2:1 says to *pay close attention*, as if speaking to the present at hand. It redirects the attention back to Scripture, sensing that a disconnect is in the works, and that's why the writer of Hebrews attempts to regain our attention by telling us to go beyond paying attention and *pay close attention*. This is not privy information; this is a herald of sorts.

Just like when the teacher is addressing the students on a calm Monday morning on a certain subject, and one or two of them aren't paying attention by drifting away from the moment, perhaps into la-la land, perhaps due to a long weekend and little sleep, and the teacher acknowledges the disconnect through observation of body language or past facts about the students. The teacher, without a doubt, must get their attention back again in order to continue administering to the entire group because that's what teachers do.

Then, the instruction follows once they are mentally back to earth so that a grasp of knowledge can reciprocate in what is taking place at that moment because—guess what—that information will come in handy on test day, and it will come (test day). Indeed, also in Christianity, we have many test days, but unfortunately, the downside of not paying *close attention* is hell bound in essence. The possibility of drifting away, just as the writer of Hebrews suggests, might happen as more than a possibility but rather a fact.

The lack of biblical revelation begs for something better than the watered-down interpretation handed down in Christian academia regarding eternal security, which is a realm where little or nothing has changed in its repetitive doctrine in decades and the like perspectives. Therefore, the controversial and quite uninformed rhetoric it's wrongly performing at unstoppable speeds, heading for the cliffs, if you will, must be redirected, or else?

Here's what Peter tells us in his second letter. At the beginning of verse one, he enlightens such misconceptions as we are finally learning about them for instruction; take a look:

> But there were also false prophets among the people, just
> as there will be false teachers among you. They will se-

cretly introduce destructive heresies, even denying the sovereign Lord who bought them—bringing swift destruction on themselves.

2 Peter 2:1 (NIV)

If I could make a case for what it is that sticks out the most about this verse, if you're an OSAS advocate, you will perhaps say it's the part about the false prophets, and that's how you avoid inter-confrontational error, and you would automatically think of prosperity preachers as false prophets.

Even though it's referring to them as a past tense, "but there were," it does speak of what will be in our midst in the future; today perhaps, and he tells us it will be false teachers, "just as there will be," not false prophets, but false *teachers*, and you know who is always focusing on the false *prophets*? Who else, the false teachers!

We call them distractions! But one of the biggest and saddest realities plaguing today's Christian society is none other than the misconception of doctrinal interpretation of Scripture. Maybe not in a cultic sort of way, but in error!

Especially about our common salvation, and from beginning to end, that's exactly what we're facing today. The many erroneous doctrinal views that are, without a doubt, the main culprits in splitting today's Christian church right in half are certainly the ones to be blamed for such saddening endeavors in today's church settings that ascend in circumspect to biblical fulfillment. As we continue to progress toward the end of the road for the ages, these attributes seemingly disguise themselves as genuine but ultimately, aren't they are expressive way of where we find ourselves as believers in these last days? Once the covers are aggressively pulled away, or another tearing of the veil, if you will, transparency will become relevant even though it has eluded the church for some time now, but for the most part, you can see it in its politics, sort of like when the veil tore in half from top to bottom in the temple while Jesus was being crucified at Golgotha (Matthew 27:51).

The religious leaders knew the Bible like the backs of their hands (literally) but lacked a relationship with the God of the Bible. The Law became their god, as I stated earlier, and the procedure to put the Messiah to death was politically inclined. They felt their cash cow was in jeopardy if Jesus remained alive; they were afraid they would be exposed, therefore killing their Messiah was a must!

The curtain, or veil, was the thing that stood between the Ark and the people in the Old Testament, except that the Ark of the covenant was no longer in the temple, neither was the presence of God, and the tear of the curtain was made from top to bottom to assert it was done by God and not a human, and also to let the priests know that they were no longer needed since access to God was now the result of the crucifixion that simultaneously took place with the veil being torn just as their ministry was. Titles and positions may very well be nice, but without the presence of God, they are no better than toilet paper after it's used! Selah!

Remember, John the Baptist, as well as Jesus, told them that they were hell bound unless they repented, and the obvious was that they didn't. Of course, except perhaps a few, like Nicodemus and Joseph of Arimathea, and this happened after the Pharisees succeeded by dividing the people against Jesus and somehow persuaded them to chant, "Crucify Him, crucify Him" before it was all but over for them, religiously speaking, and they knew what they were doing as greed and pride set in their hearts in abundance.

I'm not surprised at all at the *divisive* spirit that comes with such misguided biblical perceptions, ones that, without a doubt, must be endured but not accepted, like OSAS, if you will, so as to keep the church's composure for the sake of future generations as a solid and sanctified church that Jesus can receive to Himself for a bride.

An evolving Christianity in modern times has its place in history, which may be the last one at the pace we are going as of late. Otherwise, we would all be lost in our sins if we were to accept the error of eternal security and the like since automatic forgiveness does not require confession, let alone repentance!

Modern-day Christianity, which errs in its theology, is responsible for this unprecedented course of action and the disconnect that's heading in the wrong direction for those who have been misguided into such divisive traits. How far do the apples fall from the tree? Not very far!

In addition to that, a concept that has erupted from centuries of generations misled by such misinterpretation of God's Word are views that continue to carry on as the norm in most of today's Christian denominations who embrace the OSAS doctrine, and that is also empty in their directive in spirituality, so to speak. For the most part, they quench any move of the Holy Spirit they cannot control or understand. One that must be redirected toward a better light of biblical truth because they continually find themselves in limbo in any doctrinal predicament of scriptural truth, and unfortunately, it's taking place as we speak, and that's regardless of the many illustrations in Jesus's ministry that they read but don't believe. I'm speaking of the manifestations of demons and the like or any miracles recorded for that matter, which are as spiritual as they come.

Furthermore, such views of contradiction should be stopped as soon as possible, or we should at least try to do so for the simple fact that they do not line up with the true sense of Scripture, its virtue and main intention, as well as its formal meaning. Undoubtedly, they are self-centered to create division among denominations and Christian circles alike. This inclination definitely must be done away with before it's too late.

Views that ought to at least be revisited and promptly corrected by Christian leadership everywhere in Christian academia or should at least be considered, and they also must be aimed at the sustainability of the focus wherever there's reasoning to be re-considered, that's resulting from the error of misinterpretation of Scripture. As it misleads the faithful on such occasions, and since the book of Revelation's message to the end-times church is to *repent,* then there must be a consistency to what I'm suggesting as a solution needed for clarity so that its reasoning can completely line up with such a message of intricate truth. And we must do so before the church slips into a spiritual coma of sorts, or worse yet, ushers us into the long-awaited *Great Apostasy* that appears to be at the threshold of the times as we speak.

This, according to biblical timetables of the end times, is pre-dicted throughout the Bible by eschatological writings!

I'm speaking about the bride *fallen away* from Christ (the Great Apostasy), just as it's foretold in 2 Thessalonians, chapter two, where, unfortunately, the church takes a fall of irreparable proportions that were once predicted by Jesus and the apostles themselves and foretold throughout New Testament literature.

We are talking about a church that forsakes Christ and His teachings altogether. Watch a racial divide enhance such fallen away (Matthew 24:7)! It will be evident in the things that will be accepted as a church community loses its will to implement true Christianity, and the template will be simply forgotten, as the acceptance of vaccines leading to the mark of the beast, as well as the election of liberal politicians in the name of tolerance, equality, and equity, that are relevant to the times of Jesus, and the political circus of that day. By us embracing godless pop culture and the lie that sin is in while ushering the culmination of the end of the ages in a watered-down version of Christianity with little to no conviction, and thus, setting the table for the unavoidable apocalyptic measure of the end times, which are mentioned throughout biblical predictions with eschatological overtones now possible. Ones that even leftist Hollywood producers have warned us about through their artistic creations of motion pictures, though perhaps done indirectly, but that very much fit the bill.

The Great Apostasy is a term that the "once saved, always saved" embracers wish they were right about in its definitive sense of the word according to their views, regarding the ending of all things as we know it.

They take to the belief that the Great Apostasy is for unbelievers alone and not for believers, which strikes me as absurd in its premise, and I find it almost comical if the truth be told. But to take to such a left-fieldish belief system because the *apostasy* means the *fallen away* and to suggest that the *fallen* (the lost) will have fallen away…well, it just makes no sense whatsoever if you ask me!

John MacArthur's commentary on Hebrews 6:4-6 as well as other commentaries in the study Bible, bearing his name, are perfect examples of missing the point when interpreting Scripture and regarding certain doctrines that have been misconstrued by Christian academia over the decades, in that…he is a gem. And they are done so by a lack of personal biblical revelation, which is bent on academic education alone. These submit that knowledge without application is nonessential for Christian living, and although it may be a great idea in a theological spectrum theater of sorts, in reality, the power of God through them never sees the light of day, where it is needed most. Thus, making a manifested surge of error evident, especially when it comes to eternal security. The pages of the Bible are to be taken, where literal, literally, and allegorically, where allegorical. And without revelation, those two are crisscrossed and pointless!

It happens that way in its sequence; nothing contrary to eternal security is ever challenged by themselves or their peers. But to avoid self-contradiction regarding interpretation about salvation as already laid out in Scripture and assert *what* it means to be saved according to an authentic biblical application as well as in its interpretation of appreciation of Scripture is the reason why you are reading this now.

Especially if it's in plain sight. Or if it will stand the possibility of deeming them who have such views of error by the same people who embrace these types of erroneous teachings with little to no accountability foreseen within. Though the entire eternal security doctrine is as wrong as it can be, they will not admit it to themselves for fear of accepting the fact that they are wrong, and just like a drug addict who is the last person to concede to the idea that they have a drug problem, the OSAS subscribers and their leaders actually live under the same umbrella of denial and with the same unrealistic uncertainty of error, but in a more severe reality, no doubt.

Seared in their conscience and deep within their souls lies the error deeply seeded regarding the doctrine about the common salvation of the human soul, and this is not privy information; it is open for all to see and make a conscious choice to eternal relevancy. And as you can see by reading this book, they are the last ones to admit it's done in error, just as I'm laying this out in plain view as you see scripture after scripture telling a story in a different approach to what holiness is and why we must attempt to live in such a way daily.

Let's hope we can change that today by embracing the true meaning of Scripture as intended by the Lord Himself, especially in regard to our common salvation. Take a look at Hebrews 6:5-6 and please get an idea of what Scripture says about salvation in its purest form, not what someone thinks it means:

> For it is impossible for those who were once enlightened, and have tasted the heavenly gift, and have become partakers of the Holy Spirit, and have tasted the good word of God and the powers of the age to come, if they fall away, to renew them again to repentance, since they crucify again for themselves the Son of God, and put Him to an open shame.

> Hebrews 6:4-6 (NKJV)

I think the verses speak for themselves and are, without a doubt, quite clear and to the point, don't you agree? *Enlightenment, taste,* and *partake* are certainly three distinctive and direct actions that take place in verse four, and they require the activity of engagement, and they also identify a need for action or actions, and there's an invitation for participation as well, of course, from a Christian perspective, or a two-way street course of action if you will.

When God enlightens someone with biblical truth, *tasting* is the tangible reality of that enlightenment, which is utilizing the gift given to them by God to the fullest, but for crucial application. This, in return, causes one to believe in the impossible, and our faith expands tremendously by such enlightenment, or the miraculous if you will, which can only be embraced by faith and activated by the Holy Ghost.

It's virtually impossible to receive a miracle while not believing in one (Matthew 13:58). It's like expecting a paycheck without having a job.

That's because unbelief is the opposite of faith, and without faith, it is impossible to please God (Hebrews 11:6). There's the word *impossible* again!

In other words, if you didn't put in the forty hours required for benefits, you will have none; there may be a paycheck at the end of the week, but one without benefits. Benefits don't kick in until you decide to be a *full-time employee,* one fully invested in the company, and after a few months of dedication, you will receive your medical benefits, your pension plan, and any other perks that come with employment benefits offered by the employer. But there are requirements, just like there are requirements in the kingdom of God, except that the benefits don't benefit you any more than they do others.

When God gives gifts to someone, that gift is actually for the benefit of others; remember, Jesus said, "Surely you will quote this proverb to Me: 'Physician, heal Yourself!'" (Luke 4:23, NIV).

I get the fact that there are things in the Bible we can't understand, and there are also some we won't ever understand at all, but that does not mean we should point the lack of understanding toward a misunderstanding because we would be either adding or taking away from God's Word. And that's a no-no!

Enlightenment has to do with the supernatural, something we can't control or see on our own. In other words, an encounter with the Holy Spirit. Not with a preacher, no. An encounter with a preacher or teacher can at best inform us and educate us, biblically speaking, or do the opposite but never supernaturally empower us because they are limited individuals, outside of the laying of the hands, of course.

I remember this as if it was yesterday, back in the late '90s, I was serving time in prison for a series of crimes I committed while a member of the notorious Chicago street gang known as the Latin

Kings; I found myself between a rock and a hard place in the State of Illinois Department of Corrections.

I had quit the gang to embrace the enlightenment of knowing Jesus—I am speaking of the substance of the Gospel—which came to me a few months before being sentenced to twenty-two years in prison (thank God for a praying mother and church family) of which, by the grace of God, I ended up serving only six years. Even after catching an additional case while in prison.

I accepted Jesus as my Savior during the two short months I was out on bail. Nevertheless, things looked very good for me going into trial.

I had three paid lawyers representing me by my side, one of them who was a hotshot, African American, trial lawyer, with a great defense reputation and well connected in the circuit, one that was winning criminal cases left and right. Another one of my lawyers was someone whose father was a judge in the Cook County Jail courthouse itself; he was also a friend of the family, and that gave me the upper hand. My third lawyer used to be the prosecutor in the courtroom I had my trial in. A win-win situation, if you will.

He had shared with me that the judge who presided over my case owed him a huge favor from his former prosecuting days with this judge and that he was willing to ask for that favor on my behalf. Of course, that was music to my ears, as you can imagine.

But on the last days of trial, as a baby Christian, I asked the

Lord to show me what His will was for me, and boy, do I regret asking such a question (of course, I'm joking). I was hoping it was my freedom that His will was for me. I had assured God that no matter what the outcome was, I was ready to serve Him whole-heartedly and that He could trust me if I was found not guilty, but that I was ready to serve Him even if I was found guilty.

God's response was a question; He asked, "Are you guilty?" I answered Him, "Of course, I am!" He replied, "Then why are you trying to prove your innocence?" I paused for a few minutes while I digested such an inclination…*lump in the throat kind of moment.* Then He placed it in my heart to tell the truth and take a guilty plea. But when I shared this with my lawyers, they, of course, advised me against such an irrational decision, but lo and behold, I disagreed with them and took the plea bargain that came with the admission of guilt. I received the minimum for all five felonies, which was better than the maximum, or anything in between, I suppose!

And that chapter of my life was closed. Now, it was onto the big house where, if I can sum up in one word, that word would be *trial,* the real trial.

My spiritual trial began the minute my criminal trial ended in court that day. Someday a biography may be in the works, but for now, this is on my plate.

I waited about a month or so in county jail to be sentenced

after my unexpected guilty plea, and during that time, I ran a few buildings for the Latin Kings street gang. *I carried some juice* (power and influence) for the gang out in the streets, and one of the gang members I was arrested with, who had turned state's evidence against me, met with me in the yard to ask me for mercy. Of course, I could have had his head on a silver platter for violating the Latin Kings code of honor (to snitch on another member).

But I no longer held such convictions and felt that wasn't necessary anymore, and the need for revenge was the last thing on my mind. My conversion to Jesus and what God thought of me recently really did trump all else.

I had two bodyguards back in the unit I was assigned to at the time. It was gut-wrenching to have to run an outfit of common criminals while having the Lord in my heart, convicting me of every single step I took, until one day I couldn't take it anymore, and I asked God for a way out.

I remember sitting on my bunk, reading the Bible in secret late at night, when one of my bodyguards (another gang member) walked in unannounced to ask if I needed anything before lockdown. And he looked at my Bible and said, "I used to be a Christian before," and walked away.

I quickly rushed to the door and asked him to come back in. I confessed to Scotty that night that I no longer wanted to serve the Latin Kings' interests and that I wanted to live as a Christian. I shared with him that I got saved while I was out on bail. He smiled at my report.

Scotty explained to me why he had left the church he once attended, which made me sad; it's a true saying that Christianity is the only army that shoots their wounded.

He had gotten his girlfriend pregnant and was ousted from the church altogether; thus, he returned to the gang's lifestyle. He said it was due to that rejection. Though he was wrong in his actions, I also think the church was wrong in theirs.

He sang a few hymns he knew as our days together progressed. I had accepted Christ a few months earlier, and I didn't know any Christian songs. I still remember the song he sang in our jail cell and the enthusiasm he sang with as well, which was very encouraging.

He sang, "In the name of Jesus, in the name of Jesus, demons will have to flee, in the name of Jesus, in the name of Jesus, we have the victory…" Now that's one of my favorite hymns to this day.

And he also fed my spirit during that last month in Cook County Jail; besides having my back, he instructed me with the little that he knew. Not sure where Scotty is today, but one thing for sure: he was very instrumental during my infancy as a believer and in this journey, and for that, I'm very grateful to both God and Scotty.

GROWTH IS PROGRESSIVE!

I asked God to send people my way that could invest in the infancy of my Christianity, and since I was a baby in the faith, I knew I needed mentorship in any way possible.

The very next day, the man who was calling the shots, or the gang's leader if you will, for the Black P. Stones—a street gang affiliated with the Latin Kings, who were first cousins to the Latin Kings according to street lingo, who were both under the *five-point star* in affiliation, that is, who were called People (our enemies, who were under the six-pointed star, were called Folks, and that's regardless of skin color). Race has no barriers in Chicago street gangs?

In Chicago, you have an array of different gangs of different ethnic groups, but all belong to either the Folks or the People. Skin color is irrelevant in Chicago's thug life, but not gang colors.

Some Arab Latin Kings are called Assyrian Kings, some blacks are Latin Kings, and of course, whites who are Latin Kings are also part of the clique, and the same criteria take place in the Folks who are called Disciples for the most part.

You have Satan's Disciples, Black Gangster Disciples, Spanish Gangster Disciples, and so many other gangs affiliated with the Folks.

Back to the Black People's leader, who happened to be a Black P. Stone, who out of the blue one day, right after chow, got up on top of the table and turned the TV off, then yelled at the top of his lungs, "Listen up, y'all, I'm no longer a Black Stone, I'm a Christian now, and I'm gonna be by my cell reading my Bible. And if anyone has a problem, then bring it; if you try me, remember who I am. If you want trouble, you will find it." He climbed down from the table, and that was it…He quit the gang just like that. Left every single one of us dumbfounded.

Now, guess what was going through my mind?

What I had just witnessed was exactly what I wanted to do, and I imagined that as a way out of the gang, which would have been my answered prayer.

The man who ran the building for the Black People (black gangs under the five points of the star) just quit the gang. *What if the man who runs the building for the Latino People was to do the same?* I thought.

I did not sleep that night and waited until after chow to do a sequel of what had happened the night before. I had a one-on-one meeting with my bodyguard Scotty, and I told him my plan to exit the gang. He suggested I wait till I crossed over to the state prison system first but keep my allegiance to the Latin Kings while in county jail. But I wanted out badly, and what I saw took place with the Black P. Stone leader early that week was all I could think of doing myself.

The following day, I got on the table after chow, turned the TV off, and said, "Listen up, I'm no longer a King, I'm a Christian now, and anyone who has a problem with it, come see me." Then I held a jailhouse knife in my hand to let them know that part of me was still intact. I climbed back down from the table and went about my business.

I began spending time with Tweedy. He was the Black Stone who quit the mob the day before.

After a few days of chaos, Tweedy and I got together to read our Bibles and went to church together. My gang's name was King Cameo, and when word got around, I received a lot of backlashes from the Kings.

Nevertheless, we decided to hold a Bible study, Tweedy and I. It was always a good turnout, and since everyone feared us, every-one came to Bible study.

After a week went by, Tweedy and I announced we were going to have a prayer circle before lockdown every night, and whoever didn't come to the circle would be beaten up the next day when the doors rolled, and as you can imagine, we had a very successful prayer circle in attendance every night. After I left that dorm and went away to prison, it became the Christian dorm in Cook County Jail, and yes, I was part of that ministry though I was still very much a thug of sorts.

Unfortunately, the Latin Kings have a saying that goes, "Once you're a king, you're always a king," and that means death or default to another gang are the only ways out.

Being a high-profile gang leader, I carried some weight in the prison system for the Latin Kings, but I gave all that up to serve the Lord, though it wasn't easy, especially when your people turn on you and turn on you for no other reason than you refusing to run the prison for the gang, which will include the first two attempts at my life from the same gang *I lived for* and nearly died for several times as well since I was fifteen.

The third time my people tried to kill me was the one time that my eyes were opened to God's sovereignty and divine intervention.

I ended up in Menard Correctional Center after catching an additional case while in East Moline, IL. Menard, which is a maximum-security prison, is located at the very bottom of an old stone quarry. I spent months in solitary confinement, and once released, I was locked up twenty-three hours a day, which was not that much different from segregation. It was a fresh start, and I knew no one there.

As I was reading my Bible, and mind you, I was a baby Christian at the time, I came across a scripture that said to love my enemies and do good to those who…well, you know the rest. As I read that, the flapping from what appeared to be someone dragging their shower shoes, which was annoying, was hard to ignore. But as I was reading my Bible, a thought went through my head, *wait a minute, we don't have showers today; why are the shower shoes flapping?* And as I glanced at the walkway between the bars in my cell and the rail guard of the catwalk, the annoying sound was nearing and getting louder. I was bothered by it, and it disrupted my Bible study time.

As the person responsible for my annoyance walked past my jail cell, I remember glancing over with the corner of my eyes, and the man who was perhaps close to seven feet tall was not wearing shower shoes but torn gym shoes. He stopped next door, as the prison guard was way behind him to lead him to his assigned cell.

My next-door neighbor was running the floor for the Black Folks, so obviously, the annoying new giant was of the Folks, and that's when the scripture I'd just read jumped up at me as if it was planned. The Lord was speaking to me to buy this man some new shoes, and I did just that. I didn't know his size, but I bought the biggest pair of shoes in the commissary, and when I went back to the gallery, I went to his cell and asked him to try them on, and they were his size. I felt good inside that I heard from God to do a good thing for a change. The man asked me what I was doing with a pair of shoes that big, and I tried lying to him, but it didn't work, so I told him the truth.

That felt so good that I went to the guy who was running the gallery for the Black Folks and asked him to send me a list of any of his guys that came in on the new and guys that didn't have the essentials, and I began blessing my enemies just as I read in the Word, with cosmetics and personal items to coffee and the infamous Ramen noodle survival kit.

Well, after a few months went by, my good deeds showed up at the Latin Kings' meetings, and if things couldn't get any worse, the guy who ran the prison was sent out to do more time somewhere else for catching another case in the Menard Correctional Center. Now the Latin Kings needed a new leader, and they asked me to take over the prison, and of course, I refused.

A few days later, as I was at the weight pound trying to get a workout, a nineteen-year-old kid who had ninety-five years left to do in prison approached me and said, "We heard you're spending money on the Black Folks. Are you gay or something?" I looked straight at him and told him, "You were there the other day when y'all asked me to run the joint; why would you ask a gay guy to run things?" And he quickly changed his tone. He then said, "Well, why are you spending money on our enemies and not on the brothers?" I simply said, "God told me to, and if you have a problem with it, take it up with God!" Now the weight pound is a crowded place for the short hour we get to do recreation when we get to do recreation. That and the phones in the yard are populous places at that hour, but that day it was just a Latin King from Aurora and me, and that was it…I knew something was wrong and that it was a hit by my people.

He then picked up a twenty-five-pound dumbbell and aimed it at my temple. He was a white guy, and as he swung, aiming for my skull, a hand appeared on his forearm as if someone was holding his arm. No one was there but us, and you could clearly see the imprint of four giant fingers on his skin, and it was evident.

GROWTH IS PROGRESSIVE!

As the dumbbell was a hair away from my temple, he was making pressure on the dumbbell and swinging it my way; you could see the blood vessels pop the more he tried. And since he was making a fist holding the dumbbell, the imprint was obvious. Did I freak out? You darn right I did. But I knew this was God.

After a minute or so went by, he looked behind to see who was holding him down, and obviously, there was no one there except four fat fingers on his forearm. He yelled, "Let me go." Looking back, he saw no one there; he opened his palm and dropped the dumbbell, then asked me in fear, "What was that Cameo [my street name]? What happened? Why is this happening?" The finger marks remained in him for several minutes. I told him: "Look, I'm with God now, I do what He tells me to do, and if they sent you to hit me [kill me] and you failed, you know what awaits you. My advice is to get right with God because your hours are numbered once they see me walk away." I prayed for him and asked him to get right with God before he returned.

A few other guys were at some distance away, holding back the crowd that would otherwise be at the weight pound. Not sure what happened next to the kid, but I have a good idea!

As you can see, it would be impossible for me to ignore the tangible existence of a very real God, and I have a few more supernatural encounters with God because He chose it that way, and to be honest, I'd probably need a thousand pages to boast of how He loves me. Maybe some of you can identify with what I'm saying here regarding our God, but how many Christians know the stories and never had an encounter with the God of the stories? And I don't mean stories as if it were fiction, but the shrewd reality that God is among us to lead and guide us every step of the way, and yes, protect us even if a deadly blow heads in our direction, no matter if it's within an inch of striking distance or a thousand miles away. God can put a stop to that and more just as well. Only obey and believe.

DO WE BELIEVE WHAT WE READ FROM THE BIBLE?

Does the angel of the Lord encamp around them who fear Him?

What do you think? (Of course, he does.) I didn't see an angel, no, but an angel stopped death on my behalf, and I'm okay with that, and perhaps you'll experience something similar as me. You read some of these Bible commentaries that all sound about the same, that also interpret the same scriptures and make the same comments practically throughout the same paths, and all done in redundancy, but deny the fact that God is not secured and locked away in His little box, which infringes His perimeter within the pages of the Bible, but deny the fact that He is right here, right now, working on our behalf every single second of the day. Do I believe the angel of the Lord encamps around them that fear Him? What do you think? Did I not see it take place?

I chose these commentaries to expound on what I'm attempting to convey here because of their popularity. These men have seminaries, and that means many pupils have passed through those biblical institutions.

Now, don't misunderstand me; these men have done great exploits for the faith, but the error of eternity is way too important to ignore, and I'll show you what I mean by it.

There are a few red flags I'd like to address before exploring John MacArthur's interpretation of the following verses. One would be the word *impossible*. Just like what happened to me in prison, and the fact that God is not hindered by impossibilities because they are simply an opportunity for Him to display His power and receive glory for it, and why shouldn't He!

I admire MacArthur for his stance on the COVID-19 shutdown of churches everywhere, especially in his liberal city where he has his church. Kudos, sir!

There isn't a way out of creating a loophole for the word *impossible*. Generally speaking, the word impossible is the wall no one can climb over without God, if you will.

In Hebrews 6:18, the word *impossible* is used to describe the impossibility for God to lie, and thus, tendering the pure interpretation of the word itself is what takes place. Yet, MacArthur focuses on the word *enlightened* to reveal his doctrinal *error* on eternal security while avoiding the obvious in the resolution of his assumption to continue wrongly assessed doctrinal interpretation, and he's not alone in this by any means. By shifting the focus away from the word *impossible*, we can then build a better case for this folly in eternal security. Take a look at this passage beginning with

Hebrews 6:4:

6:4 enlightened. They had received instruction in biblical truth which was accomplished by intellectual perception. Understanding the gospel is not the equivalent of regeneration (cf. 10:26, 32). In John 1:9, it is clear that enlightening is not the equivalent of salvation. Cf. 10:29. *tasted the heavenly gift.* Tasting in the figurative sense in the NT refers to consciously experiencing something (cf. 2:9). The experience might be momentary or continuing. Christ's "tasting" of death (2:9) was obviously momentary and not continuing or permanent. All men experience the goodness of God, but that does not mean they are all saved [...] Many Jews, during the Lord's earthly ministry experienced the blessings from heaven He brought—in healings and deliverance from demons, as well as eating the food He created miraculously (John 6). Whether the gift refers to Christ (cf. John 6:51; 2 Cor. 9:15) or to the Holy Spirit (cf. Acts 2:38, 1 Pet. 1:12), experiencing either one was not the equivalent of salvation (cf. John 16:8; Acts 7:51). *partakers of the Holy Spirit.* [...] Even though the concept of partaking is used in 3:1; 3:14; and 12:28 of a relationship that believers have, the context must be the final determining factor. This context and verses 4-6 seems to preclude a reference to true believers. It could

165

be a reference to their participation, as noted above, in the miraculous ministry of Jesus who was empowered by the Spirit [...] or in the convincing ministry of the Holy Spirit (John 16:18) which obviously can be resisted without experiencing salvation (cf. Acts 7:51).[1]

If we were to take a look at a different Bible commentary from the very same set of scriptures but varying from its theological ideology of an approach and its interpretation altogether, we would be able to see the polarization of both distinctive views in regard to their unique approach to Scripture, this one in particular.

Also, consider *one* of them to be genuine in content, as well as the biblical context in keeping up with Scripture and its true meaning as its intended end so that it makes sense when presented for its value.

Just as intended by the writer of Hebrews, who was of course inspired by the Holy Spirit in its definitive consistency for such biblical teachings, we too feel we were led by God's Holy Spirit. And if so, we would then question the former interpretation on almost every ideological, biblical issue it presents in error in our view as well. When someone is *off* (in error) on the interpretation of Scripture in one area of the Bible, chances are they are "off" in several other doctrines as well, sort of like a rule of thumb, per se. And both schools of thought feel they are spot-on on all counts.

The writer of Hebrews was not focusing on those whom the

Lord or the disciples healed and empowered by the laying of hands, the writer of Hebrews was focusing on those who did the healing and other miracles as portrayed in this particular biblical setting in the first two verses of the chapter.

Partaking of the Holy Spirit has nothing to do with receiving a miracle of any magnitude coming from the Holy Spirit. It's evident that when Jesus healed someone or cast a demon out of them, they were the beneficiaries, not Christ.

Partaking of the Holy Spirit only happens by coming to Christ as a believer and by receiving an anointing to do a particular task for the Lord, i.e., a miracle of some sort. Whether it be healing or casting out demons, this is what we refer to as gifts of the ministry. In other words, this was directed to those who were once enlightened, those who were creating the miracles themselves or were the vessels being used to implement them for the Lord if you will, and by the direction of the Holy Spirit and not themselves.

They are partaking in one of the spiritual gifts given them by God (1 Corinthians 12:10). Those who were healed or delivered by the apostles, who were the recipients of such miracles, make it clear that they did not have the same spiritual power, nor did they have the faith to heal and deliver themselves. Right from the beginning, they were receivers; otherwise, they wouldn't need the disciples and their anointing if they could have accomplished the miraculous for themselves. Makes sense, right?

Their faith was only that of expectation. Having a need and believing in a miracle was all they needed for the manifestation of a miracle in their lives. They believed, period!

The need for a miracle is just as tangible as the miracle itself for that need, and faith and expectation have to be parallel to allow for the manifestation of the impossible to take place in our lives. Otherwise, God will not move on our behalf without faith in Him.

To be clear: without expecting a miracle or not believing in one, you have the exact sentiment of doubt, and doubt will never make room for a miracle, and that would be the equivalent of not having any faith in the impossible. Remember that it only takes a mustard seed of faith to move a mountain!

Jesus rejected the demoniac from following Him after de-livering him from demonic oppression that had taken place only God knows how long (Mark 5:18-19). Someone had to be praying for that man because he was not enlightened with the Gospel, as MacArthur suggests.

The demoniac was shown mercy, which has absolutely nothing to do with the enlightenment of the Gospel, and if he was enlight-ened, he was rejected to follow Jesus closely and rejected by Jesus Himself, and the obvious is that we cannot second-guess Christ's decision to reject this individual for whatever reason He decided to reject him.

In essence, if being enlightened does not pertain to salvation, or regeneration for that matter, how then is tasting of the Holy Spirit something temporary, *unless you make it temporary yourself* and that alone will annul the OSAS doctrine?

Furthermore, do so by rejecting the gift, and most importantly, the Gifter.

Just like Judas and King Saul decided to reject God as they both did by later rejecting their calling, as well as the anointing in their lives, and by forfeiting their position in God's kingdom as two men called by God to do His will. One as a king, and the other as an apostle or disciple.

We know that both were Spirit-filled. Therefore, such admission and the display of their sinful actions in rejecting their calling…is by far the best example we have that you've lost your salvation, just like these two once-upon-a-time anointed men did, who both ended up taking their own lives in the end as proof of God abandoning them because of their sins.

Partaking in something is not a drive-through emotion of the moment; thus, tasting of the Holy Spirit is not something just anyone can attain nonchalantly. Also, the prescribed sequence in which it was said that it took place here leaves no doubt that the writer of Hebrews was addressing someone who was indeed partaking of spiritual power, just like Saul and Judas did.

Someone who was at one point in their walk with God a devout Christian, or someone who was all the way in with the Lord and acting out in the miraculous as bearing fruit as well. Just as Saul and Judas were both, there is absolutely no way that Saul and Judas were never saved since they were both filled with the Holy Spirit, and both performed the impossible while filled with God's Holy Spirit: for God knows how many years (see 1 Samuel 11:6 and Matthew 10:1-15). Yet, both committed suicides. Both were rejected by God. Both were Spirit-filled. In the same way, a Christian can't have the Holy Spirit moving in power one day and plunging to their self-death the next. That is the opposite of going from glory to glory as we should.

Otherwise, people can contend that Judas and Saul were never saved to protect the OSAS's erroneous doctrine, though we read in Scripture that Satan entered Judas while Judas was next to Jesus as He addressed his betrayal at the last supper in front of the rest of the disciples. Somehow, the error leads to Judas as he was never saved, a man that, for three and a half long years, kept the purse for Jesus, cast out demons, preached the Gospel, and healed the sick, just like the other eleven did. And there is absolutely no biblical proof that denies my statement that Judas was saved but only confirms it. To think he was not saved. I mean, Jesus did say that you can only cast out demons by the Holy Spirit (Matthew 12:28) when accused of casting out demons by Beelzebub by the religious fringe, remember?

And what about King Saul, who spoke to a demon by way of the witch of Endor (1 Samuel 28)? A demon who made it clear where Saul would end up the following day, as Saul fell on his sword as he trembled (1 Samuel 3:4) and took his own life on the battlefield in *fear* (Revelation 21:8) of desecration from his enemies. Just like the spirit of an old man that came from the earth had predicted would happen. And this took place after King Saul had been experiencing the fellowship of the Holy Spirit for years (1 Samuel 1:16), and that also once upon a time in his early ministry he did God's bidding because He was endowed by the Holy Ghost for such performances.

It is also clear that they were not only once enlightened by the Gospel's truth but also tasted the heavenly gift; both Judas and Saul were partakers of the Holy Spirit as well. Saul was also among the prophets. Or so we read.

These are three characteristics you can't dismiss as ineffective in being chosen for ministry by the Lord for the simple fact that there were three of them. The writer made sure he pounded that sentiment in its clarity. Thus, making it obvious for the reader to receive what he wanted to convey in his message.

If a person is not saved, they aren't by any means enlightened; they cannot taste any gift of the Holy Spirit outside of our common salvation without receiving Christ, and receiving a miracle is not a spiritual gift but an act of mercy on the part of God, as I stated before.

Maybe if we took a closer look at the things that the writer of Hebrews laid down for us in verse four for our enlightenment, we might be able to exponentially line them up with other scriptures and compare the similarities thereof, dissect them in a better light in contrast to their due reality so that we could make more sense of it all because a holy life is the lifeline of a believer who believes in a holy God.

"It is impossible for those who were once enlightened" (Hebrews 6:4a, NKJV). Compare:

> That the God of our Lord Jesus Christ, the Father of glory, may give you the spirit of wisdom and revelation in the knowledge of Him, the eyes of your understanding being *enlightened;* that you may know what is the hope of his calling, what are the riches of His glory of His inheritance in the saints, and what is the exceeding greatness of His power toward us who believe, according to the working of His mighty power.

> Ephesians 1:17-19 (NKJV), emphasis added

There is no better way to reveal what *enlightenment* means in the Bible than to do it with another set of scriptures that amplify the true meaning of enlightenment.

The qualities of enlightenment and its intentions target the needs predetermined for their solutions, whether spiritual or physical, since both derive from an omniscient perspective prescribed only by God's Holy Spirit, who then redirects the anointing wherever He wants it to rest on—speaking of an individual, of course.

There is absolutely no way God is unaware of whom He should gift when He chooses to do so, spiritually speaking. Otherwise, God would have given the *one* talent individual five talents so that he could bury them all just like he did the one talent he was given.

And we can argue that God gifted King Saul at some point, and yes, He surely did, but Saul was the product of Israel's pop culture's entanglement with the trend of monarchy. They wanted to keep up with their neighbors who surrounded them, who all had kings as rulers, and thus, they wanted their king.

God's filling of King Saul with His Holy Spirit was done because of where Israel was at that point. They are God's chosen people throughout history without a doubt, and up to this point, God had raised for Himself devout Jews who were anointed to lead, as well as to minister to the Lord and His people.

Israel felt that God was no longer enough for them; they wanted flesh (Saul) to be their ruler and not Spirit (God). Thus, as a nation, they rejected the true King of Israel who lived amongst them since the Exodus from Egypt (God).

According to the verses above, the Bible tells us that enlightenment has to do with the hope of our calling, or His calling of us as believers, framed by a life of devotion. It also says that after receiving that calling, we receive His revelation of what the riches of

His glory are all about, which is something for us to look forward to. He dives further into the thought process of enlightenment with meticulous detail, and he also explains how enlightenment is about an inheritance for the saints and that that inheritance is none other than salvation itself.

That salvation does not take place at conversion; conversion is only the portal to the spirit realm, which gives us access to the things of God. Accepting Christ is the initiation of salvation, not the culmination thereof. Accepting Jesus as Savior is leaving Satan behind for a better life in Christ. It's leaving the realm of sin for the realm of worship. In other words, acceptance is only the down payment, and if you stop paying your mortgage, you more than likely will lose your home, right? Likewise, here, if you stop worshipping God (paying homage), you lose your salvation because the further away one gets from God, the closer one is to Satan and sin.

Salvation gives us access to God through prayer, and prayer gives us manipulative power to change a bad situation for the good of others, ourselves, and the kingdom of God (we call it the prayer of the righteous). But the culmination of that salvation is at the end of a faithful journey for us all, or when we die, that is (Hebrews 1:14).

Paul puts it this way as he is about to be beheaded for his faith in Christ, thus fulfilling the Word from the Lord to Ananias regarding Paul's expected end (Acts 9:10-19).

For I am already being poured out as a drink offering, and the time of my departure is at hand. I have fought the good fight, I have finished the race, I have kept the faith. Finally, there is laid out for me a crown of righteousness, which the Lord, the righteous Judge, will give to me on that Day, and not to me only but also all who loved his appearing.

2 Timothy 4:6-8 (NKJV)

"I have kept the faith" is a statement of a ceaseless course of action of faith. Why keep something you cannot lose? The word *finally* comes after he expresses that he has kept the faith.

Paul is about to face his executioner. He speaks about receiving his crown of righteousness; he mentions that we too can receive one if we persist and if we *loved* His (Jesus's) appearing. What Paul means is the inner appearance of Christ in us, of the One who changed who we were, the One that's inside of us (Christlike), and the way we portray such appearing outwardly by imitating God as His dear children in doing His will as much as it is up to us (Ephesians 5:1).

The inheritance of salvation happens as we transition from physical death to spiritual death and inherit such promise when we die and step into eternal life deriving from physical death, just like we went from spiritual death to be alive in the Spirit when we accepted Jesus as Savior. Or, in layman's terms, we are saved when we die (Hebrews 1:14). But unless we view all biblical entries regarding the stage in which the culmination of our faith finally takes place, we will continue to indulge in sin by thinking eternal security is real and biblical. And it's not!

The writer of Hebrews destroys the "once saved, always saved" doctrine in almost every chapter in this letter. Just read the excerpt when salvation takes place as written in Hebrews 9:28: "So Christ was sacrificed once to take away the sins of many; and He will appear a second time, not to bear sin, *but to bring salvation* to those who are waiting for Him" (Hebrews 9:28, NIV; emphasis added).

The clarity of when salvation takes place is missed *internationally* to protect the said erroneous doctrine. And only because of errors. That would be until today because today, you are receiving the truth, not a doctrinal error regarding eternity for all believers.

And as you saw the above scripture in Hebrews 9:28, the culmination of salvation happens at the end of our journey, not at the beginning. Yes, salvation is free, but it'll cost you your life of sin… and that is the exchange for every one of us. Remember, you were bought at a price, and you are not your own (1 Corinthians 6:20).

In 1 Peter 1:4-5, the Bible speaks about the salvation of the saints: it's stored for us in heaven and is to be revealed in *the last days*. The misconception that we obtain salvation at conversion is inaccurate. We obtain access to salvation at conversion, but the culmination happens just like we see in the verses above—at the end of the journey. Otherwise, apostasy would not have had a mention in the Bible.

Sort of like a race: you don't get the trophy at the start. That would be cheating. You get the trophy at the end, after overcoming all the hurdles life throws at you, but the finish line is when we are ready to be poured as a drink offering, just as Paul explains in 2 Timothy, chapter four.

There is a very thin line between the spirit realm and the physical realm, and the spirit realm has two different dimensions of itself. One is in the realm of sin, and one isn't. The realm of sin is a place that God does not dwell in, nor has He ever abided in. God cannot live in a sinful dimension; God can't dwell in sin, but we surely can but shouldn't. Especially as believers. We're perhaps the only part of His creation who can experience both realms, though not simultaneously, but we can.

If we sin, we automatically enter a dimension unknown to God, that's why we are encouraged to confess that sin immediately, and Satan is the god of that dimension. He knows that once upon a time we lived there with him too, before we met Christ as Savior, and now that we return there, as we adopt a sinful lifestyle after knowing and walking with Jesus for some time, the devil's craftiness will make you think you're still saved. And shame and condemnation await just to create confusion and separation from God, which translates into spiritual death.

Satan will allow you to attend church and act "saved," but as soon as you walk out of that service, the Word you just received will be stolen by Satan, just in case you were thinking of getting right with God, as it stated in the parable of the Sower (Matthew 13). Satan rules the realm of sin, not us. When we confess our sin, God hears, "Help!" and gets us out of that mess.

We become completely vulnerable when in sin, and living in sin is a place of darkness that manipulates anyone's frame of thinking to the likes of confusion. Remember that light and darkness never abide together.

The Bible talks about us being the light of the world (Matthew 5:14), and Jesus said that we are a lamp and that we shouldn't keep it under the bed, but on a table, and visible. The Bible also calls God the Father of lights (James 1:17), and we are supposed to be a guide to the blind, a light to those who are in darkness (Romans 2:19). We were called out of darkness into His marvelous light (1 Peter 2:9b), and the way we came out of that darkness was by confessing our past sins (1 Corinthians 18:11) and not our future sins because future sins do not exist (Hebrews 3:15). Therefore, there is no need to forgive what is not yet a reality; what is a reality, though, is the fact that we are identified as the light from God, the Father of lights, not the father of lies!

Think of it this way: God, the Father of lights, lives in the third heaven as stated by Paul, and He watches the earth where His lights (us) are shining in a dark and perverse world. You and I are to shine or should be shining for the world to see (2 Chronicles 16:9). And when we fall into sin, our light turns off, we then enter the realm of sin as discussed earlier, and He no longer sees us until we plug ourselves back in, and that's only by way of confession (1 John 1:9).

Picture for a moment, if you will, God in heaven watching you from His heavenly window. You walk into a motel after you've planned for some time to have an illicit encounter with perhaps a coworker, or maybe another Christian from church, whom by the way, you have no business being with because you're not married to them, and you allow yourself to get to a place where conviction is no longer active inside of you, but rather the desire to sin due to temptation's takeover, which is now in the driver's seat. Since you have been texting back and forth to that effect, and for some time now, and let's not forget planning such an event takes two because affairs aren't easy for believers, and the truth is they sound stressful, to begin with, what you are now facing is without doubt predisposed. It has become a goal of yours and theirs, and that's sex outside of God's will, and it was planned by you both by an idea of the enemy and your own desires, as James puts it.

Once we are engaged in a sinful act, our light goes completely out. (It's not "flee to sexual immorality," it's "flee *from* sexual immorality" [1 Corinthians 6:16]). At that point, God can no longer see us; the Holy Spirit leaves immediately. If you don't believe me, I'll prove it to you with Scripture to help you understand that God does not see anyone who is in sin, and the reason being because their light goes out due to that particular sin, and we know God cannot see sin or saints who decide to be sinners, for that matter!

We can understand this from Scripture since the Bible's entire message of discouraging sinfulness is evident. No better picture to paint than that of Jesus at the cross when He took on the sin of all humanity. Jesus said to the Father, "*My God, My God, why have You forsaken Me?*" (Matthew 27:46b, NKJV). God could no longer see Jesus as He bore our sins. And if Jesus felt forsaken, what do you suppose will happen to you and me if we decide to die in our sin? It's clear that Jesus went to hell for that sin, and it will be the exact same for us, though Judas was an apostle and, of course, once a believer in Christ and then as a deceived by Satan.

In Judas's case, where God rejected his repentance for obvious reasons and to show us the thin line between sin and righteousness as a model of what could happen if we are not careful, is a reality because we know he tried repenting but could no longer find repentance within himself (Matthew 27:3).

Jesus died immediately thereafter, which means He went to hell because sin was set upon Him to be consistent with Scripture. Our sin, not His sin. And that tells us that if we die in our sin, we too will immediately end up in hell just like Jesus did (Matthew 12:40). He was able to break free from hell and death because He was sinless on His own, but we won't be able to because we will be bearing our unconfessed sin if we happened to die, let's just say in the act of sexual immorality category, which is the church's biggest issue today.

I know many preachers love to teach the all-inclusive, "nothing can separate us from the love of God" cliché of a half-truth, as they make it a cliché themselves, but the real verse reads differently, "who," not "what," "shall separate us from the love of Christ" (Romans 8:35a, NKJV). The *who* is us, we, ourselves. The same individual who can confess Jesus as Savior is the same individual who can embrace a lifestyle of sin thereafter, and the lie that they were never saved only insults the Holy Spirit's work even more, as it suggests that the Holy Spirit was not active in a, perhaps, pastor who, after twenty-plus years pastoring a megachurch, decided to sleep around with his sheep (church members), after Bible college and decades of ministry. And to suggest he was never saved would be some amazing deceitful traits in such an individual, and I wonder if the scores of people he led to the Lord over the years are even genuine converts and truly saved since he was never saved according to the lies of the OSAS doctrine that applies only to others and not themselves. That's not an example; this happened to a pastor in Florida, actually!

Romans chapter eight ends by saying that *all the things mentioned in context* cannot separate us *from the love of God that is in Christ Jesus, our Lord.* But that's a statement of who Jesus is to us, not a statement of who we are to ourselves, or to Him for that matter!

The example of the pastor above is a real story of a real pastor who put into practice such atrocities and much more, and he was an OSAS enthusiast. My question is: Can you really spend four-plus years in Bible college, get married, start a family, then begin a church with a handful of people and watch it grow over the decades through many sacrifices, go from a few members, and grow to close to thirty thousand members, and one day decide you want to have sex with the women in your church, and he also frequented prostitutes thereafter? Suggesting that person is still saved while doing all that sinfulness, or suggesting he was never saved is not only as preposterous as the former, but it annuls Romans 10:13 in expressing *whosoever* in that verse by cheapening the saving power of God's Holy Spirit. Is Revelation 21:8 not clear in what is the outcome of the adulterer?

Furthermore, that pastor should not be allowed anywhere near a pulpit until he has humbled himself and not before confessing his sin and after going through the process of restoration as if he was a new convert.

I don't think Revelation 21:8 meant unsaved adulterers only, and to my knowledge, all adulterers are unsaved, but what do I know…right? Sexual sin is the only sin that is sinning against one's own body (1 Corinthians 6:18). We saw it in King David's affair with Bathsheba, where the prophet told David that the Lord was going to spare his life, which meant that that was going to be his punishment in the first place, but instead, God said his son's life was going to cost David his sin's consequence for that sin. Not to mention the rest of the friction he put his children through for that particular act of rebellion (2 Samuel 12).

The light goes out!

Remember when Adam and Eve sinned in the Garden, and God came through asking Adam where he was? Why would an all-knowing God ask someone where they are?

The answer is He cannot see a sinner who once was a saint due to that sin, which brings separation from God every single time we sin.

There is overwhelming evidence in the first incident of the fall of man back in the Garden of Eden, where it tells us that from the very beginning, God could not see sin or sinners, if you will. God walked in the Garden, asking Adam where he was (Genesis 3:9). God can hear a sinner because He gives us a chance to confess and repent from our sins. Remember that "Out of the abundance of the heart his mouth speaks" (Luke 6:45, NKJV). But in Genesis 2:21, God performed surgery on Adam, which means He was that close to His creation. There was no sin as of yet, but as soon as sin entered into the first humans, the relationship between God and men was severed thanks to sin.

Adam and Eve chose to play the blaming game after getting caught with their hands in the cookie jar, and that's not confession, that's, well, the blame game, and that's exactly what got them kicked out of the Garden indefinitely. Had they confessed their sin and repented immediately, they could have perhaps changed things a little since God no longer trusted them with the other tree, the tree of life. Then, they would have eaten from it and lived forever. Imagine that, eternal life for sinners?

Expelling from the presence of God is the consequence of unconfessed sin. It only means "we might want to remain in sin" as the only possibility for not confessing what we know is wicked, which includes a man after God's own heart!

Furthermore, are you ready for this? Sin did not originate in the garden of Eden, no! Sin originated in heaven, the same heaven you and I are trying to someday end up in; that's the same heaven where sin began. That is the truth about sin, and that heavenly sin by Lucifer was *pride* (Luke 10:18 and Revelation 12:12).

We are not sure what led to sin in heaven but are told in Scripture it was pride, but a third of the angels were also ousted from heaven for believing Lucifer's lie of a takeover; he was a liar from the beginning. The question remains: What happened in heaven?

But here on earth, something happens to us the moment we sin. One of those things is the Holy Spirit leaving our bodies thanks to that sin, and the longer we go without confessing that certain sin, the deeper we go into that realm of sin, which is unknown to God, and we then live without the Holy Spirit until we repent.

The light that once was is not, and God can no longer see those two individuals in that motel room, engaging in sexual immorality, and what follows that illicit affair is despair and separation from God; shame and condemnation follow, and sadly, at times divorce, or worse, spousal abuse, even into a fatality. What once illuminated a community no longer does, although God knows where we are always. God, who has better GPS than Google, like Google without a signal, can't see you either, He too can't see our location until the signal returns, and that's what we call confession.

Either we die to sin, or we die to Spirit! And don't think for a moment that going to church means you're okay with God just by attending. Imagine if churches weren't allowed to open, it could happen, or it will, at some point. So, church attendance does not make you saved. If being in the ocean does not make you a fish, I hardly believe being in the church will make you a Christian. A churchgoer, maybe, but that's it.

Just think about a sin you struggled with in the past and how hard it was to overcome. You have perhaps called it a bad habit or something cute like a pet sin, and as you very well know, bad habits are hard to break!

But when we ignore the spirit realm as believers, we become more vulnerable to sin and its clutches and perhaps prone to it if we go on without confessing them indefinitely. Though we quote Scripture where demons talked to people, like in Acts 19:15 (NKJV), "Jesus I know, and Paul I know; but who are you?" And we honestly have no idea what that even means, and as we become desensitized to our former reality of sanctification, it definitely

185

does play a huge role in how we view the subject of sin.

We know it's real because we read it in the Bible, but do we believe it? How many Christians do you know that have had the opportunity to testify of casting out a demon from someone who was possessed by a demon(s)?

Or how many Christians do you know who have been part of miraculous healing? The answer should at least be one! Or are you around a pastor who prays for healing and begins with the words, "God, if it's Your will..."? I think God's will is laid out perfectly, loud and clear in Mark (16:16-18), so if you ever hear a prayer that begins with those words, then you're in the presence of a power-less individual, and prayer without expectation means that prayer is DOA!

Can you imagine if the devil asked for permission to entice two individuals to engage in an out-of-God's-will sexual extravaganza and end by asking for permission to cause an abortion to take place if a pregnancy resulted from such a sinful practice?

Sounds ridiculous, right?

Well, so does asking God if it's okay for Him to perform His will. Do we not remember the catchy biblical phrase, "Your will be done on earth as it is in heaven" (Matthew 6:10, NKJV)? I don't think there are sick people in heaven, do you?

Now that we have covered what being enlightened is, that's

not a word pretty much defaced by MacArthur's commentary but rather an exponential eye-opener for us to see, and that's to see what God sees as it should be. But we also need to look at the word *partake* and inspect its true meaning and application thereof.

- "…and have become partakers of the Holy Spirit" (4b).

Here are some definitions of what, *to partake* is: (1) participate, (2) receive, (3) nature or character of something. But my favorite would be Ephesians 5:1. And you cannot partake of something you have no access to; otherwise, it would be cheating or stealing. Did not someone anger the disciples for thinking the Holy Spirit can be bought? (Acts 8:20).

- "Therefore, holy brethren, partakers of the heavenly calling" (Hebrews 3:1a, NKJV).

There is no introduction needed to explain what a partaker is, it is most obvious that when someone is a partaker of the gifts of God, they are without a doubt saved and sanctified, and the gifts remain even after the Holy Spirit leaves, but they are no longer anointed. In other words, God does not validate them anymore. Pots without water, if you will.

Furthermore, partaking in the Holy Spirit only happens by a true relationship with Jesus Christ and way past the initial conversion. This means that the writer of Hebrews was making a bold statement that it is impossible to renew someone who knew the truth, worked in the truth, lived in the truth, tasted the truth, then walked away from the truth and embraced a lie and a lifestyle of sin, not just a fall, but a fall away, or perpetual falling.

That's what the writer of Hebrews was conveying to us through the first half of the letter, and to think someone else can write about the same thing and see completely different reasoning is beyond me. Take a look:

(Hebrews 6:4-6)

Christians can backslide, tear down the foundation of repentance that is already laid. Should they ever again be admitted into the church, they will have to build again the foundation of repentance and do their first works again (v 1-2; 2:1-4; Rev. 2:5).

Christians can fully apostatize from Christ, completely reject Him and His atoning work, so that is impossible to renew them again to repentance (v 4:9; 10;26-29; 2nd Peter 2:20-22).[2]

I have to agree with Mr. Dake's interpretation because apostasy is the epitome of a believer forsaking Christ and not only embracing a lifestyle of sin but denying who paid for their sins once upon a time. Furthermore, its doctrinal application in OSAS, for the most part, has been repro, from revelation dating back to decades into the 1930s to 1950s at best.

This leaves us with the unfortunate notion that there is no real *evolutionary* approach to any type of new revelation from a limitless God. A God who renews our mercies every single morning as He reveals Himself to us daily and in countless ways shapes or not of forms that are beyond our comprehension as intellects.

Yet, by a single dash of a revelation of God's will, it suddenly becomes a game changer delivered in a whole new light and done so for our edification as His children and for our personal growth, which is beyond the scope of reality as we know it.

That revelation continues to speak to us today in more ways than ever before, but if we were only to ask God for it to be revealed. It would be a game changer, no doubt, if we were only mindful to pay close attention and listen to what God is trying to say to us through His amazing Word. We would get far more things accomplished when it comes to ushering the Lord's inevitable return if we were only to hold onto the unadulterated truth of the Word of God, which should without a doubt be our main focus as believers. As for the redundant stagnancy of such watered-down theological misrepresentations as OSAS and its erroneous misconception of prophecy that continues to spawn out of focus from the lie of eternal security, it's quite evident that it's accomplishing little to nothing when it comes to unity in the body of Christ, as well as its standards for the most part, which have veered into the wrong direction as of late and for some time now. Unfortunately, those standards are getting worse as we progress toward the end times, which are knocking on the door, even now, just as it's talked about in eschatological Scripture regarding the Great Apostasy.

You can see the evident similarities of at least 80 percent of all Bible commentaries in the past fifty years, and it makes one question why do we need so much of the same over and over again? Also, this erroneous interpretation of Scripture, which is by far the main issue we face today as believers, time and time again has prompted a decline of unity in the body of Christ, but also it has been negatively effective in personal spiritual growth over the decades on in, and wherever this is taught, OSAS, and without a doubt has shaped the body's inner warfare in its divisive intent in the name of doctrine. It's done by content not endorsed in true biblical revelation, and concluding that the "once saved always saved" theology has created scores of demonic oppression where taught since it refuses to teach confession and repentance after conversion and look no further than suicide as, in my view, the worst example of error.

In my view, that's the biggest issue I have regarding this doctrine and the faith we know, which should be an oxymoron of a statement, but it isn't. Being that *suicide* in the body of Christ is one of the biggest issues we face today since the Bible tells us in Deuteronomy to choose life, and the OSAS base isn't trying to save those people killing themselves, who essentially chose death in the name of eternal security!

All the churches who teach about eternal security do not see it because spirituality is not welcome in their midst, one they cannot control. Under the flag of "we do not want to attract any attention away from the Holy Spirit," they are translated as, "We are powerless and are afraid we might look stupid if things were to get out of control, and we'd have no idea what to do then." That is the reality we live in because if you never enter spiritual warfare, you'll never have to fight the demons who oppress us!

You have never heard of a single deliverance from demonic oppression taking place in their services or miraculous healing by the laying of the hands. That's because they don't understand the Holy Spirit because they are satisfied with knowing Jesus, and not the God who was left behind by the Son of God to convict us of sin and empower us to bring life onto others who don't know God as Savior, Deliverer, Provider, or Healer (Luke 10:18-19).

These doctrines have been characterized in error throughout the last century and have gone ignored for the most part because pretty much nothing has been fulfilled biblically until now, and unless premeditated (?) and done so by scholar after scholar, which is mind-boggling by itself. It makes it almost hard to blame the pupils in their midst because these issues were perpetrated by a lack of personal encounters with the God of creation; there was plenty of Bible knowledge, very little revelation, and a lack of personal relationship. Not many preachers are looking for prophecies to come to pass perhaps since these various commentaries began circulating and making their way into Christian academia, as they have been propagated there, as well as in bookstores everywhere you can think of, not to mention the online availability of materials that have shaped what we know today as the "once saved, always saved" indoctrination fringe.

Perhaps because of the centrality in the OSAS doctrine that denies the existence of the spirit realm but in deeds, not in admission! One that pivots pretty much the rest of all other misguided doctrines that follow circumspectly, but that's for another time and another book. And they are prospectively waltzed in conjunction with the chief misconception that eternal security is, and thus, it leads to the same wrong direction, and just like a snowball effect, they take their place in aligning themselves in error, one after the other like clockwork.

Doctrines that are unchecked themselves are passed as the norm, though they're far from it, such as women in ministry, tithing, blasphemy of the Holy Spirit, and the Sabbath, just to name a few, but many others as well. Believe me: it's a hot mess in today's church circles when it comes to doctrine and its constant resurgence.

Usually, when *one* is off in interpretation in one doctrine, chances are *one* is off on several others, as is the case in the centrality of such doctrine as OSAS.

Not only that, but it also has so many believers numbed to the idea of the church's false sense of unity and has done so by creating an elitist (I'm better than you) individual whose framework looks down on those who do not fit their agenda, agree with them in their perspective, or fall into their criteria of what they deem to be faith. Unfortunately, humility as a whole takes a hit because of the selfish embrace of church elitism, and that's devastating in today's Christian culture because there are a lot of good people out there that have been deceived by such negative religious beliefs and are convinced in indoctrination, who also refuse to hear the voice of reason!

A perfect example is a man whom I met through a popular social media outlet, who is a believer, of course, and as our social media friendship grew, we decided to meet on one of my visits to California. That time I went to do a taping at Almavision TV network. And we met in an attempt to escalate the friendship.

After my taping, we got together for lunch. Everything was fine until sometime after we met as I was scrolling down the newsfeed, I saw him at the Azusa Street Revival centennial celebration, which happened several months later after we had met. As I was scrolling down the newsfeed, there he was, and he was posting live videos about how this was not the Holy Spirit moving in this event. He was asking the audience who jumped right into the live feed and told this man to leave because their Spirit also sensed it wasn't of God, imagine that?

He was, of course, not used to any of this, coming from a church that has a cut-and-dry program of half-hour worship, the usual five-minute announcements, and topped off by the proverbial twenty-minute teaching. Perhaps because of the several services at his church, but you get my drift, and that's okay. But to attend an event with the sole purpose of demonizing it for selfish gain due to spiritual shallowness because that's exactly what it was, and not understand the church's historical Azusa Street Revival's heritage and what it meant to the many who attended then, especially those who traveled across the country to attend this event and did so just to be part of history once again, as well as their desire to see yet another Holy Ghost explosion because God knows we so desperately need one, and I'm sure you can agree as well, but to attend with impure intentions is what worried me!

How sad it is to know someone who has no spiritual power or any idea of how it works who goes to an event just to make himself the would-be hero to the rest of the spiritually anemic and uninformed.

A man who had the guts to enter a place he deemed as *empty in spirituality w*hen in reality the circumspect of his biblical views of expression are as divisive from his part and as unconvincing as these views are. Not to mention that it was the other way around, from not only this individual's point of view but also the many who have been indoctrinated by such hate toward a spirituality unknown to them as well. And one taught in their circles.

The confusion he caused in my inbox was phenomenal, as well as creepy, as many brothers and sisters were asking if the revival was authentic or not, especially the babes in Christ!

What a disservice to Christianity this was, especially to truth seekers abroad, and also when conveying the message of real biblical interpretation—when it comes to the subject of eternity—it's as far off from the reservation as it can possibly be. A total miss of the mark.

As you just read above on the lengths some people are willing to go through when sympathizing with the erroneous doctrine of OSAS, and simply because they have been indoctrinated to the core, it makes one wonder why the division we face today as believers is as prevalent as it is?

Now imagine what else can be happening out there in such Christian circles because of biblical error. The only hero in Christianity is Jesus Christ, not someone who can enter an event that is clearly above his spiritual pay grade, and that's an understatement, to show up solely to wrongly criticize the event for sheer misconception and the ignorance of spirituality, or for personal attention for that matter, and perhaps the proverbial Facebook likes. For the most part, this error continues with no end in sight, and it's growing each day that passes by; this is just another example of adding more hate through spiritual prejudice that is happening every single day, equal to that of the Pharisees of old, but within the body itself, which is the worst part in my personal view of things!

HOW BAD IS THE PROBLEM?

Jesus said that *a bad tree bears bad fruit*, and the issue is like an out-of-control avalanche moving down a mountain at unstoppable speeds. Unfortunately, as you very well know, avalanches have only one thing in mind, and that's to devastate whatever gets in their way, thus, unleashing discordant rhetoric of sorts that needs to be curved at once and curved before it's too late for the body of Christ in its divisive overtones, especially for the many believers already caught up in this web of deceptive indoctrination.

I pray they receive insight before it is too late; I really do (Mark 3:24).

Overall, doctrine is by far the number one cause of division in today's Christian denominations, and in my desperate attempt of pointing out its origins, of where it's going to raise a red flag, making it quite evident wherever you look. But for the most part, we can see the eventful evidence taking place in almost every social media outlet you can think of, just as I explained in the Facebook story in the previous chapter.

You can actually sense a split taking place in the faith, getting close because of these false core beliefs and an indoctrination of the masses, which is at hand even now, beliefs that are constantly paraded through social media day in and day out, and to think that these beliefs originate in their pulpits! Things that are being taught in most churches all over the spectrum that evidently show up in these social media outlets as a result of indoctrination, at times making idols of these teachers, and rather than promoting unity, a division is a draconian of a caveat instead, and perhaps unintentional. This is due to this faulty belief system of erroneous indoctrination, as well as other beliefs that err in conjunction with such beliefs.

An axiom that couples itself together and is aligned in a divisive nature of doctrinal misconception with an overwhelming alliance. "How bad is it?" you may ask. Well, keep reading! Such misconception has misguided way too many believers in "the blind leading the blind" turn of events that's exactly how Jesus experienced as well the error of the then biblical contemporaries of His times, who were fixed on the idea of eternal security as well, and all to find out they were utterly wrong about such misconceptions, as Jesus explained to them over and over again how they had it so wrong for so long (Matthew 21:43).

Contemporaries that today are unfortunately misleading the masses outside of the gates as well, and thus, becoming a curse that's no longer invisible (Hebrews 6:8) for the last-day church, and just as it was predicted in Scripture to usher in the end of the ages where the light goes out in masses, it is a feat that is looking more and more like a reality in today's church circles.

HOW BAD IS THE PROBLEM?

Instead of launching the net into the deep for fresh souls, those of them that are on the boat who are indoctrinated as well are jumping off the boat and drowning for lack of sanctification, mainly those who take the way out in suicide, but that's thanks to the false sense of eternal security being taught. They dive into their sinful demise and catapult themselves directly to judgment, and some of the blame should find its way back to these teachers who advocate the OSAS lie of indoctrination, which makes suicide attractive, rather than hope in Christ for a better day tomorrow.

Perhaps in ignorance, perhaps a plan of the enemy. Who knows, really, but the bottom line is this: it's happening now, and it needs to be stopped, or at the very least, be addressed!

The disconnect is very real, and what's worse is that most division comes from an erroneous doctrinal interpretation of Scripture from people who've learned it at Bible school, or other Christian academic establishments, who then turned around, taught others, and practiced for themselves the same error that they learned in their past academic experiences.

An error that has over the decades recycled itself circumspectly and overall has invited a spirit of division as that of a doomsday invasion that continues to grow stronger as the days go by. And just as biblical misinformation continues to be presented by such contemporaries, and as the conversation continues to progressively resume as the same, such rhetoric is uttered in these divisive circles of the OSAS academic realm with no end in sight. For the most part, this belief system will remain unchanged unless true revelation gets implemented, or maybe the Lord will make something happen along the lines of awakening to unite the body at last, though as painful as it may be, needful it is.

The curriculum of such erroneous belief systems has adopted a false interpretation of Scripture as their basic teachings in every academic endeavor regulated as normal, but are far from it, and thus, the necessity to begin a much-needed revolution of a new and fresh revelation is prescribed in a *revivallution* of biblical correctness that is a must to enhance that which is what's wrong with this picture. This undoubtedly leads more people to repentance, just as it's intended in the opening chapters of the book of Revelation and its clear message to the churches, which is to repent. I know it sounds redundant, but so did the seven letters to the churches, and then we can fervently line up with the call of repentance taught by Jesus when addressing the seven churches, as it was one of biblical and spiritual balance. And again, wasn't the message to the seven churches of Revelation to *repent?*

Sadly, that's our reality today as a body of believers; it seems as if culture is running game on us, and error continues to curb any spiritual growth within the body of Christ, which is very unfortunate, to say the least. We can see the moral decline of today's church circles as a common thing. A decline that, whenever we look at the surrealistic state of Christianity, especially when it comes to church leadership, is found in want. And when we tend to search for a deep path for answers as part of the solution to repercussions we embrace as the church, answers are nowhere to be found or are unsatisfactory at best, and its light is progressively dimming like that of the five foolish virgins of old, which Jesus mentioned in Matthew, twenty-five, in the infamous parable of the ten virgins, as exactly what we expect as our day nears, thus putting a hold on spiritual sustainability in record numbers.

This division flows from error, an error that allows for the belittling of those who disagree with the theological pedigree in the Bible beltway, that in my personal opinion is irresponsible on the part of the educators of that particular sect, who have pushed such doctrines onto their pupils and beyond, and as they continue to do so today, judging those who don't act as they do, which makes it somewhat prejudiced (spiritually speaking) if the truth be told. This is nothing short of ridiculous, and those who disagree with them are viewed in most cases as second-class citizens. We can continue to ignore the real issue in Christianity if we like, but if we do, who then can be saved, and who then can stay saved?

Core beliefs are very important in our faith, especially in the church's overall fundamental values. While some may believe that one can lose one's salvation due to a newly adopted and extremely sinful lifestyle after conversion, unfortunately, others believe that eternal security is pretty much sinch, and according to them and their emissaries, whose core beliefs suggest that simply by coming to Christ as believers in principle is the way that seals the deal, and it's passed down as a *gimme* with low to no accountability whatsoever, and it's exactly what is wrong with having such core beliefs.

There are extremists on both sides of the coin, but when you advocate for the enemy, suggesting suicide is a sin God can forgive is suggesting an atrocity not found in Scripture.

I often ask God why they push such a fallacy, and in my frustration, I sometimes have to find whatever hope possible to shed some light on the subject. Remember that bad habits are hard to break, and this one is no different.

I keep telling myself, "Help is on the way," and in order to keep hope alive, I have to stay focused, but not without feeling the despair of finding out that another Christian has taken their own life. It happens every day, and whether I hear about it or not, I know it takes place even though I'm not in the loop of each attempt.

May God awaken the individuals responsible for such events of despair and traumatic conjunctions. We are not perfect, I get that part, but if Christ is the hope of glory, I happen to think it's for those who want to live for Him. I really do!

If the church is going to hit revival, it must develop soon because I see the hand of the enemy advancing on all fronts. We must do our best to counterattack the enemy's tactics by being proactive and united in one spirit.

Therefore, it comes down to this: Do we believe the Bible and its eschatological predictions, or do we not? If we do, and we should, then we need to prepare to live what we believe. If not, life will go on as it does, and unfortunately, we may have to learn the hard way, and that's living on the outside looking in. Salvation has its place in such decisions no matter what side of the coin you land on.

The first letter from Peter plainly explains the journey of salvation for believers. Furthermore, when it is that we are saved; take a look:

> whom having not seen you love [Jesus]. Though now you do not see Him, yet believing, you rejoice with joy inexpressible and full of glory, receiving the end of your faith—the salvation of your souls.

1 Peter 1:8-9 (NKJV), emphasis and brackets added

Peter was not speaking of himself and the other apostles here. They walked with Jesus, so the obvious is he was speaking to us, today's Christians, and since they saw the Lord, he was not addressing that day's believers either. And our salvation is not attained by confessing Christ as Savior alone, but that it's initiated at that start-up point, and we obtain salvation at the end of our faith journey, which is when we die, and only if we die in Christ.

The premise that we are completely saved and sealed at conversion by the Holy Spirit is untrue. There is not a one-time filling of the Spirit; the Bible is quite clear about that. Otherwise, we could continue to sin and not worry about a thing, pretty much "no harm, no foul," and confession is irrelevant then, which is the lie

OSAS tells those who commit suicide and eventually end up lost and in hell, and that is my biggest concern in that regard.

When someone commits suicide, they are tempted by the devil, just as Jesus was tempted by the devil to commit suicide in the wilderness experience. If Jesus made it clear that suicide is tempting God, what makes you think that has changed?

Death by suicide ends every relationship with friends and loved ones; it also ends our relationship with God, and that relationship is one of growth; therefore, death kills any opportunity for growth, especially when speaking of sanctification or spiritual growth. And it is pretty much how OSAS followers perceive Christianity to be, "Don't worry about it, you're covered by the blood of Jesus." And you are, but only if you confess your sins, that is!

They center their erroneous beliefs on one or two verses that were not speaking to the church of today, perhaps to the disciples or to the church of that day in general.

Jesus said, "I am the way," which means the journey. He also said, "Behold, I stand at the door and knock" (Revelation 3:20, NKJV). If we let Him in, we will enjoy His presence, but if we deliberately sin, or better yet, if we plan our sin and embrace a sinful lifestyle after conversion, He has to leave our presence because light and darkness cannot abide together!

But don't take my word for it, take Peter's:

to an inheritance incorruptible and undefiled and that does not fade away, reserved in heaven for you, who are kept by the power of God through faith for a salvation ready to be revealed in the last days.

1 Peter 1:4-5 (NKJV)

Allow me to break down these verses to see them clearer, and the disclaimer is there is no disclaimer:

- *to an inheritance*: This is something someone gets, with or without having anything to do with getting it, and simply being named in the inheritance, or a will, qualifies them to receive it. In this case, it is salvation. And Jesus left it for anyone who will confess His name after repenting. The repenting part is conditional because John, chapter one, says it is.

- *incorruptible and undefiled*: Though these words are self-explanatory, I feel a need to explain them all over again. *Incorruptible* is something that only God can demand from us; if we attempt to corrupt this format administered by God's Holy Spirit, we lose! Ananias and Sapphira are perfect examples of an attempt to corrupt something that cannot be corrupted without God's intervention. And if you're not convinced, we also have a Simon the Sorcerer's case who wanted to buy the anointing to heal, or Saul who went to ask a witch to talk to God on his behalf. It didn't end well for any of these people, and don't think for a moment it will not end that way for you as well if we pull a fast one as they did. And *undefiled* is the very nature of God; we can't accept that God who only asks us to confess our sins when we fall short so that we can be reconciled to Him for no other reason than that of stopping the enemy from infiltrating what Jesus has made holy and defiling it all over again by flooding us with the enticement of sin, a sin that cannot be embraced by a holy God, has no place in such state.

- *that does not fade away* (because it's God's): Just think how long it took God to bring to fruition a prophecy born in Genesis 3:15 during the fall of men. Though it took a long time, it did not fade away. Snakes crawl, women have excruciating birth pains, and well, brother, sister, you're probably at work reading this book. I'm sure you get the point.

- *reserved in heaven for you:* The reservation is in heaven, and it has to be filled. Right now, it depends on our obedience to His expectations, and if we (and at times we will fail) confess our sin, then the next step is repentance, and these are what keeps that reservation afloat. We have to get there because we have the ticket to get in, and we require transportation, and Jesus is clear which train leads to downtown paradise and which one leads away from it and into outer darkness.

- *who is kept by the power of God:* This is a no-brainer? If we are kept because we want to be kept, we are kept because He can keep us, and if He says we are kept, it's because there is a downside to keeping something, and that's keeping what we think it's worth keeping, and if we want to be kept, then how is being kept done?

- *through faith*: Aren't we convinced yet that we are saved by grace through faith? It is *impossible* to please God without faith, we are told, and that's because faith is the prerequisite that it takes to keep pace with God. The entire Bible is built on such faith of the most amazing miracles ever recorded, but it was said by the Lord that greater things than these we should do. One only can read about God's amazing power, but do we not know faith will guide us away from the accounts Jesus warned us about in Matthew, chapter twenty-four, and without fear of the unexpected?

- *for a salvation ready to be revealed in the last days:* This tells us when salvation is revealed, not when it was acquired, but whether it's speaking of the end of the age or the end of a believer's journey, it makes no difference. We must keep our eyes on Jesus throughout our entire journey, but if it's personal, then this verse says we will get a warning that we are checking out so that we are not caught by surprise. "The thief," Jesus says, "will come at an hour you didn't expect" (Revelation 3:3, paraphrased).

There is no way possible that Jesus will be in your bedroom if you were in bed with someone you're not married to, someone you have no business being in bed with. Remember that light and darkness cannot abide together. Therefore, it will be Satan who will be in the room with you and the other, or others, who are there with you, which is what's inside anyone who sleeps around. I'm referring to soul ties! But if you were to decide to continue in such a sinful lifestyle after knowing the truth, then you've lost your salvation, and if you were to die as such, you would be doomed and hellhound, guaranteed!

When we are saved, our names are written in the Lamb's book of life, but if we walk away from Christ, due to a *lifestyle* of sin, then they are erased, "He who overcomes […] I will not blot out his name from the [Lamb's] Book of Life" (Revelation 3:5, NKJV). The word *blot out* means *erase*. Yes, our names can be written in at conversion, but this is Jesus speaking about erasing names in the book of Revelation, and He is referring to them that do not overcome or that fall away (apostates). Too many preachers teach the false sense of eternal security that hangs on the premise of one scripture, and that's, "and no one can snatch them out of My Father's hands" (John 10:29, NKJV). But they never bothered taking a look at the fact that losing one's salvation isn't predetermined on getting snatched out of God's hands but falling off of God's hands rather or jumping out, and it's done voluntarily!

It's not like Scripture didn't submit such possibilities. Take a look for yourself: "But the ones on the rock are those who, when they hear, receive the word with joy; and these have no root, who believe for a while and in time of temptation fall away" (Luke 8:13, NKJV).

Nowhere in this verse is their salvation put into question by Jesus, but it's their sanctification that is the problem. *Fall away* means apostasy; we cannot minimize what Jesus was conveying to us in the name of protecting erroneous doctrine. We know James said that when we are tempted, we are tempted by our own evil desires, and that means that the devil simply supplies such temptations according to our liking. Or how about this one: "Let no one deceive you by any means; for that day will not come unless the falling away comes first" (2 Thessalonians 2:3, NKJV).

Again, there is nothing here that even hints to snatch anyone away, but the clarity of falling away is truthfully executed. We don't have a problem with people getting saved; we have a problem with people staying saved!

Here is yet another reminder of the fallout:

> For it is impossible for those who were once enlightened [saved] and have tasted the heavenly gift [The Holy Spirit], and have become partakers of the Holy Spirit [the anointing], and have tasted the good word of God and the powers of the age to come, *if they fall away,* to renew them again to repentance.
>
> Hebrews 6:4-6 (NKJV), emphasis and brackets added

Talk about clarity!

The misconception of hanging an erroneous doctrine on the premise of no one having the power of *snatching* a believer out of God's hands completely ignores the fact that no one forces you or snatches you into His hand in the first place, and therefore, makes it impersonal when speaking of snatching someone out of God's hands when in reality, it's very personal since it took accepting Christ as Savior by the leading of the Holy Spirit. And it will take accepting whatever the enemy is offering to snatch yourself away from God's hands.

Therefore, just as the Holy Spirit led you to Christ and into the hands of God, so will the devil lead you out of the hands of God, and not by snatching you out of His hands but by voluntary participation. Or, as the Bible calls it, "the falling away." Not convinced yet? Take a look:

> You, therefore, beloved [speaking to the saved], since you know *this beforehand*, beware lest you also fall from your own steadfastness [loss of salvation], being led away with the error of the wicked [which is sin].
>
> 2 Peter 3:17 (NKJV), emphasis and brackets added

This is a biblical conclusion that addresses the downward spiral condition of anyone who walks away and should exemplify the willingness of falling from grace, but rather than making *the*

210

snatching away a means to ignore an educated guess to fall away from God's hand as a personal choice, jumping out a third-story window is a feat of volunteerism when you are alone in the room, and unfortunately for them that made that decision, they have lost their salvation, at least for that time, and that's if God does not turn away from them, as we read in chapter six of Hebrews.

Furthermore, an entire Bible is negating such contradictory beliefs and actions, and perhaps an inevitable *rain on their parade feat* of sorts, and since making the snatching out of God's hand part of their central biblical view which the OSAS erroneous doctrine hangs their entire theology on, and has done so for far too long, it's time someone called them out.

But who's wrong and who's right about this most controversial and divisive endeavor of both truth and error?

A controversy that's splitting the church of the Lord Jesus Christ right in half brings about such disruptive ways, ways that have gone ignored for far too long by Christian academia, that for the most part, and perhaps in an elusive justification of sorts, suggests that sanctification and holiness are unnecessary once the initial confession is made unto salvation in Christ and that simply by confessing Christ initially as Savior pretty much does the job completely for the rest of the journey. And that, my friends, is the dilemma!

Though Jesus made it clear that only "he who endures till the end will be saved" (Matthew 10:22, NKJV), it's scriptures like this one that OSAS followers often quote in their all-too-common cliché, "That's taking Scripture out of context!" and there we are, back to square one once again!

A perfect example would be how Islam and Christianity both believe in similar eschatological signs to some extent: eternal security, as well as the loss of salvation, per se. Though only one of them can be right, of course, the other must be wrong without a doubt. The Mahdi, an individual who is also the same character as the Antichrist of Christianity according to Scripture, is a shrewd reality in both known faiths, but the question is, will both Mahdi, Islamic and Christianity, fulfill themselves simultaneously in the same character, which is a phenomenon of itself? These two-in-one characters fulfill two different religious roles in the same *individual* as a prophecy that is awaiting fulfillment to end all things as we know it, and that will soon take place, again, according to Scripture. It is said that the Mahdi will offer Islam to Christianity and Judaism, and if they accept, they will be spared, and if not, they will be killed.

This event lies at the threshold of fruition. To Islam, the twelfth Imam is their returning messiah, or the Mahdi, if you will. To Christians (not including Catholics), he is the Antichrist (1 John 4:3 and 2 John 1:7). "How so?" you may ask. "How can the same character produce the fulfillment of both religious faith's prophetic prognostications simultaneously?"

HOW BAD IS THE PROBLEM?

The answer is quite simple: by *deception*!

Islam is a religion that got its origins from the infamous prophet Muhammad, his vision and his interaction with an angel of some sort, as explained according to Islamic tradition.

I, for one, would put into question what kind of angel it was that Muhammad had an encounter with, perhaps a fallen one? Also, the mere fact that God would send an angel to a man whose last wife was but a child (Aisha, the daughter of Abu Bakr) who was six years old when she married Muhammad and eight or nine when the marriage was consummated (that's pedophilia in any century), according to most Islamic historians, that's the belief they pass onto new converts, would at least make such claims of this angelic visitation very suspicious, to say the least. Nevertheless, opening a Pandora's box of the insatiable practices of child brides of today's Iran and other Muslim nations worldwide is a sad reality because of this tragic event of Muhammad's misguided preferences of his last wife, who was but a child. This child had to undoubtedly endure traumatic events kids are not fashioned for. Then or now. Things that are considered criminal in western societies, at least for now, but only God knows what liberalism has in store for the innocent. Not to mention the other radical, problematic Muslim nations under the same sharia law of deceptive practices that places these small children at risk as well, and in so many other nations.

Females in particular because of the child bride practices taking place, and these are all religious practices found in the Quran, as practiced by the prophet himself and practiced by Islamists from all over the world, publicly and secretly, perhaps except for America's Muslims.

Not only are they putting children at risk, as I said before, but to have the audacity to insist that God has signed off on this most outrageous and criminal behavior of a belief system is preposterous and insidious in any light. Practices that unfortunately and gradually continue to gain support by liberal politicians who savor the idea of legalizing pedophilia in exchange for power, just as it happened in the EU. Even if it meant the destruction of innocence just to make a buck (or billions) since child pornography would be legal when this happens and would rack in the big bucks more so than now, and that is desired by the Washington leftists that one day might get their wish in an Islamic takeover of the world, and when it does take place as progressives yearn for communism in the US as their utopia, we will face the times Christ referred to as the *never before times*. For whatever reason, they are open to accepting pedophilia and perhaps making it legal soon. But this revelation to Muhammad came way after the Old and New Testaments were completely written, which makes Islam just another religion after the death and resurrection of Christ.

And the simple fact that it devalues the already formatted pattern of God's Word as established by Jesus to the Jews and Gentiles alike is what allows us to conclude that Islam is another false religion to add to the collection of AD would-be-faith systems. I am undoubtedly suggesting that the angel's encounter with the prophet was but an actual encounter with a demon instead; that's the only expression of truth viewed under the filter of a biblical stance. Like it or not, it's a fact, and that's because of sanctification requirements in such a high-profile position of a prophet as it is in any religion. Wasn't Warren Jeffs a prophet? Therefore, the laws that govern are culpable in their design. Imagine what perversion can come from a one-sided leftist government?

Especially after Jesus made it clear that if we *cause a little one to sin, it would be better to tie a rope around our neck with a millstone attached to it and thrown then into the sea*, rather than to cause a child to sin, in which sex with one would be the culprit of such deserving outcome of a biblical punishment (Matthew 18:6).

The radical Muslim who may very well be a suicide bomber in the making since youth and groomed to do just that due to tradition and instilled hatred for infidels and the belief that it's an honor killing—that alone justifies his actions, per se, and the training that gets underway, perhaps since childhood, will undoubtedly develop this Muslim into the kind of monster we see during acts of terror every single day they're implemented around the Middle East and some here in America as well. As the case was during the Obama administration, where we saw terrorist attacks every year of his presidency on American soil.

Perhaps suicide bombers do such acts of violence because of sheer ignorance of Scripture on their part, to say the least, but when carrying out an assignment of such devastation, they do so…

simply because of *illiteracy* of God's Word, like I said before, and altogether out of ignorance of the truth, and definitely because of a lack of love for humanity as a whole. Though they see it in a different way, it remains wrong.

We as believers have a huge responsibility in getting the Gospel out to these lost individuals in these Middle East, war-torn countries. They do such things as suicide bombings because they don't find it morally wrong to kill infidels because to them this is the norm, and that alone justifies their actions, but normality that suggests killing those who disagree with their religious views is pretty much all we need to know to deem such a religion as false, as radical Islam is.

Although the outcome is always the same for a suicide bomber...to them, the duplicity in the act of fidelity is no doubt an act of heroism on their part, as well as an act of worship to Allah, their god, as an act of war on the infidels prescribed as the norm.

Of course, as wrong as it may be, and that's the case every single time this depredation of truth takes place in their midst and their mindsets, the bottom line is that these individuals have mistaken death and devastation for worship and fidelity as a parallel.

Though being wrong as it may be, it's what they know, it's what they breathe, and it's what they live and die for, and it's because their conscious has been *seared* with the notion of an erroneous religious belief system, one that's conjectured and seared with

216

a hot iron of falsehood.

Who knows how long they've had this insidious belief system of solecism?

One thing is for sure: it's wrong, and there is no debating that sentiment from a realistic biblical view!

Its erratum may very well be obvious to us all, but to them…to them is part of their worship to their god, sadly, but true, and this devastation continues every time we turn on the ten o'clock news regarding the Middle East and its unfortunate ongoing civil wars. As more terror attacks on Israel, as well as among themselves and others continue, these attacks that appear to be without end, until the end that is, will continue to bring a takeover of Islam by fear-mongering, which is consistent with Jesus's view of terror and fear predicted in Matthew, chapter twenty-four.

In the case of *eternal security,* the similarity also presents itself in plain view when regarding the *searing* of the mind. It has been translated repeatedly but religiously speaking, though it condemns suicide bombers, not only does it embrace suicide within its own perimeters, but it also suggests it indirectly. And it's time to embrace the truth for a change. After all, isn't that what we are after?

HOW AND WHERE DOES DECEPTION FIND ITS ROOTS?

Deception begins taking place by ill interpretation of Scripture, and most of us in our infancy will fall for anything anyone sounding deep will tell us, just like radical Islam does in their midst. But this time, this time in sorts of spiritual sciolism of beliefs, a theorem that suggests that suicide is okay with God as "all things doctrine" hang in the error of eternal security.

This makes room for indoctrination in the worst kind of way! Galatians 3:13 (NKJV) tells us that "cursed is everyone who hangs on a tree." And those who commit suicide by way of hanging put on such a curse for themselves in the act alone. But are there other ways to be cursed as well?

One belief system takes the approach of what I call "Samson's curse." Samson's curse derives from taking one's life for the sake of heroism and also a way to make amends for perhaps an infraction of great design or an array of infractions that this course of action, which derived from a lifestyle of rebellion, would be the only alternative for the restoring of the individual's reputation back to a society of faith and perhaps in right standing with God as well, as was the case with Samson, but done in the act of war for all the right reasons. A curse because once you die, what does it matter what people may think of you?

In Judges 16:28-31, we see Samson's intentions for ending his life totally opposite to that of what Saul and Judas did to end theirs, which were also suicides and raise questions of intent. Suicide in the OSAS sect is an entirely different story. I call it the "Judas–Saul effect."

Two individuals with personal knowledge of God. Two individuals with spiritual power from God. And two individuals who defaulted from the faith in a similar fashion and walked away from God. Who once had a personal relationship with God, without a doubt, and let's not forget that Judas talked with Him for three and a half years until his betrayal?

When a believer, who wants out of this race we call life, finds justification through some spiritual authority whom they love and trust, it makes much more sense to them in taking the proverbial plunge because of validation. And since the assurance is attained by such unveiling of error via a trusted source, this belief system of sorts conducts itself into the intellect of the individual that is driven by audible repetitive and erroneous doctrinal antidotes that are conducive to that effect and that usually come after they have already been struggling with suicidal thoughts in the first place. And I'm sure depression and the error of OSAS validate and indirectly encourage such actions. "Salvation is of the Jews," said

Jesus (John 4:22b, NKJV), which meant the Jews had salvation locked in; therefore, they were heaven-bound no matter what. At least, that's what we get from Scripture. But because of that assurance, the Jews made salvation a common thing; then they lost it by literally killing their own Messiah after shaming Him in an execrable way and perhaps devalued His life by not understanding what was in front of them, as they had no clue to what He was saying to them. We see it in John 8:22 (NKJV), take a look: "So the Jews said, 'Will He kill Himself, because He says, "Where I go you cannot come"?'"

The Jews were heaven-bound, salvation was for the Jews, as we saw in John 4:22, and that's why the Jews thought Jesus was saying He would commit suicide because suicide is a sure ticket to hell, and they did not think He was one of them though they called Him Teacher and thought they had eternal security on lockdown. They were suggesting Jesus was going to hell because of the ultimate consequences of suicide. Oh, He did go to hell all right, but to preach to the spirits in prison (1 Peter 3:19) and to bring out of Abraham's bosom every Old Testament believer whom He has translated into heaven the minute He arrived in the lower depths of the earth (Ephesians 4:8).

Therefore, the constant and unimaginable download of negativity into the recipient being tempted to commit suicide births simultaneous *hate through error*, combined with contempt of self, and at times the supremacy of sorts, thus creating confusion and self-righteousness that is now evaluated by erroneous misconceptions of Scripture. And once it begins advocating the implementation of spiritual separation from God, it now dictates a command to the one thing only God should control, and that's life and death. The aftermath is never addressed when told he or she is right with God, even if he or she kills himself or herself.

Then, the belittling of those who disagree with them coevally insists it's a righteous decision to plunge into suicide mode and out of God's will in an instant. They validate this inalienable behavior of someone who needs the entire opposite for survival of what they're contemplating doing in wanting out of this world and out of it by their means to exit. Though it happens gradually…it happens! And usually unnoticed by the conferrer!

This takes place when an individual continues to hear something repeatedly, time and time and again, all the time, and unfortunately, hears it from a most trusted source of religious esprit de corps: their pastor!

This pastor repeats what he has learned over the years in seminary or Bible college. Then, as this pastor begins feeding his sheep with this erroneous rhetoric, something begins to form, and once the domino effect is set up, it begins to run its course, especially when these things are spoken from the pulpit, a place we all take very seriously, or should.

The individual who wants out of life is living in spiritual confusion because I guarantee you God is trying to reach them, and for whatever reason, they are numb to His voice, and once they begin to feel a false sense of peace and security instilled by men who they trust that relationship with God masquerades itself as a righteous decision that's coerced by biblical error and no longer in holiness. Though the reality of this falsehood is quite the opposite if the truth be told, the thought of suicide is what implements this false peace that this trusted source has validated by way of errone-ous biblical interpretation.

I remember once having a conversation with a young man in my youth group back when I was a youth pastor in the Chicagoland area, where I began my ministry as perhaps most of us do, as youth workers. I felt as if this kid's life was in the trench-es. Me being street-smart because I came from the very streets he was now in, and the same gang as well, is what gave me intuition about this young fella and what felt as if he were at wit's end. Well, it was right on the money, so I pulled him to the side the night in question and had a heart-to-heart with him; of course, he denied any concerns on his part. But since I was in those shoes before, I was able to remain prayerful about it.

He was a very handsome young man and very popular in the youth group, as well as the streets, and it's obvious those things are almost impossible to overcome when involved in a gang. Lo and behold, after youth service, this young man was involved in a shooting that led to a murder late that night.

When I heard the news, all I could think of was telling him

how life in a gang can change overnight and the overwhelming void it will leave in his mother's heart, his siblings, and the church community as well. And that's exactly what happened.

But when I went to see him in county jail a few days later, the first thing he told me was, "You were right, pastor Al, you were right!" As he sobbed on the other side of the thick plexiglass that divided our last conversation, it broke my heart to see him there. It brought back memories as well. I myself had only been out of prison a few years, but I knew he had an opportunity to stay free and simply passed on it.

After our visit, as I was leaving the county jail, I ran into an old friend from the streets; he was now a doctor and lived out in Indiana, where he practiced medicine.

He told me he was visiting a colleague who was locked up for kidnapping his children; this was way before the Amber Alert's days. And he asked why I was there. I told him I went to see a kid from my youth group, and he looked at me funny and said, "You're a Christian?" Then he laughed hysterically because we were both growing up in the same gang, and well, he knew my reputation as a gang leader. Not to mention him being a doctor was just as absurd as me being in ministry, but we were who we were, and now we are who we are, and that's what counts, and that we made it out of the neighborhood alive is all that matters.

But he then, in a stern voice, said, "Don't waste your time, there is no God," and added he was writing a book on the subject of disproving God's existence. Obviously, not only was I stunned, but I was at a loss for words as well.

In my confusion, I softly asked, "What do you mean?"

He boldly began to quote Scripture; he knew his stuff, and I am not lying: he almost convinced me there is no God. Simply because of the way he spoke and because he was Word wise and educated, then somehow, I began praying in the spirit silently, and I said to him, "Here you are, visiting a friend in Cook County Jail, and the county jail is full of criminals, and there is no God? Tony," I said, "if there is no God, then there is no devil, and if there is no devil, then, by that premise alone, there is no evil, and if there is no evil, then why are Cook County Jail buildings full of criminals?"

We were standing across the street from the new construction of an annex to the county jail, which was underway, I believe it was the third division to house women, and we were debating the existence of evil.

I said, "Brother, let me pray for you, and if God doesn't show up, I'll believe what you believe." I had to get his attention somehow, and pushing God against the corner, figuratively speaking, seemed to be the only alternative I could think of at that moment.

He agreed, and I began laying hands on my friend. I felt the presence of God immediately, and boy did I need to feel that. I think even more so than my friend!

After I prayed, he settled down some; he looked me right in the eye and said, "I was a Christian too, but I walked away because my brother committed suicide. His wife was a Christian, and she always bothered him with her I'm-better-than-you nonsense, and nothing he ever did was good enough.

"One day, he felt he had enough and jumped from a ten-story building he was selling on the market. He was a successful commercial realtor. He left a suicide note expressing his love for us all and apologizing to his kids."

I was stunned when I heard that, but I replied, "Brother, you don't express your love for your kids by jumping out of the rooftop of a ten-floor building. Brother, that wasn't love; that was an act of cowardness. Love doesn't make you leave your loved ones behind, especially kids. Love makes you want to see your kids grow up, not grow up without you."

Before I could get a word out, he said, "It happened on my birthday!" Tears rolled down from his eyes, and I choked up quickly as well. I was searching for words when he continued, "You know what happened on my next birthday?"

I honestly didn't even want to ask…but I did, "What happened?"

"My sister, who has been a Christian her entire life, who had been battling cancer, decided to cut her veins and end everything because she wanted to be with Jesus since she couldn't handle her pain anymore, and I know she is not with Jesus, and neither is my brother, and her pastor told her she could go to heaven even if she killed herself, and that is a lie, and that's why there is no God. That's why I will prove to the world God isn't real!" he said in a loud voice.

Now, how do you comfort or say anything positive about such catastrophic events in a man's life? What do you tell a man who connects the deaths of his only siblings to a nonexistent God?

I thought I was there to see a young man who refused to take heed to a life-changing decision a few nights before. It turned out I was there to encourage a friend from doing the very thing he was blaming God for.

I said, "Brother, there is nothing I can say that will change what happened to your brother and sister. What I do know is that all of us are tempted to commit suicide because Jesus was tempted to commit suicide!"

He said, "He was?"

"Yes!" I replied. "One of the temptations was when the devil took Jesus to the highest point of the temple and asked Him to jump, saying that God would send angels to catch Him, but Jesus said that *we should not tempt God*! God won't stop a person from taking their own life any more than He won't stop a person from taking another person's life. We have choices, and, you know we made some really bad choices running the streets, and no one forced us, and we cannot go around blaming God for what we should be accountable for. Well, does suicide run in your family?" I asked.

"Yes! My mom's dad and two of his brothers committed suicide."

"Well, it's time to end that curse because your nephews and nieces will end up in the same steps, and I think your love for them should empower you to make sure they don't end up in the same predicament as their parents. By the way, millions of people must deal with cancer, millions of people have to deal with mean spouses, but punishing the rest of your family for how things in life turn out to be, taking your life, isn't the answer. Your brother's wife is probably still mean—"

"She is," he said.

"Your sister's death did not cure cancer...did it?"

"No!" He said.

"Look, God loves you, and deep down inside, you know He does, but He is not going to knock the pen out of your hand to not write this book, no more than He didn't knock the *apple* out of Eve's hand."

He smiled and said, "You're right!"

I prayed for him one last time at his request, and all I can remember from both prayers was that I said that before he crossed the Indiana–Illinois state line, He would have an encounter with God once again.

He never followed through with the book; I guess our conversation had something to do with it.

And it not only seems that life's struggles and adding bad teaching to them can cause a person to do the unimaginable but that the root of the result comes from the searing of the mind, and that's why this book is so important for today's Christian, so make sure you tell your friends about it. Heck, tell your enemies too! The searing of the mind can set you up for the continual error of religion. Perhaps even suicide!

Let's examine 1 Timothy, chapter four, and try and understand how the searing of the mind forms in a person's mindset, just as I presented the two views earlier on (radical Islam and OSAS).

According to Scripture, this is what that means; take a look:

> Now the Spirit expressly says that in latter times some will depart from the faith, giving heed to deceiving spirits and doctrines of demons, speaking lies in hypocrisy, having their own conscience *seared* with a hot iron.
>
> 1 Timothy 4:1-2 (NKJV), emphasis added

Misusing the pulpit for the sake of doctrine is something I totally disagree with and quite frankly despise overall on a very personal level.

It forces the entire Bible to fit a progressive erroneous view of Scripture that has been handed down through decades of watered-down beliefs in Christian academia, as well as in local churches everywhere, and that's not preaching the Gospel as intended by God. A Gospel of power by a sanctified and sacrificial life cannot end in suicide; it just can't. God's Gospel is a choose-life Gospel.

Verse one begins by undoubtedly placing a revelatory expression of the Holy Spirit, not man, as an emphasis on who is to be our guide and source regarding all biblical things, as well as spiritual. It is a statement of certainty of what the expectation will be from the Spirit's revelation standpoint, right onto the believer and the defaulted individual as well.

There's no missing the point here unless, of course, you purposely want to.

He (the Spirit, not the writer) makes a statement of when this account would begin to take place, in this case, it relates to the *latter times*, or the end times if you will, which leaves Islam out of the picture due to its commencement in AD 600, and the *action* that would take place when it does happen is, "some will depart from the faith." But OSAS must abrogate this statement to preserve its abrupt biblical error, clearly. If the Holy Spirit says that in the last days, people are leaving the faith, we need to not second-guess God or God's Word on this issue, for that matter.

This foretells the condition of the last-day church more than anything, and it's undeniably, vividly being played out in today's Christian society, making it noticeable that something bad is taking place, and it doesn't look good, not at all. This is about us! The obvious would be that if you're not in the faith, you cannot depart from it; that would be impossible, absurd, and incoherent of its own, and that's not conventional wisdom; that's the shrewd reality. But OSAS simply writes off anyone who walks away from Christ, as "They were never saved."

Just like they proclaim Judas was never saved, though he was given the power to heal and cast out demons just like the other eleven disciples did (Matthew 10:10). The argument that the Spirit wasn't given holds no water whatsoever, we know from Scripture that John the Baptist was filled with the Holy Ghost from his mother's womb, as she had been filled with the Spirit herself simultaneously when she was in the presence of Mary, who was caring the Messiah within her (Luke 1:15).

Also, we know from Scripture that Jesus was accused of casting out demons by Satan (Beelzebub), and Jesus reassured them that the casting out of demons can only be done by the influential power of the Holy Spirit (Matthew 12:28).

In any case, this concept of eternal security cheapens salvation and minimizes its true intention, to say the least!

Suggesting people aren't saved when they walk away from God and into the open arms of sin is suggesting God is not good enough, powerful enough, or worthy enough for people to hang around Him, with a believer as if in an unattractive journey of undesired expected ends that deny His existence as a need and not a mere want, as if God is a common commodity that can be measured!

I think that's pretty simple, don't you? OSAS also suggests that departing from the faith dates back to some dispensational period sometime in AD 70, which means that the "fallen away," or the Great Apostasy, is not a real account since one cannot lose one's salvation.

This error is more or less to circle the wagon around a subject they cannot comprehend or contain, and thus, they avoid confrontation regarding eternal security. A plain and perpetual error!

Or that apostasy pertains to the unsaved according to some, but the unsaved are not bound by the Word of God. They are in darkness even as you're reading this book. Therefore, the unsaved are not affected by the promises of God but are afflicted by His premises instead (John 3:18b), and since they are out of God's will, there is no directive on them unless they repent, well, other than repenting.

To say that the unchurched must obey the biblical standards we're called to abide by as believers is preposterous and disingenuous of itself. They are not part of the kingdom of God at this point, or His covenant for that matter, until conversion. Thus, not bound by kingdom rules.

It's like saying you bought a ticket going downtown on a downtown train and expecting to get to your destination, but without ever getting on the train itself, thinking that it can still get you downtown won't get you there on time simply because you've purchased a ticket for this train. There are some prerequisites to make it to the said destination in this moving train, and that's if you opt to get on it and stay on it until you reach your desired destination, which is the end of the line.

The conductor simply instructs you on how to get there but will not leave his position to physically place you on the train itself. You must do the heavy lifting all on your own, even if the ticket was a gift to you.

Though Jesus said, "For My yoke is easy and My burden is light" (Matthew 11:30, NKJV), there's still a yoke, and there's still a burden.

The announcement is made of the train's departure and destination, the estimated time of arrival, and once we are on the train, every single stop after boarding is announced (in the same way God warns us throughout our walk) to keep us informed of where we are always, and to help us get to where we're going is what the train's main objective is all about. It's done by updating us of its progress and nearness to our final destination (by eschatological writings).

We are discouraged from doing certain things that could impede the process of making our final destination a probability, like leaving the train prematurely before the last stop. It's possible to fall on a moving train because of its unpredictable speeds and sudden stops. A great number of things can take place on that moving train itself, and it's almost certain they will, but regardless of the accounts that might go on while you're on it, you know that the train has a responsibility to get you to your final destination, and the only way to get there is by you staying on a moving train, and also if you abide by the train's rules as well. Then, and only then, can you accomplish your goal and reach your final destination, which is downtown (heaven).

If you happened to get off, let's just say, one stop before the downtown stop, and then decided to walk the rest of the way, being that you're so close to your final destination, then you're no longer under the jurisdiction of the conductor because you *willingly* opted out of your final destination and disconnected completely with your means of transportation for a journey you were well aware of in great detail. You've defaulted and decided to get there on your own. And if you're going to use the ninety-nine sheep analogy, do remember the one-hundredth sheep comes back on a stretcher!

Yes, you came really close but fell short, and just like how you made a choice to get on…getting off was a choice as well.

At this stage of the journey, the journey did not matter much to you, and obviously, neither did the destination. Or perhaps you thought you could get there by your means (self-sufficiency), and simply because you once were on the train, you may have thought that that was the caveat. Perhaps you met someone on the train who enticed you to get off (Matthew 13:30). Maybe you saw something through the window that was worth exploring, apparently worth jumping off for.

But rest assured, that train will make it downtown with or without you because that train has other passengers that are determined about getting downtown as their final destination. In poor words, *a free ticket to downtown was offered*, and you simply decided to *depart* from the moving train and did so willingly. Yes, you got on the train, but somehow you decided to get off before reaching your final destination, and to deny that you were once on the train is to deny the truth. Just like denying a saved person was never saved because they are no longer walking with Jesus, and that's because they left the train too! Jesus tells them, "I never knew you," because their names were blotted out, meaning there is no record of you even though you answer, "Did I not cast demons out in Your name?" Leaving Jesus for Satan comes with a price!

It's imperative for us to remain focused on the truth and reality of life's most essential details. Jesus said, "But he who endures to the end will be saved" (Matthew 10:22b, NKJV). There is no reward before that.

It takes faith and dedication, courage and loyalty, patience and submission, and so many more spiritual fruits and attributes to reach downtown goals, and faith is by far the most important of them all.

The reality of *departing* means "to take off from point A to point B." Leaving the trajectory between points is an unwise decision, one we must live with, perhaps for all eternity. Leaving a place of origin and going onto another place entirely different from your previous environment is sort of like a transformation: you crawl like a caterpillar but will fly like a butterfly at some point, and returning to our own vomit is discouraged since only dogs perform such disgusting acts (2 Peter 2:22). And no butterfly ever returns to being a caterpillar unless it dies, and over time, its wings dry up first. This process takes months, but eventually, the butterfly is seen as a caterpillar only because it died!

In essence, a caterpillar can potentially mutate into a butterfly, but a butterfly cannot mutate back into a caterpillar no matter how hard it tries. While it lives and the entire time thereafter, a butterfly acts like a butterfly and never again as a caterpillar; if it did, that butterfly would be attacked by predators it faced in its crawling stages, enemies a butterfly should never have to face again in its new environment, and we simulate the same course of action, or should, as believers.

In this case, *leaving* the faith or departing from the faith to something *other* than the faith or outside of the faith, to some extent, is a lifestyle of sin observed as the norm once again. It's obvious that that's what took place here (abandonment), and OSAS ignores the very position of such a departure. This is done to attempt to keep intact its erroneous interpretation of their doctrine. Not the means of salvation, but the means to hold on to that salvation, which they contend is works. Not the means of getting in, no! But the misinterpretation thereof. Once you're in, rather! Take a look at what the late Chuck Smith had to say about Hebrews 3:12-14 regarding the departed (abandon).

"Beware, brethren, lest there be in any of you an evil heart of unbelief in departing from the living God" (Hebrews 3:12).

Again, departing from God. These people had been delivered from Egypt. They'd come out of the bondage of Egypt. The issue isn't the deliverance from sin, the issue is entering into the fullness God has for you [...]

And so they wandered for forty years as an example of what happens when we, by our unbelief, fail to receive the promises of God. So, we are needing to take heed that we do not depart from the living God.[3]

This interpretation of Chuck Smith's view of *departing from God* had nothing to do with *sin* by Chuck's own admission in his interpretation of the passage.

As you can see, the way he described it in this commentary and attested that *sin* wasn't the issue, though he was reading the words *evil heart* in the text, includes "unbelief," meaning that God can take you home despite your sin, which is pretty much what he meant.

Except that the writer of Hebrews began his discourse with the words "Beware, brethren." So, to kick the can down the road as Smith suggests, it's irrational of its own, to say the least, and the verse calls them *brethren*, and that means that they were part of the brotherhood in Christ and not the unsaved.

Furthermore, the scripture goes on to say, "Lest there be *in any of you* an evil heart of unbelief in departing from the living God."

Now the word *departs* means "to go away," "to deviate," "to pass away" (die). In essence, what the writer of Hebrews was saying here, was that a gradual disconnect might take place because of an evil heart, and an evil heart causes unbelief. It gravitates to departing as its main intention or walking away from God and deviating from the truth of God, then ending up passing away spiritually because of it. Which is a gradual account that ends up as spiritual death, or better yet, loss of salvation, and that happens from a lack of confession of sin, which deters on repentance's stance, and sin then accumulates until there is no longer any evidence of God other than verbal (Matthew 15:8), and now the only thing left is judgment.

This discourse does not point to any other past generation of faithful individuals, as Smith suggests. It addresses the brethren, not the ancient Hebrews. I say that because the writer uses them as an example to warn all of us today, the readers, the believers of that day, and all whom he was speaking to at the time.

Chuck Smith is utterly wrong in his perception of Scripture when it comes to eternal security because, as I said before, it perverts the truth of God to fit the OSAS agenda, and thus, makes anyone promoting it as being *seared* with a hot iron, and he's not alone in this, by any means, as you will see if you continue reading.

How much clearer can it get if we accept that salvation is that serious to retain since it was very serious to attain because Someone paid the ultimate price for us at the cross, and that to entertain the idea that salvation is not all that serious is an error? One that no one can afford to make, and that's regardless of position or title of an individual, and to think that Smith and others advised the cowardly act of suicide to take place and that it's okay with God because of the error of eternal security makes one question what's in these leaders' hearts. And how many people who have taken the plunge of suicide will ultimately be laid as their responsibility for advocating and advising the cowardly to end a life only God reserves a right to take?

When it comes to suicide, Jesus made it clear for us to keep up with the commandments He left for us to follow. Take a look: "Whoever therefore breaks one of the least of these commandments, and teaches men so, shall be called least in the kingdom of heaven" (Matthew 5:19a, NKJV).

If suicide is murder, then "You should not commit murder" applies here, and that is one of the Ten Commandments. And if you kill yourself, how can you repent after the fact?

Jesus said that if you break and teach others to break one of the *least* of these commandments, and murder is a top ten, then you will be least in the kingdom of heaven, and the way this is spun by someone who advocates OSAS, focuses not on what Jesus was centrally portraying, no! But on the loophole, which are the words "least in the kingdom."

John Macarthur puts it this way in his commentary of Matthew 5:19:

> *5:19 shall be called least…shall be called great.* The consequence of practicing or teaching disobedience of any of God's Word is to be called least in the kingdom of heaven […] Determining rank in the kingdom of heaven is entirely God's prerogative […], and Jesus declares He will hold those in lowest esteem who hold His Word in low esteem. There is no impunity for believers who disobey, discredit

or belittle God's law [...] That Jesus does not refer to the loss of salvation is clear from the fact that, though offenders will be called least, they will still be in the kingdom of heaven.[4]

Perhaps Mr. MacArthur didn't read his own commentary, but it looks to me that his emphasis on the word *least* is sort of like a bronze medal, if you will, but that is not what Jesus meant.

Furthermore, MacArthur makes the statement that there is no impunity for anyone who disobeys the Lord in teaching in such divisive ways. Then he goes on to say that that he does not mean the loss of salvation. So, if there is no impunity, which means no forgiveness, how then can one retain salvation?

It sounds like a contradiction of sorts, don't you agree?

Jesus meant more than just a rank from top to bottom; maybe we should ask this man what "weeping and gnashing of teeth" means or being placed in outer darkness. Being least was the outcome of someone who knew the law, or in today's standards, the Bible, and broke the law and taught that breaking that law was okay with Jesus, especially on the subject of eternal security, which is what OSAS does and teaches by constantly instructing people who are at their wit's end, advising them to go ahead and commit suicide because God knows their hearts, and the fact that they cannot lose their salvation is then affirmed. But that is a complete lie from the pit of hell. Unless Mac Arthur sees no virtue in "be holy for I am holy!"

The Pharisees wanted to excuse themselves from judgment, though it was clear that Jesus was here to make evident who they were. Jesus said, "For judgment I have come into this world, that those who do not see may see, and those who see might be made blind" (John 9:39, NKJV). This also applies to OSAS leaders.

The Pharisees asked, "Are we also blind?" in verse forty, and Jesus answered them, "If you were blind, you would have no sin; but now you say, 'We see.' Therefore, your sin remains" (John 9:41, NKJV). This means there is no security of sin, and they did not confess their sins as they were supposed to because Jesus made it clear they retained them! He called them sinners!

Yet, Jesus Himself said in Mark 7:21 and 23 (NKJV), "Out of the heart of men, proceed evil thoughts, adulteries, fornications, murders [...] All these evil things come from within a defiled man." And suicide is murder, and that, according to Jesus, is an idea coming from a defiled man!

We then can conclude based on what Jesus said, suicide being murder, it derives from a defiled individual's heart, and how is that a person saved when they can breed murder from within?

Doesn't the Bible teach us to *choose life?* (Deuteronomy 30:19). Being not saved means you started the race but went in a completely different direction, one opposite from Jesus's teachings. Kind of like, "You ran well. Who hindered you from obeying the truth?" (Galatians 5:7, NKJV). That kind of deal.

Verse eight goes on to say, "This persuasion does not come from Him who calls you." Then where does that persuasion come from? Satan. When preachers and teachers teach people to commit suicide, they are teaching the opposite of *choose life*, and that is 100 percent satanic. Not teaching against is teaching for it!

The reason why MacArthur, Smith, Lutzer, and everyone who attains and teaches OSAS are utterly wrong about the retention part of salvation is that what Jesus says in the very next verse in Matthew 5:20 (NKJV): "For I say to you, that unless your righteousness exceeds the righteousness of the scribes and Pharisees, you will by no means enter the kingdom of heaven."

This is the end of the Beatitudes discourse, and Jesus was speaking to the masses, which means it applies to us all. Go ahead and read the verse again and understand that the end of that verse is not up for debate. If it wasn't so, the truth of Scripture would take a back seat to their erroneous doctrinal beliefs, exactly as you see here and in other commentaries equally wrong, and as we continue to expand on Hebrews, chapter three, more warnings rather than excuses pop up to admit suicide is somehow not blasphemy of the Holy Spirit, coming from a group who can't tell the east from the west when it comes to revelation. I hardly believe they know what blasphemy of the Holy Spirit is. That is exactly why many believers have plunged to their self-inflicted deaths, just like my friend, the Doctor, unfortunately experienced it with his siblings.

But exhort one another daily, while it is called *Today* lest any of you be *hardened* through the *deceitfulness* of *sin*. For we have become partakers of Christ *if we hold* the *beginning* of our confidence steadfast *to the end*.

Hebrews 3:13-14 (NKJV), emphasis added

You can almost see the writer of Hebrews attempting to make a connection to the ancient Jews so as to make an example of how one may deviate from the premise of the promise, or in layman's words, what not to do, and his conclusion was none other than *sin*.

- He suggested we exhort each other daily. How often? Daily! Have you called your brother or sister in Christ to encourage them today?

- He emphasized the importance of "today" so as to re-mind us of where our focus needs to be at all times. That's because tomorrow isn't promised. Therefore, your future sins, which Jesus forgave, don't exist! Today is the day of salvation, not tomorrow!

- And if we don't take those two steps, then he warns us of a hardened heart in the making due to the deceitfulness of *sin*. No one walks away from God in the twinkling of an eye. Take Joshua Harris, who for twenty-plus years pastored a church that, when he decided to leave Jesus to embrace a gay lifestyle, was at over twenty thousand members. Selah! Oh yeah, he was never saved, right?

- The reality of it is that the conditional clause "if" comes into play after "becoming partakers," and in essence, it means that if you want to continue to partake, "if" is what gets it done because it ends by saying that is necessary to have one's confidence to remain steadfast to the end. Where in this verse does he say we are sealed? Because if we are *sealed*, then this verse is irrelevant, but if you get down to the nitty-gritty, being sealed requires remaining sealed, and that's our part, and if you don't believe me, then look for Joshua Harris and see if a guy who advocated for OSAS has a problem telling you he is no longer a Christian, and if you're going to use the "he was never saved" card, you're more naive than you look!

What else can *the deceitfulness of sin mean*?

Today ignores the beatdowns of yesterday; it aligns the hope of tomorrow thanks to forgiveness, but under no circumstances are we to boast about tomorrow because Jesus said so. And that should be enough for us all to take in, and if tomorrow is not promised, suggesting our future sins are forgiven is suggesting the irony of error!

OSAS suggests that Jesus has paid for our past, present, and future sins, and that is not true!

The only past sins God forgives are *confessed sins.* Just as it's stated in 1 John 1:8-10, and in reality, any future sins do not yet exist. How is it then that we need forgiveness for something that hasn't taken place? It's like telling the bank, "Hey, that eighty thousand I borrowed" or "that car loan last year is paid in full. I paid it next month; can you please give me the title today?" That makes absolutely no sense whatsoever, right?

Furthermore, Jesus Himself said that tomorrow isn't promised to anyone, and tomorrow is irrelevant according to Him (Matthew 6:34 and James 4:14). That's why the focus is only on *today*.

How then is it that our sins that aren't yet sins are forgiven if tomorrow is a day we cannot worry about because it's not promised and when we are told specifically that we need to focus on today by our Lord, why then worry about tomorrow?

In essence, what Chuck Smith is doing here, and many others like him, by the way, is attempting to disconnect the issue by making it impersonal, when in reality, it is very personal.

> Again, the exhortation towards perseverance twice here in the text. Actually, three times within the text. "If we hold our confidence steadfast to the end."

> It is important for us to notice their failure was the failure of faith. They did not believe God was able to bring them into the land.[5]

HOW AND WHERE DOES DECEPTION FIND ITS ROOTS?

Referring to the lack of faith that the wilderness experience brought about in the Jewish community in the Exodus is pretty much denying the reason there was a wilderness experience to begin with. I mean, the journey was supposed to be an eleven-day journey, not forty years of bickering!

Remember the *downtown train* analogy I introduced earlier? Well, it's the same archetype as the wilderness experience, at least in my perspective.

JOURNEYS

Israel's eleven-day trip out of Egypt turned out to be a forty-year journey of redundancy and delusion, and the cause of it pretty much was rebellion, or sin. Not at all a lack of faith as wrongly put by Chuck Smith in the previous chapter.

They knew God was there; they just ignored it. Never live life like God is not in the room!

Moses failed to make it into the promised land not because of a lack of faith. Moses did not make it into the promised land because of *sin*. He struck the Rock when he was supposed to speak to the Rock for the yielding of water. That Rock was Christ Jesus according to 1 Corinthians 10:4.

This tells us that the higher you go in God, the less tolerance for sin God has! It then makes perfect sense to see the unfortunate demise of Judas, the apostle, disciple, and treasurer of Jesus Himself!

Judas was a *dual office* recipient type of individual. Does he remind you of someone else who had two offices?

That's right, Lucifer was the covering cherub, as well as the worship leader in heaven, and saying Judas wasn't saved is the same as saying Lucifer was never an angel in heaven who had access to the throne of God and was the best-looking creation God ever put together (Ezekiel 28:12).

We know what Lucifer did wrong and it did not happen at a motel or a nightclub; what Lucifer did wrong, along with one-third of the angels, actually took place in the same heaven you and I are trying to get into.

But *sin in heaven* got all those angels ousted from God's presence. Sin got Adam and Eve evicted from the Garden of Eden for good. Sin got Israel into bondage after they were delivered from their oppressors in Egypt, and it is that sin that can cause a believer to lose their salvation as well because, as you can see, God deals with sin the same way He dealt with sin even in heaven itself.

Did Lucifer get back into heaven?

Did Adam and Eve get back in the Garden?

Is Israel saved?

Let's ask the Bible, shall we?

Take the letter to the Hebrews, for example, where the condition left for us from Hebrews 3:14 (NIV) is, "If indeed we hold our original conviction firmly to the very end." Something the children of Israel failed to do, and I mean miserably so, and that same dismal confession applies to us all today as well.

Sin is the ugly thing that keeps us from being in communion with a holy God. Not a lack of faith, as Chuck Smith wrongly suggested. A lack of faith always results in a sinful lifestyle of some sort, that much we know.

I'm also positive that God forgives sins when we confess them. Not sure He forgives sinful lifestyles when we embrace them? He did tell the prostitute, "Go and sin no more" (John 8:11, NKJV). I say this simply because sinful lifestyles pretty much exemplify unruliness in an individual's life, and at the same time, they amplify the course of action of a (negative) reaction to sin, or its embrace thereof, and also the direction one may take when making the subtle wrongful decision of departing from God to embrace such a lifestyle other than an exemplary faith walk.

Which isn't easy by any means! Christianity is by far the toughest faith to follow because of its self-denial and admonition to holy living. Therefore, Israel chose to rebel rather than submit, which is the case with all those who willingly depart from God. Regardless of title, place, or position, those who go on to sadly embrace a lifestyle of sin and do so willingly are those who depart from the faith and embrace carnality.

Sin always carries consequences much more exorbitant than what we can afford, and the result of those consequences is never considering a passiveness we can imagine and definitely never a good thing for the individuals at fault, who can't even afford its due payment when a judgment for such sin finally arrives and arrive it will. Furthermore, sin hangs out around us way past its overstated welcome, and we are never in control when in sin, never!

King David did not write some of the psalms thinking it would someday make a great read, no! King David wrote the psalms from, at times, a bleeding heart, and he was well acquainted with grief; he also expressed the notion of losing touch with God, as he exclaims that very sentiment in psalm fifty-one, especially when we know that he was as close to God as one can be, according to Scripture (2 Samuel 11:14-16).

David painted a picture of despair, a season of dissolution, in an extravagant place of dismay he found himself in and to his own hurt. And the aridness he felt from separation from God surely brings melancholy that David acknowledged he was not right with God. He viewed himself as an outsider by choice, a choice he later regretted since he was dubbed a man after God's own heart early in his ministry, and that was God's title of David, not self-proclaimed. God referred to him as such because of David's unique way of accepting his wrongdoing and the ability to repent. Not perfect, but open to perfection, which is what correction does.

God did not change His mind about David, but the other way around. David addressed his transgression and iniquity by classifying his sins as an admission not warranted or open for debate. In other words: guilty as charged, and this attitude of repentance which perhaps took months or years, who knows really, but that he finally made the connection between his heart and his mind, just as we read in Psalm fifty-one. The confession of a repentant and a bleeding heart that wanted a second chance to be close to God was finally a reality for the King:

> Have mercy upon me, O God, according to Your lovingkindness; according to the multitude of Your tender mercies, blot out my transgressions. Wash me thoroughly from my iniquity, and cleanse me from my sin.

> Psalm 51:1-2 (NKJV)

Sins that depicted the infamous *staying home from the battlefield* (2 Samuel 11) incident of David's only disconnect with God, or at least that we know of, and a disconnect in a substantial way that ended up rewriting the king's already bright future into the nightmare it came to be for not only him but his entire family and community, giving us an example of the importance it is to stay connected to God as our source for being.

Just like David's obedience was connected to so many people's destinies, so was his disobedience, and both have an impact on the reshaping of our environment, which derives from the consequences of that sin, and those vicissitudes are a product of our decisions. Just like it happened with David, where his family was cursed, and God no longer had the confidence of allowing David to build Him a dwelling place, and that was the result of sin, by the way.

What man sentences another man to die and sends the death notice with the dead man walking himself, as he had no clue what was about to take place because sometimes loyalty is the attraction of betrayal? It happened with Uriah carrying a letter with instructions to his death. Among other things the king did to this righteous man, this was by far the worst, and by being clueless about it, Uriah made the trespass that much more macabre, if you will.

In essence, iniquity is treating someone bad though they treat you good, or unequal treatment, one unreciprocated. Iniquity also means to treat a person with contempt, and not in a vindictive kind of way, but in an initially well-calculated attempt to destroy that person through hidden and premeditated deception with tabs on its progress, as in Uriah's and David's case, especially when expecting the result to go as planned, and treating it as if it was shocking news when informed of its execution, knowing well what the animus was all along. And what's worse, David included others to share in that same detestable sin, as well as its prospective agenda of infringement, a well-calculated move of ill intentions for the purpose of selfish gain.

David concludes verse two by saying, "Cleanse me from my sin." He was apparently sick to his stomach by what he had done, even if it was because he was caught, and all of us know that exact feeling, and when we no longer care, we are no longer saved and perhaps in a sinful lifestyle by now.

How many of us wish someone would call us out when in sin? When we take on sin, we can't shake it off as if our life depended on it. We should want to be right, but in verse three, David takes responsibility for his actions. Again, even if it was because he was caught with his hands in the cookie jar, which is one of the things that made him a man after God's own heart, that he repented and never went back to do the same fallacy again.

Unfortunately, this is where most of us miss the mark. We do so by not understanding God's grace at all or simply by believing in err of the truth of God's Word, which comforts us when we repent. And by abusing grace in a nutshell, we sometimes make it the result that plays against us because of the sheer disconnect with God, which is what sin leads to every time it goes unchecked. And when we do, the sin that ensnares us will continue to do so because of our unrepentant heart, one that progresses in a downward spiral as we drift further from our first love (Jesus).

In verse four, David made the incident more of a "me and You, God" thing. When he says, "Against You, You only have I sinned," he personalizes the incident by fessing up to his wrongdoing; though it took a while, he eventually got it right.

David left Joab, Bathsheba, and Uriah out of the equation here. I doubt that he was trying to minimize his actions by any means, but by owning up to his fallacy, he was pretty much asking God not to make this an issue outside of the king's rendition, and thus, covering his accomplices and sparing them from God's wrath regarding the Uriah incident, as much as it was up to him, that is!

David pleads with his Maker to create in him a new heart, just

as it is stated in verse ten. He understood that the heart he had
had been tainted with some of the vilest and perverse sins one can
imagine, especially for a man as close to God as David was.

A parade of sins resulted from waking up in the wrong place at
the wrong time, as we learned in 1 Samuel, chapter eleven, speaking of David's playing hooky from the battlefield days, only to find
himself walking into a life-changing view of a naked, gorgeous
woman bathing right outside of his palace terrace, as Bathsheba
was a woman who was too beautiful to pass up, I suppose. The
Bible calls her beautiful to behold, which introduced a battle of the
mind that David lost before it even got started, one that altered his
entire future and gave his ego the keys to the car, then opened the
floodgates of destruction, especially that for his family.

We learned that just what the prophet said would happen to
King David because of his sin ended up happening. The sword
did not depart from his house, and sexual sin destroyed Tamar, his
daughter, who was raped by her half-brother; his concubines and
wives were ravished by Absalom, his son, and it was done openly
and in plain view of daylight, as Absalom defiled them by engaging them into sex in front of all Israel at the city gates (2 Samuel
16:22).

David's son Amnon raped his half-sister Tamar, and Tamar's
brother Absalom killed his half-brother Amnon in retaliation for
the rape. King Solomon killed his half-brother Adonijah who
had made himself king while they awaited David's death, and we

somehow think God no longer judges sin because of a confession we later forsake due to sinful lifestyles. Give me a break!

David concluded that his current heart needed not a change but a replacement. He was asking God for a heart transplant of sorts when he said, "Create in me a clean heart" (Psalm 51:10, NKJV), and that's because the heart is deceitful to the core (Jeremiah 17:9).

He added, "Renew a steadfast spirit within me" in the latter part of verse ten. In other words, David wanted for God to give him an abiding spirit so that it would yield to God according to the Holy Spirit's instructions, and after failing God miserably, David needed a change of heart.

One just like the one he once had, and that was how he accumulated victory after victory by seeking God for His favor and with a clean heart. Nevertheless, the disconnect happened, and it happened because of sin, which is always the case in any believer who embraces it and takes a chance at abandonment. Then and now, and with no reservations because sin is the resolve that separates us from God's presence, and it happens every single time we do it. Sinful lifestyles are independent of God's will. And it's always the same people who pick and choose the error regarding the interpretation of Scripture, people who abruptly apply it in total bias, as the intention is evident for whatever the situation may be in circumspection to favor their agenda, their own will, and not God's will, one not up for debate.

They say nothing can separate us from the love of God, not even death; then, they separate from their wives and credit the death of the marriage as grounds for divorce, favorably dead, and do so to remarry. The death of the marriage is what they simulate, as Jesus stated: unless the spouse dies, if you marry someone, you can live in adultery when you or they are divorced, and I'm paraphrasing, of course. Total hypocrisy, if you ask me!

So many believers today quote Scripture without having an ounce of revelation for the Scripture they recite. In other words, they merely read the Bible as if it were an ordinary book off the shelf, or at best, repeat what they heard in church on Sunday or from some indoctrinated circle of some sort, never understanding that one must read between the lines because the overall intention of the Bible is to introduce a holy living, to bring revelation, and do so as to give understanding that for every implication in the Bible, there's an *application* in the real world, and it's to be followed in that manner. We know that actions speak louder than words and also that there's another side to that coin as well or somewhat of a "finish the sentence" challenge, if you will!

Let me show you what I mean by this: When the Bible tells us to do something we can utilize for our benefit somewhere down the road as we grow in Christ, we must use common sense to advert that message and find biblical clarity within it to not be carried away with every wind of doctrine as the Bible instructs us not to (Ephesians 4:14).

For example: How many times have we gone in a direction opposite to where the Holy Spirit wanted to lead us, and in the aftermath of such nonsense, we acted surprised at the outcome? Once we were caught, we somehow went around, finding someone to place some of the blame on to avoid full responsibility for our actions, knowing well that we are as guilty as they come. Adam and Eve are perfect examples of kicking the can down the road. Adam said to God, "the woman," and Eve said to God, "the serpent." You get my drift!

So many people find refuge in false hope, and God does forgive sin, but we have to repent from whatever it was that came between God and us, and it begins by way of confession. Try getting money out of an ATM after you insert your card without entering a password…good luck with that!

Likewise, having Jesus but no confession is having a card but without the password. There is no withdrawal in either case. Therefore, unconfessed sin is unforgiven sin, and that does not lead to repentance or deliverance, for that matter, and confession is there so that we never return to that prior mess when we sincerely confess our sins and not be subject to it. But when unconfessed, and if it's not forgiven, then sin is retained until forgiveness comes, and it only comes by confession.

Then, after two or three days go by, the enemy will make sure we add to that unconfessed sin some more sin. Church services begin to be skipped, church leadership is talked about, the blame game points to everyone else but us, and we begin to attract evil influences all the time now to make us feel at home. And so they can make us feel pious because we're better than them, so we think.

That's called spiritual death 101 in the making, and it happens gradually and without notice; here is where people begin to question God's reality of holy living, which is a requisite in Christianity so to continue in Him, and apostasy now becomes a reality and more evident by the minute. Separation from God is now ever near, but OSAS suggests such individuals were never saved.

That statement says, "Either the Holy Spirit has no idea what He's doing or doesn't have the power to keep someone saved," and it also makes the confession of conversion illegitimate, even if a person walks with God for years on end. Just like Judas did for three and a half years with Jesus. They say he was never saved, though he was no different than the other eleven disciples before Satan entered him and, after that, was never allowed to shake him off anymore (Matthew 10:6-8).

Though they read that Judas was just as anointed as the other eleven by casting out demons, healing the sick, etc., except that Judas had an extra calling in his life; Judas kept the purse, or was the treasurer of the Lord, and suggesting that he was never saved would be suggesting that Jesus was a simpleton for trusting an unsaved person to keep the church's money! What pastor that you know lets a thief have control of the church's finances and an unsaved one at that?

But it appears that the OSAS frenzy assumes Judas wasn't saved and does so to protect the eternal security lie they've subscribed to for centuries and the error they accumulated over time. Not to mention that it also makes Jesus a terrible judge of character for having Judas carry the purse.

How many of us can say that Jesus had no clue Judas was not saved? He did say He chose the twelve.

The transaction of transgression is a sure denial for access to God, and if there's no confession, according to 1 John 1:9, there's only judgment without justification. And that's because not confessing your sin is as if you didn't sin, which will make Him a liar, and that's what OSAS teaches: that past, present, and future sins are forgiven virtually and automatically.

That is why so many people misquote Romans 8:35 (NKJV), "Who shall separate us from the love of Christ?" And the only answer is, "Sin"! Not who, but *what*.

When we retain and accumulate any amounts of sin in our daily lives, the paradigm of the consequences is just as broad as the sin itself, and mercy does not take place until after the trial ends as far as the law is concerned or is part of the sentencing that later takes place when a guilty verdict is pronounced, or a confession of guilt is uttered. This is what we know as *judgment day.*

A just God has to deal with injustice, and sin is an injustice against God Himself. Just as David puts it in Psalm 51:4 (NKJV),

"Against You, You only, have I sinned."

Nowhere in the Bible can you find a sinner who was not dealt with by God, and that individual's position was irrelevant to the outcome, except that the punishment was always greater than the average Joe.

What people seem to forget is that Romans 8:25 lists several things that cannot separate us from the love of God, but sin was not on that short list because there's an assumption that we as believers should know sin and God are on two different parallels, but if you read Romans, chapter eight, beginning at verse one, where the conditional clauses begin, it's not a *free-for-all* as some would have you to believe, no!

And we will break down everything that suggests that "once saved, always saved" is a perpetuated lie that protects an erroneous doctrine that is most dangerous and disingenuous. There are rules and regulations to retain what was given for free (salvation); it may cost you nothing to be saved, but it will cost you everything to stay saved, and you can quote me!

There is no condemnation for those who are in Christ Jesus, but it also says that it applies to those who do not walk according to the flesh, but according to the Spirit, which means that if you walk according to the flesh, there is condemnation, by default there must be some.

One cannot stay a baby Christian any more than a baby can

remain a baby for more than two years. A baby becomes a toddler, then a child, after that, turns into a preteen, and goes on to be a teenager, transitioning to a young adult, and will eventually graduate into adulthood, and finally evolve into an elderly person.

In like manner, believers need to grow spiritually, and the older you are as a believer, the less tolerance for sin God accepts in your life because you know better as a seasoned believer or should.

Romans 8:5 clarifies that those whose minds are focused on the things of the flesh actually live according to the flesh, and those led by the Spirit, live in the Spirit. Verse six ends the confusion by saying that carnality simply means you're dead in the Spirit.

Carnality is against God and is sheer lawlessness (verse seven), so then those who are in the flesh cannot please God (Romans 8:7). Romans 8:9 is a statement of affirmation of past, present, and post behavior for a believer. Take a look:

"But you are not in the flesh but the Spirit, if indeed the Spirit of God dwells in you [?]. Now if anyone does not have the Spirit of Christ [?], he is not His [!]" (Romans 8:9, NKJV; brackets added).

- Past: "but you are not in the flesh but in the Spirit..." (conversion).

- Present: "if indeed the Spirit of God dwells in you..." (continual sanctification).

- Post: "Now if anyone does not have the Spirit of Christ, he is not His" (loss or failure of retention of salvation).

There is no way possible that the writer of the book of Romans was addressing this particular piece of writing to unbelievers, but to all believers instead.

Not convinced yet? Take a look:

> Therefore, *brethren,* we are debtors—not to the flesh, to live according to the flesh. For if you live according to the flesh you will die; but if by the Spirit you put to death the deeds of the body, you will live.

> Romans 8:12-13 (NKJV), emphasis added

Paul addresses the *brethren,* not unbelievers; look at what he says, "we are debtors"; we owe!

Who do we owe? God! What do we owe? Our very lives!

We were bought at a price, and he suggests that because we owe, we are not to live in the flesh because we are no longer carnal or should not be, and if we continue to feed the flesh, we will die, just like the verse suggests!

He concludes by saying that if we are saved, we must stay saved, act saved, and live saved, and live by the Spirit if we want to live, and not live a mere carnal life but a life alive in the Spirit, one that requires continual change, progressive sanctification and growth, one that requires holiness daily, even to our own hurt because denying the flesh isn't a joke.

Take a look at a Bible commentary from the *MacArthur Study Bible* regarding Romans, chapter eight. This is in response to verse one.

> *8:1 therefore*. The result or consequence of the truth just taught. Normally, it marks the conclusion of the verses immediately preceding it. But here it introduces the staggering results of Paul's teaching in the first seven chapters: that justification is by faith alone based on God's overwhelming grace.[6]

One cannot disagree with Mr. MacArthur one bit…After all, the Bible does say that *the just shall live by faith* (Romans 1:17), but how is someone *just* if they live in sin on the premise of eternal security?

It's like getting a brand-new car, but never putting gas in it, or oil in it; the result is the car will die regardless of its prestige, make, or model, or accolades for that matter, and if we are talking about believers, it's all one and the same.

A believer that doesn't feed themselves will also die in the same manner from spiritual malnourishment, and sin is what kills an individual who refuses to invest in their spiritual growth. Don't believe me: read King Saul's chronicles.

Unless we simulate psalm fifty-one after our mess-ups, which are a reality, and all too common events for that matter, we can end up as King Saul did after God rejected him as king and also as a believer, an all because of Saul's embrace of sin and his sheer rebellion against God. You can't be a mountain-of-transfigura-tion-experience kind of Christian and act like a valley Christian worshipping a golden calf!

But as I kept on reading the commentary further down the page, it became more suspicious as I went along, and as I was read-ing along the thread, it presented its conspicuous agenda of which I am finally unmasking its theme of error; take a look:

> *no condemnation.* "condemnation" is used exclusively in judicial settings as the opposite of justification. It refers to a verdict of guilty and the penalty that the verdict de-mands. No sin a believer can commit—past, present, or future—can be held against him, since the penalty was paid by Christ and righteousness was imputed to the be-liever. And no sin will ever reverse this divine legal de-cision.[7]

Not sure how someone can write a Bible commentary and have no clue to what he's saying or trying to convey a message of hope, biblically speaking, that utterly disagrees with Scripture on the matter. I understand up to a certain point, but unfortunately, these types of heresies are taught in seminary and Bible colleges everywhere, but misleading believers at this altitude, as it is writing a Bible commentary, is a huge offense in God's eyes if you ask me.

Making the statement that no sin can reverse a legal decision for God's disapproval of an unruly individual based on the embrace of a sinful lifestyle, but a right-out lie of itself, and it also says God will not punish sin. Just wondering why Jesus's second coming is necessary.

Did not sin get Lucifer and a third of the angels ousted from heaven?

Did not sin get Adam and Eve evicted from the Garden of Eden?

Did not sin keep the children of Israel forty long years in the wilderness and from entering the promised land altogether, except for two of the original pilgrims?

Did not sin end up being the reason why Israel lost the covenant and was later offered to the Gentiles (us) to inherit the promises by way of the cross? What gives MacArthur the right to deny the consequence of sin in a believer's life to be *nonchalant and irrelevant*? Not one book in the Bible suggests it's okay to keep sinning after our conversion, not one!

There may be plenty of commentaries that do, but not God's

Word. Furthermore, we know that blasphemy of the Holy Spirit is an unpardonable sin. The Bible is very clear about that. That alone nullifies MacArthur's statement or anyone who believes along those same lines, and the OSAS approach to that is "only unbelievers are capable of blasphemy of the Holy Spirit," but ask yourself this: If unbelievers are not saved, they are going to hell anyway, what difference does it make if they blaspheme against the Holy Spirit or not?

Jesus made it clear that blasphemy of the Holy Spirit is when someone gives credit to Satan for what the Holy Spirit is doing and vice versa (Matthew 12:22-32).

The religious leaders of that day, or the Pharisees, if you will, made the statement that Jesus was casting out demons by Beelzebub (grand lord of the house). Now, this happened in the synagogue (inside the church) where Jesus cast a demon out of a person who was possessed, and by them saying to Jesus that He casts out demons by the *lord of the house* (Beelzebub), and because the incident happened at church (the house), what they were saying pretty much was that Satan was the lord of their house.

Remember Jesus said to them, "You are of your father the devil." He wasn't just trying to insult them; He was pulling the covers from them (John 8:44). Now you know why He said it!

They were omitting that at best. And thus, Jesus was right, the Law was their god, but Jesus was clear on who their father was.

Just like the OSAS doctrine has become the god of those who believe such a lie and not only—but teach and practice it! They made their Bible their god and not the God of the Bible.

To say that God tolerates sin in a believer's life is to say that the letter to the Hebrews is unnecessary. As we all know, Hebrews, Romans, or the Gospels for that matter, deal with the limitless consequences of sin, and that's because the Bible contains scores of repercussions citing to that effect. Of course, it can happen to anyone who walks away from the faith, should they choose to.

Furthermore, why would the Bible be needed after conversion if you cannot lose your salvation? Why not just use John 3:16 and Romans 10:9 and discard the rest of the Bible? That would be staying consistent with the lie of eternal security.

This is not to make John MacArthur, the late Chuck Smith, or Erwin Lutzer look bad in no way, shape, or form, but simply so that they and everyone else who teaches OSAS as well can also receive the truth of God's revelation of His Word and not have to face judgment because of complete error about such wrongful theology handed down over time. And the judgment that follows it, due to the many who have committed suicide because of this false teaching and those who will, and these teachers (James 3:1) are in danger of hellfire themselves (Luke 13:25-28).

Every single suicide that has ever taken place in the church because it was told to them that you can commit suicide and still go to heaven will be charged to that teacher or preacher who said it, and the suicide's blood will be on their hands, guaranteed!

Just imagine getting to heaven after preaching God's Word for twenty, thirty, or forty years, and having to face the reality that, "Thanks to you, thirty-nine," or "seventy-nine," or "eight hundred and ninety-nine more people took their own life because you said it was okay to, because you said that not even death can separate you from the love of God," while leaving out that it's God's love for them, not our love for God, will annul their relationship with God as they play god themselves and take a life that is for God only to take and not an individual, even if it's their own!

"You shall not murder, and whoever murders will be in danger of the judgment" (Matthew 5:21b, NKJV).

How much clearer can it get? Jesus said if you murder, you will be in danger of judgment, and I'm sure He meant every word, and suicide is murder and an act of cowardness. MacArthur needs to visit this verse.

The Bible is not shy when addressing the subject of murder, and that includes suicide, "For out of the heart proceed evil thoughts, murders..." (Matthew 15:19a, NKJV). This nonsense that God knows your heart, and if you commit suicide, it's okay because God knows your heart has no place in Scripture, and the response shouldn't be regurgitated as if it was a clear call.

Furthermore, Revelation 21:8 lists a series of sins that will lead people into the lake of fire, and one is "the cowardly," that's people who commit suicide because suicide is the biggest act of cowardness, and another one is "murderers," that's people who commit suicide who fit this category as well.

Our love for God is displayed by living in His will and obeying His Word; suicide, therefore, is rebellion against God. Suicide makes the individual take the place of God, a God who is a life giver, and the only One who reserves the right to take that life back is God. In essence, committing suicide is playing God.

The Bible is very clear that we must love God with all our strength, all our mind, and all our soul and strength (Mark 12:30). Suicide is having *no strength*; it's being *out of your mind*, and it's an act of *weakness* in the worse way. Suicide violates all the above!

Not having faith that God can turn the situation around tomorrow is giving up on God today, and it's also an act of *cowardness*. This is what Revelation 21:8 had in mind: "But the cowardly, unbelieving, abominable, murderers [...] shall have their part in the lake which burns with fire and brimstone, which is the second death."

Let's view these observations of who are the people that fit such descriptions:

- *Cowardly*: Suicide is by far the number one act of cowardness in our society. There is no bigger coward than one who has absolutely no value for life, especially of self. A life was given to them by God for a special purpose and not to end it this way because no one wins with suicide, and the life of a believer should only be taken by God. There is one suicide for every twenty-five attempts, and approximately 123 suicides per day, perhaps more, according to American Foundation for Suicide Prevention.

- *Unbelieving*: When a person refuses to believe that God can turn a situation around because that's what He does best, just as recorded in the entire Bible, from parting the Red Sea to holding the sun still, to killing giants, bears, and lions. Knowing this and not believing God for a personal breakthrough means *losing* your faith. *Unbelief is the loss of faith*. How can a person believe Jesus can save you but not deliver you from whatever the situation may be at the time, like being some form of depression to the point of self-death?

- *Abominable*: This is the state of an individual's life when God walks away from them, and He does. As in King Saul's case. Also, Revelation 21:7 tells us who God will accept in the end and those He won't. Abominable is someone who makes God sick to His stomach, for lack of a better analogy. An abominable person walks into a curse. This happens when an individual no longer identifies with God at any level. God no longer sees Himself in that individual's life; thus, God walks away from such people because an all-knowing God surely knows that person will never embrace His precepts ever again (Malachi 1:3), as was the case with Saul and Judas! Two suicides from two men who once *walked* with God at intimate levels but later walked away from God indefinitely.

- *Murderers*: This is simply a person who plans to end a life, not in self-defense, not in an accident, not in war but with premeditation. Murder happens as the *ultimate* act of hatred to the affected. Whether that hatred is for someone else or self, murder is the ultimate way of expressing that hatred at its best. And taking your life is hatred toward God as well, not just yourself.

My question is: where is God as someone loads a gun or ties a rope around their neck as they plan to carry on the act to commit murder, *self-murder* (suicide)? Why doesn't God stop them?

No Bible verse reads, "And Jesus told the spirit of suicide in Judas, 'I rebuke you,' and Judas's rope around his neck broke off, and Judas lived." But we do read: "Now after the piece of bread, Satan entered him [Judas]. Then Jesus said to him, 'What you do, do quickly'" (John 13:27, NKJV, brackets added).

There is no reference to Jesus trying to stop Judas from betraying Him, as there is a reference to stopping Peter, who denied Jesus three times. We know that Jesus told Peter, "Get thee behind me, Satan," and that Satan had asked to sift Peter as wheat. Let that sink in...Satan asked God for permission to go after Peter, but access was denied, and Jesus told Peter that He was praying for him. Why not Judas—what was so bad about Judas that he was beyond repair? Did Jesus green-light Judas to kill himself? Or was Jesus simply referring to the betrayal?

And the answer is God knew the outcome, and He simply allowed it because He gave us this thing called free will. That's what makes Him God; his attributes are beyond our comprehension. From scriptures like, "My thoughts are not your thoughts, nor are your ways My ways" (Isaiah 55:8, NKJV) to this: "I will have mercy on whomever I will have mercy." (Romans 9:15, NKJV). That tells us God has no qualms about giving us free will and not interfering with it at all. Just not His way of doing things. Unless, of course, prayer is involved on behalf of that individual who attempts suicide, which is pivotal. Prayer changes things!

Verse eight of Revelation, chapter twenty-one, begins with these four bullet points you read a few minutes ago, so as to make a statement of where such bad decisions may lead if we decided to go that route, and "the lake of fire is the second death." There is no denying that these sins are that result *and how can someone mislead* an individual who requires the biggest miracle in their life and some hope, as it is trying to turn someone back from attempting such a sin, but instead, denying the only hope of giving God a chance to fix what's broken by telling such individuals to take the plunge and guarantee them heaven through a lie fabricated by an erroneous doctrine as is "once saved always saved," which is a perfect example of a doctrine of demons!

How can we ignore Scriptures like, "Weeping may endure for a night, but joy comes in the morning" (Psalm 30:5b, NKJV)? This verse is built on hope for tomorrow, and we have to make it our business to convey the message of such hope for the hopeless! Why instruct someone to enter the lake of fire by morning rather than offer God's hope during the night?

The suicide rate in the Christian community is the same as the suicide rate in the secular world, even throughout the pandemic's lockdowns. There is no distinction whatsoever in this awful category between the two. That means that 24.5 thousand believers are taking the plunge into eternity, but for the other team; not understanding the consequences by believing the lie of eternal security is wrong, and those who advocate such acts of despair and terror are responsible for the loss of life of every single individual who killed themselves because it was told to them that suicide is part of God's will for them or advocated the result thereof, and it's not!

How can anyone make the statement that future sins are forgiven, and where is that in the Bible?

Sin happens only when we break God's law. God never said, "Because you will sin, I will cast you out." But He does say, "If you sin, I will cast you out." That statement of having future sins forgiven makes absolutely no common sense whatsoever.

The definition of sin is "breaking God's law." That much we know. The preacher said, "Do not boast about tomorrow, for you do not know what a day may bring forth" (Proverbs 27:1, NKJV).

Wouldn't ignoring the ugly thing that keeps us from God (sin) that has not happened yet but addressing it as if it did and boasting that we are forgiven from it, though not a reality yet…wouldn't that constitute a violation of this proverb? I believe it will! Jesus said, "Don't boast that the spirits are subject to you but boast rather because your names are written in the book of life" (Luke 10:20, paraphrased). These names can be blotted out as well according to Jesus Himself (Revelation 3:5).

James, chapter four, is clear that we do not know what will happen tomorrow; he called it boasting as well (James 4:16). James said such boasting is evil; in other words, boasting about your future sins being forgiven is a sin, according to James. Jesus also said in Matthew, chapter six, that today has its own problems; why worry about tomorrow? In fact, tomorrow is not promised to man, so we read.

How then can we make such a statement of having forgiveness for something that does not yet exist?

It's like saying once you get your driver's license, you'll never have to worry about road infractions; you took the test, you passed it, and therefore, you can just drive any old way you want and never have repercussions to such erroneous behavior as reckless driving, which is what suicide is, recklessness.

If we are forgiven without sinning, it's not only ambiguous

thinking, but it also cheapens the sacrifice that it took for the sin that was and the one that is now actually being committed today. We are forgiven for past sins by accepting *that* sacrifice at conversion and confessing Jesus as Lord and the Savior gets it done, but that deals with past sin. We are well aware we've committed such sins, and confessing them got it done because they were exposed.

Present sins are those we committed today and can only be forgiven *if* we confess them, just like past sins were. And that's exactly what 1 John 1:9-10 declares. The premise of sending Jesus to die for our sins was because the Law had failed.

> *If* we *confess* our sins, He is *faithful* and *just* to *forgive* us our sins and to *cleanse* us from all unrighteousness. *If* we say that we have not sinned, we make Him a liar, and His word is not in us.

> 1 John 1:9-10 (NKJV), emphasis added

Beginning at the conditional clause "if," here we go once again with the "*ifs*," and this time that conditional clause is at the start of the verse and pertaining to a believer who has already made the initial confession of acceptance to Christ as Savior because John said "if we" so to include himself as well.

The condition is *if* we confess! Leaving room for nothing other than true interpretation; *if* we do not confess our sin, what are the consequences then?

Well, *if* we confess it, He is faithful and just to forgive us our sin, and the downside of that is, meaning that *if* we do not confess our sins, He remains faithful and just, and the *just* part, which is the root word for *justice*, means God has to judge the sin whether we confess it or not. But if we confess it, He will forgive us, and it's up to God to either impute judgment at whatever level for the caliber of the sin itself or show us mercy, meaning we get off scot-free if the latter takes place, but *if* we do not confess our sin, the only outcome is judgment, and that's judgment without mercy.

This is because if we choose to retain our sin, it means we're enjoying a sinful lifestyle, and when we do so with joy, we have replaced God with the sin, even if it's for the moment.

Daily confession means there's a struggle, but we are not content with our actions and ask God for reconciliation ("oh wretched man that I am" mode), and not confessing your sin means the struggle with sin is over, and sin is our master once again.

MacArthur suggests the forgiveness of sin is automatic, and simply put, a free-for-all at conversion. Except that, this erroneous theology leaves sanctification out of the equation altogether. And the ignorance behind an attempt to eradicate sanctification, which is unbiblical, to say the least, has to be done away with because we need confession followed by sanctification to be a present help in our daily lives without reservations, and I mean a sanctified life so as to keep us close to our Lord at all times.

Verse ten of 1 John, chapter one, says that if we say that we have not sinned, we make Him a liar, and also that His Holy Word is not in us. This is exactly what the issue is with the erroneous doctrine of eternal security. They don't understand the sanctification process after conversion!

If our past, present, and future sins are forgiven, then there is a suggestion that we do not have to confess our sins. For what? It would be pointless. Especially since, just as MacArthur and others suggest their sins are forgiven simply by accepting Jesus as Savior, I get it if we are talking about the baggage we initially bring to the cross with us at conversion. But after we've been walking with Jesus for some time, to believe sins are forgiven even before they take place, and therefore there's no need to worry about sin, let alone confessing it, falls into what 1 John was aiming at by saying that if we say we have no sin, we make Him (Jesus) a liar. That's exactly what the suggestion is: if our past and present sins are automatically forgiven, then there's no need for confession or a sign of sanctification; furthermore, there is no need for 1 John 1:9-10, and what a disservice to Romans, chapter eight, this is as well.

MacArthur's analogy of condemnation is on point. One can only be condemned if one is first arrested for a crime. One must also be found guilty of that crime to continue the process, then and only then can one be condemned during the sentencing, but as believers, confessing our sin does not guarantee mercy. Forgiveness, yes, but not mercy. The Lord is very clear that He will show mercy on whom He will show mercy (Romans 9:15). So, to say that sin does not harm a believer's life is misleading the masses.

We saw how David was judged for his sins once the prophet Nathan paid him an unwanted visit. The only thing that was left intact after that was the promise of the Messiah coming through his bloodline, but the journey was disrupted to a degree, regrettably so in a disadvantage for David and his family, and that due to the initial adultery sin with Bathsheba.

David got to see every bit of judgment take place that Nathan pronounced to him, and because of his disobedience, he saw it all before he finally closed his eyes and took his last breath.

CONSIDER TRUE WISDOM!

King Solomon, who was the wisest man alive, regarding money that is, ended up walking away from God due to his rebellion in idol worship as God warned him about it. Even though God instructed him against the women Solomon frequented because they were going to lead him away from God, Solomon persisted in his pleasurable ways and ended up an idol worshiper, just as God predicted he would (1 Kings 11:4).

Sanctification is the continual upkeeping of our common salvation; it's just like doing laundry: you wear it, you wash it, and unless you're homeless, I'm pretty sure you wash your dirty laundry as needed. Confession is doing laundry, and when we refuse to confess our sins as the Bible instructs us to do (James 5:16), we fail to wear that sweet-smelling aroma God is so moved by, and just like a clean linen scent to us, so is sanctification to our holy Lord.

In Romans, chapter two, the Bible speaks of what was taking place in chapter one, but here, Paul placed a mirror in front of the believer when he said,

And do you think this, O man [you and I], you who judge

those practicing such things [homosexuality and idolatry], and doing the same [and not confessing it], that you'll escape the judgment of God? [And the answer is no!]

Romans 2:3 (NKJV), brackets added

How many people do you suppose are guilty of this judgment? Maybe you're not a closet homosexual, but are you a closet fornicator or a closet adulterer?

I happen to think that a Christian who is having sex outside of God's will is way more detestable than that a homosexual or any sexually immoral unsaved person, and I say this because we expect homosexuals and the unsaved to behave as they do, but believers are not supposed to do such unimaginable things, and what do you suppose is the number one problem in Christianity today? Because it's not prosperity preaching, no! Picking on prosperity preaching constantly and the men and women who are labeled as such is what distracts from the real issue in the church, or the number one issue, if you will, *which is sexual immorality*!

At the end of the verse, Paul boldly tells us that by living in sin while judging those who also are living in sin but are not believers, if we think God will not bring judgment on us for living a lie, we pretty much have lost our minds and in danger of losing our salvation, and that is exactly what he meant by that.

Romans, chapter two, is filled with information discouraging eternal security altogether.

Romans 2:4 (NKJV, brackets added) reads: "Or do *you* [he is not talking to those who are living in sin, he is talking to those who are judging those living in sin—while in sin themselves] *despise* the riches of His goodness [this is directed to believers who feel there is no need to embrace the said attributes of God], forbearance and longsuffering, not knowing that the goodness of God leads to repentance? [thinking that there is no need for confession of sin is thinking that there is no need for repentance]" and that's exactly what's wrong with OSAS!

OSAS teaches that there is no need for sanctification, though they won't admit it. It is the continual act of confession that *reconnects* the believer who falls into sin against the God who forgives that sin when confessed, and *eternal security* suggests that repentance or confession, when is theorized it admits that sin automatically disappears without confession, which is entirely wrong, or better yet, a lie!

Contending that even future sin is forgiven, though it hasn't happened yet, is unfathomable of itself. Just as we read MacArthur's analogy on the subject, and he's not alone, unfortunately!

But in accordance with *your* hardness and *your* impenitent heart [or stubbornness just as the Israelites had when in the wilderness] *you* are treasuring [because of lack of confession accumulation] up for *yourself* wrath in the day of wrath and revelation of the righteous judgment [God has to judge all sin] of God, who "will render to each according to his deeds." [If the deed was not brought up to Jesus by confessing it, it will be brought up as the individual's sin.]

Romans 2:5-6 (NKJV), emphasis and brackets added

Not convinced yet? Well, take a look at the very next verse then: "Eternal life to *those* [not everyone] who by patient continuance [living holy] in doing good seek for glory, honor, and immortality [eternal life]" (Romans 2:7, NKJV, emphasis and brackets added).

Paul changes gears from verse six to verse seven. He talks about a hard heart developing in a believer's life (see Hebrews 3:12) to readjust the qualification that's necessary for why we're in this thing, to begin with (eternal life!). But it doesn't come automatically, as OSAS wrongly suggests. It comes just like the verse says it comes, "by patient continuance in doing good."

Why else would Paul begin his letter to the Romans by addressing the letter to those in Rome called to be saints (or Christians), which means a continual attitude (Romans 1:6)? Paul was laying down a strategic plan to keep them saved; he knew that there was hypocrisy amongst them. He knew that there was sin that

284

needed to be dealt with.

He knew that discrimination would not end at conversion, just like you see today, as many minorities in the faith refuse to let go of racism or a victim mentality by keeping themselves bound by choice. And he addressed it as such, though we seem to have ignored the antidote for a different high, one fueled by hatred and racism, and without resolution for those who embrace it yet call themselves believers and gladly support domestic terrorism like the Black Lives Matter riots, simply because of color, when wrong is no longer wrong and good is no longer good. Woke-ism dictates the flavor of the day; we have crossed the line (Isaiah 5:20).

It is a typical move by the liberal left who uses racism to pretend they care about minorities though that's not at all true since they keep minorities by killing them in the womb and allowing interracial crime to flourish while they tie the police hands to prevent them from performing their duties in stopping crime. No religion, no nation, no political party, no skin color, and no ethnicity paid the price for the forgiveness of sin. Only Christ did, and when we accept that sacrifice and become His followers, we are no longer driven by the color of our flesh, the same flesh we all know that no good thing dwells in it.

Paul pretty much meant, "Don't belittle the unsaved without giving them a chance to try Jesus for themselves." What's worse is that they were doing the same thing they were judging others for, or kind of like the pot calling the kettle black, if you will. The problem is that too many denominations know Jesus but not the Holy Spirit!

I don't want to be condescending, but the reality of a spiritual disconnect due to spurious doctrine is nothing short of brass tacks, and the fact that such doctrinal errors are repetitive is because Christian academia hasn't changed one bit over the centuries, maybe only in the technological sense.

They continually create unspiritual candidates who have never experienced an encounter with God, and everything they learn is from a textbook, and the only miracles they encounter are in the pages of the Bible, but they have never seen that manifestation due to unbelief (see Matthew 13:58).

Paul seemed to think that it was the problem with the Roman church. Paul made it clear he wanted to see them for that purpose. He knew that without the Holy Spirit's gifts, the church is nothing but a country club full of *do-gooders*.

Thus, his words resonate in his letter, and should today as well,

> For I long to *see* you [he knew there was a lack, one that had to be personally addressed] that I may *impart* [*meta-didomi*, Greek, derived from metamorphosis, or complete change] [...] to you some *spiritual gift* [*charisma*, Greek, not learned] so that you may be *established* [*sterizo*, Greek, fix].
>
> Romans 1:11 (NKJV), emphasis and brackets added

Paul knew that books can only inform you, and yes, even books like the Bible. This means that without the Spirit's revelation of the Word, it's only an academic feat of sorts, and this regardless of how much information one may retain as a good biblical scholar. Without the Spirit, it is just school because revelation suggests application due to an instructive set of values that must be displayed tangibly. Otherwise, God would not have given such a revelation for no reason. I don't think any of us know the Bible quite as Satan does, and he is not a saint!

Paul (Saul) is the best example of Word knowledge without the Spirit (see Acts 23:6).

It took Paul to have an encounter with Jesus on the road to Damascus (see Acts 22:10) to understand that books can only inform you, and it is by the Spirit that the Bible can transform your knowledge into power, which is what was needed in Rome, and it's exactly what's lacking in today's churches who hold the OSAS misguided doctrine as canon. They are powerless though well informed!

The Upper Room experience has to take place in every believer's life to know the Spirit of God's purpose, because without it, there is only knowledge without power, and the more knowledge you have, the smarter you think you are, and knowledge can only do one thing, "puff up" (1 Corinthians 8:1). And the Bible is a book of accounts where the only thing that parted seas, shut the mouths of lions, raised the dead, held still the sundial, confused the enemies of God's people, and resurrected a Savior was based on the Holy Spirit's powers and impartation, which was prophesied by revelation given to men and women like you and me, eons before the events took place (see Luke 3:16).

Paul said he wanted to see them to *impart* a spiritual gift in them. The impartation can only happen by one who was imparted by someone himself then passing it to someone else in the direction of the Holy Spirit and not the flesh. Having a spiritual gift is the difference between a doer and a hearer. In Mark, chapter sixteen, he ends his Gospel by telling us what a follower of Jesus looks like *if* they believe. Take a look at what impartation is:

> And these signs will follow those who believe: In My Name they will cast out demons; they will speak with new tongues; they will take up serpents; and if they drink anything deadly, it will by no means hurt them; they will lay hands on the sick, and they will recover.

> Mark 16:17-18 (NKJV)

Are you under the impression that Jesus didn't mean what He said in the above verses because, to me, He meant exactly what He said, but He did place a limit to this conditional clause? He said, "These signs will *follow* those who *believe*," which means that He will never give you a gift you don't believe in.

288

Parakoloutheo is what the Greek uses for "will follow" (*shall* in NKJV), and some of the translations are very interesting, so I'll share a few with you just to keep it fresh:

so, to follow one, as to *always* be by his side.

to *follow close*, accompany.

to be always present, to attend one wherever he goes.

to follow up a thing in mind to *attain to the knowledge of it.*

to understand (follow a matter up, *trace its course*).

to examine thoroughly, investigate.

to follow faithfully, i.e., a standard or rule, to conform one's self to.[8]

As we jump over to read Hebrews, chapter three, the tremendous findings of watchfulness regarding the faith as a whole are nothing short of screaming, "Be careful" in walking away from the living God, and to be consistent with "will follow" as explained above, it goes something like this, take a look:

Verse one of Hebrews, chapter three, engages the reader by the assertive yet well-calculated embrace of the faith. He uses the words "holy brethren," "partakers of the heavenly calling," which are engaging words of affirmation of someone connected to the faith. Like that of Jesus's vine and branches parable in John, chapter fifteen, because the Gentile church is grafted into the Vine.

The word "holy" comes before the word "partaking," and if you remember covering what partaking is, you will cruise with ease to where it should be leading us to, and the clarity of the calling is that it's undoubtedly heavenly and being holy is a requirement to stay afloat and connected, and that requirement can only come by sanctification, which is what we've been discussing all along. The confessing of sin!

In verse two, he talks about Jesus being faithful to His heavenly calling, and then, he refers to Moses as doing the same, and he portrays Moses as someone being faithful in his household.

As we go down to verses five and six of Hebrews, chapter three, we see that Moses was faithful in his own house, as was Christ. Then he talks about our faith toward Jesus and makes it personal for application, "Whose house *we are* if we hold fast the confidence and the rejoicing of the hope firm to the end" (Hebrews 3:6, NKJV).

What if we decided not to hold onto that confidence until the end, as prescribed by the writer?

Then the only thing left is the conditional clause in verse six, "If," and it would play a huge role of negative impact to anyone who opted out of the two-sided coin at hand. Here is the downside to that. If we do not hold fast our confidence till the end, then we are not His house! The writer did not present a statement that singled out everyone and left himself at a disconnect, assuming he had already arrived because he hadn't, and I assure you that none of us have either!

The writer said, "Whose house *we* are if *we* hold fast." He included himself to remain connected to the end, which suggests that salvation is never complete until the last day we spend on the earth serving God, and it ends in our death, or until we meet our Maker for the first time face to face since our arrival here on planet Earth, and that is what we're dealing with in life; then, and only then, can we say we are saved in the full context of the word.

Sadly, you can turn on Christian radio daily and hear an erroneous message on eternal security almost guaranteed. And perhaps you might hear it several times a day by different *men* teaching on different subjects but the same error, from coast to coast, north to south, east to west, teaching that you cannot lose your salvation, which is biblically wrong in any light if you ask me!

My question is this: Why advertise it daily if it's true?

Taking the Bible out of context is usually done by those who claim that others are taking the Bible out of context themselves, and the more I read the Gospels, especially the parables of Jesus, the more I'm convinced that Jesus was portraying a message contrary to that of eternal security. A debacle by the OSAS frenzy, no doubt!

Radio preachers have gone way too far in their error on the

subject of eternal security, to the point of telling their listeners that they can commit suicide and still go to heaven, and this because God knows their hearts, and yes, He does, but no, they can't (commit suicide), and remember that these messages originate from some pulpit in a Christian church somewhere in our midst, and it is Satan's mindset.

Scripture entirely contradicts such specious beliefs, and the more I hear them, the more I'm convinced that enlightening God's people with biblical truth is a must.

Take a look, please:

> Then the devil took Him to the holy city and had Him stand on the highest point of the temple. "If You are the Son of God," he said, "throw Yourself down. For it is written: 'He will command his Angels concerning You, and they will lift You up in their hands, so that You will not strike Your foot against a Stone.'" Jesus answered him, "It is also written: 'Do not put the Lord your God to the test.'"

> Matthew 4:5-7 (NIV)

How can anyone with spiritual authority advise an individual that wants to end their own life to go ahead and do it and tell them to rest assured because they will meet their Maker at the pearly gates and meet Him with open arms despite their wrong decision, especially after knowing this verse in Scripture, which by the way originated in the Psalms?

The verse in Matthew, chapter four, talks about a suicide attempt. The tempter is Satan, who suggests to Jesus to go ahead and take the plunge from the highest peak of the temple and to not worry about a thing because God would send angels to His rescue, and no harm, no foul. Pretty much God knew His heart, right?

But what did Jesus say to the tempter regarding the temptation to jump onto His death?

Verse seven, "Do not tempt God." Essentially, when these radio preachers suggest to their listeners and parishioners to go ahead and commit suicide because God knows their hearts, what they are doing is giving these individuals satanic advice because that's who tempts suicide, according to what we just read above!

Individuals who are at their wit's end, and there are way too many out there, who for whatever reason life has handed such a devastation blow, for them to even consider such an end, and these men who are giving advice that is contrary to how Jesus dealt with suicide in His situation when tempted to jump off the temple's pinnacle is beyond ill-advised, and more so, demonic.

We are to act just as He acted and shun such temptation. Not accommodate it or excuse it to preserve an erroneous perverse view of doctrine not in line with the Word of God, as is eternal security!

Anyone regardless of title or position who entices or con-
dones suicide is *playing* the part of Satan. Just like we saw in the
Scripture at hand. Jesus not only did not jump but also quoted
scripture of His own, and it was not to tempt God! Which is what
suicide essentially is, a temptation of God.

Nowhere in Scripture did He ever agree that suicide is permissible. Directing someone to commit suicide is tempting God,
which was discouraged by Jesus. So, these men who act on behalf
of Satan on Christian radio are mimicking the enemy twofold, not
Jesus! One: by telling people it's okay to kill themselves when the
going gets tough, and two: by tempting God once they go through
with it, as they will be held accountable for the lost souls embedded in suicide.

That leads me to one conclusion: every single victim of suicide
who's ever taken the plunge because one of these preachers who
lied to them and promised them false heaven will have to face God
for their deaths, and the bloodshed of every man, woman, and child
whose lives and souls were lost to suicides, suicides that were advocated by these *false teachers*, their blood will be on their hands
without a doubt and based on the passage in Matthew, chapter four,
it will be so!

No wonder the message to the end times churches is to repent!

Dr. Erwin W. Lutzer of the Moody Church wrote an online
article in regard to suicide and salvation.

If you were to read his introduction, you might think that he's completely against the act itself, that is, until he concludes with the erroneous idea of eternal security in finalizing his closing point. And that's always the premise to protect their erroneous doctrine of eternal security daily, which denies the truth and points out the consequence of such a horrendous act as it is suicide's sequence. Take a look:

> Suicide is self-murder. Though suicide is sometimes masked by words of good intention, it is selfishness (often mingled with convenience, unfaithfulness, depression, or impatience) that underlines the suicidal motive. It is no accident that Saul, with his proclivities toward selfishness and arrogance, chose suicide […] Suicide is putting a period where God intended that there be a comma […]

> Is it possible for a believer to commit suicide? We believe the answer is yes. First, we know that the temptations which assail believers (from within or without) can be immense. We do not always take advantage of the way out of our burdens God provides (1 Corinthians 10:13). Does a Christian who commits suicide lose his/her salvation? No, because as believers, nothing can sever us from the love of Christ.

Believers are "sealed with the promised Holy Spirit, who is the guarantee of our inheritance until we acquire possession of it, to the praise of His glory" (Ephesians 1:13-14). A believer who commits suicide enters heaven on the coattails of failure and might deserve few rewards, for he/she has neglected the presence of the Spirit, the words of Christ, and the aid of the church which God has mercifully provided for every believer. However, all who have been justified by faith in Christ belong to Him, and He will take them to be with Him forever.[9]

I was shocked to read such instructions from the leader of the Moody Church himself!

Lutzer mentioned Saul as an example of someone who committed suicide in the Bible. He pointed out his actions were due to Saul's proclivities, but Saul did not arrive at this intersection overnight, no!

Saul had a long journey of disappointment after disappointment. From David's victories overshadowing his, ending up at a witch's home, and asking for godly advice, which is impossible of its own, but without a doubt, his biggest blunder was God's departure from his life. Saul fell into the hands of the living god.

This is a great story to gauge the presence of God in our very own lives as well, and any individual who refuses to maintain his or her relationship with God, and do so on a daily basis, a tight-knit one at that, if not, will undergo some severities for those bad decisions made, and do not doubt me on this one.

The Bible tells us in 1 Samuel 10:6 that Samuel told Saul he would prophesy when the Spirit will come upon him ("as the occasion demands," the latter part of verse seven); it also says he would be turned into another man.

This is the same idea Paul the Apostle expressed in 2 Corinthians 5:17-18 (a new creation).

The Holy Spirit would come upon Saul powerfully. This tells us that Saul was Spirit-filled, and the misconception about the Holy Spirit's ministry in the Old Testament and the New Testament being different is absurd.

If God never changes and is always the same, then that applies to the Holy Spirit as well. The Holy Spirit is always there. Once a person is filled with Him, He never leaves unless *sin* enters into that individual's life by him or her embracing a sinful lifestyle or if God rejects him or her because of the same premise. Saul is a perfect example of that premise. And the confession of sin allows the Holy Spirit to return to us again; that's why we have to immediately confess our sins.

1 Samuel 16:16 displays God's rejection of Saul. We read that Saul was prophesying as well as the other prophets when under the Spirit. In 1 Samuel 11:6, the Spirit came upon Saul again and gave him unimaginable physical strength, enough strength to chop up

oxen into twelve individual pieces, which means that the infilling or the capacity needed for the task at hand or the reason why He was filled with the Spirit was what was necessary for the task itself. The Spirit knows exactly what we need and for what. That's why God reveals Himself to people He chooses to, and how! And once the individual is aware of that revelation, God will direct them the rest of the way, but the revelation comes with a task, meaning an action must follow such revelation.

In Saul's case, God gave him the strength to perform a necessary feat that would raise awareness for the evil that was attempting to manifest itself as the ruler of that particular demographic area. Demons are territorial in nature. In other words, a greater outpouring takes place according to the work assignment at hand. God, the Holy Spirit, wants to have something done at whatever level He sees fit. He simply does it!

"And let it be, when these signs come to you, that you do *as the occasion demands*" (1 Samuel 10:7, NKJV; emphasis added).

In Saul's first encounter with the Holy Spirit, Saul chopped animals up in bits and pieces. It looks to me like Saul had an amazing conversion, to say the least; don't you agree?

So, to suggest that the Holy Spirit came and went in Old Testament believers is to wrongly suggest the ministry and outpour of the Holy Spirit—simply because it's what's being taught in seminary, and it's the wrong approach.

CONSIDER TRUE WISDOM!

Think of it this way: When a car runs out of gas, that car goes nowhere, but as soon as you refuel it, you can continue on your journey. If you fill the tank to its fullest capacity, you can get further down the road. The less fuel you put into it, the fewer miles you can travel under such circumstances. If you want to go the distance, it's obvious you would fill the tank.

In like manner, the Spirit fills the people He called but to whatever capacity He sees fit, for whatever task He has for them. But when we insist on traveling roads, we have no business being on, at some point, God will allow us to run dry on gasoline and will not give us any gas money. And in some instances, God decides to abandon His purpose in us because of the adoption of a sinful lifestyle on our part. If we spend our gas money on other things that don't move a car, we are expressing a lack of interest in God. Who's in the car with us?

Saul and Judas are perfect examples of this analogy; they had a witch and the Pharisees (whom Jesus said their father was Satan) in their cars.

Though the OSAS lie suggests Judas was never saved, it is not only wrong to accept such a lie but is an insult to God, who chose the twelve and filled them all to the capacity they needed to be filled with. Every single one of them was anointed for a task, except that Judas, like Saul, decided to embrace sin rather than to embrace the God who called them in their perspective callings, to begin with, as is the case with anyone who adopts a sinful lifestyle

299

after tasting the goodness of the Holy Spirit.

> For if we sin willfully after we have received the knowl-
> edge of the truth, there no longer remains a sacrifice for
> sins, but a certain fearful expectation of judgment, and
> fiery indignation which will devour the adversaries.
>
> Hebrews 10:26-27 (NKJV)

If "we sin willfully" *includes the writer*, he was, as Judas was, saved. And just like in the story of Samson, Samson was not abandoned by God; God was abandoned by Samson.

We read in the book of Judges that Samson was a product of God's visitation to his parents. The Bible tells us in Judges 13:1 that the children of Israel *again* did evil in the sight of the Lord, and God delivered them over to the Philistines.

In the meantime, God was forging a deliverer for Israel because they were about to experience oppression due to their sinful behavior. Unfortunately, Israel's deliverer was full of himself and forgot who gave him strength, like that of an army.

In the end, Samson ended up in bondage just like Israel was and was also subject to the same Philistines Israel was subject to, whom he was sent to destroy because he was sent to destroy them, not sleep with their women!

Although in the end Samson repented from his sin and was granted a chance to redeem himself and the opportunity to destroy the Philistine rulers as was the plan from the get-go, his death happened as an act of war, and not a suicide as some teach, but it happened that way because of Samson's destructive behavior, and not because God planned it that way.

God had to improvise the method, not the outcome. Samson was supposed to kill those men and then go home and smoke a cigar. Killing those men and dying with them…there is no victory lap there!

Just like you see the many men and women of God today falling into licentious sin and leave the confines of their calling for that tasty trifle, forgetting that they were sent to deliver someone in bondage, and perhaps they did, but now, they need a deliverer themselves because the tempter never stops tempting.

God deals with sin, we saw in the Garden as He encountered a hiding Adam, who, when confronted, simply passed the buck, and Eve did the same as well, blaming the snake. We saw it in the wilderness during the forty-year rebellion. We saw it in the palace as King David took the forbidden fruit. We saw it in the prophets. We saw it in the Gospels, and we see it now.

No one gets away, no one, including a man after God's own heart, and you and I won't either!

David's fiasco with Bathsheba opened a door for the enemy to come into David's life and wreak havoc due to a season of rebellion on David's part, but once he repented, God used him once again, but notice that the damage he did to his family went as God said it would, and all Israel as well had to suffer defeat because of his sin. And it wasn't until genuine repentance took place from David's part that David began seeing the Spirit take residence in his life all over again, though it was no longer the same outpouring as the initial infilling was; he no longer had what he had before the Bathsheba effect!

Sin has many consequences even after we repent!

WHAT DO WE KNOW ABOUT GRACE AND MERCY?

We can't deny that sin changes courses in God's calling, and King David is a perfect example. Today, many people in ministry view sin as if grace is the Mr. Clean of sorts, but it's not!

Grace is simply a period between sin and the judgment of that sin, though mercy is sometimes God's way of dealing with us when we sin and only after we repent, and thank God for that, because we do lose intimacy with God's Holy Spirit.

He is not a doormat!

We saw it in the confusion that followed Saul's extensive history of disobedience that eventually led to Saul taking his own life in fear of what God had already given him power over (the Philistines).

Eventually, Saul took matters into his own hands because of fear. Therefore, Samuel told him that God would have established him as king over Israel forever if he had *obeyed* the Lord's commandment, and that's a big "*if*." That task could no longer rest in

King Saul's calling; therefore, God, through Samuel, let Saul know He had raised for Himself another king to replace him and a man after God's own heart at that.

God did establish this promise to David later after Saul took his own life. This tells me that Saul lost his kingdom because of sin, his calling because of rebellion, and his salvation because of suicide (1 Samuel 13:13). In verse fourteen, Samuel told Saul that God had already found a replacement for the throne (in King David).

From this day forward, Saul's downward spiral began a snowball effect of unprecedented circumstances not in his favor, and at unstoppable speeds, might I add, and something that was definitely not in his control. The snowball effect eventually rolled over Israel's first king.

Saul went from anointed to annoyed, from zero to sixty in just two seconds.

In chapter fifteen and verse eleven, God regrets making Saul king because of his rebellion. Saul was supposed to annihilate the Amalekites, but instead, he took the spoils of war and also took king Agag alive as a prisoner. Perhaps to boast?

Although Saul acknowledged his sin in verse thirty, it was a little too late because it wasn't just anyone sinning, it was the king of Israel sinning, and may I add that his grace ran out that fast because of who he was and what he had done regarding his sin.

Just as it happened to Judas as well, *the calling dictates the measure of judgment*, just as Jesus said it in Luke 12:48. In other words, the higher the calling, the less tolerance for sin from God is available for that monumental calling.

As David began gaining prestige with not only God but also God's people, Saul's downward spiral accelerated into high gear, and to add insult to injury, Saul's son Jonathan became David's best friend, or his inside man, if you will. As David's battles began buying him popularity, Saul's washed-down crown began dreading its replacement. That caused King Saul to repent from what he knew to do when in trouble and take a different approach to spiritual insight, and that was to pray and not visit a witch. Soon he began chasing David for his very life.

Saul turned on lunatic mode. Meanwhile, David is winning battle after battle, and Saul pretty much becomes yesterday's news.

David passes up a few opportunities to kill Saul because he was God's king, and David would not dare touch God's anointed king because he knew the consequences, which shows the respect David had for the throne and for the king who sat on that throne, regardless of Saul's attempts on David's life.

How then did Saul end up in a place of rejection? I mean, rejection from people is one thing, but when God rejects you, what can you do?

Here's why Saul was rejected; take a look:

"For *rebellion* is as the sin of witchcraft, and stubbornness is as iniquity and idolatry. Because you have *rejected* the word of the Lord, He also has rejected you from being king" (1 Samuel 15:23, NKJV; emphasis added).

A righteous God has to punish the unrighteousness of sin…has to! The rebellion ended up in a witch's house, and you can call it a coincidence if you like, but rebellion is witchcraft, and Saul ended up with a witch, and that's the parallel.

That's what makes Him (God) righteous because He is compelled by His nature to do the right thing, and sin is the wrong thing and must be dealt with. But notice what Samuel tells Saul, "Because you have rejected the word of the Lord, He also has rejected you from being king." Saul rejected God before God rejected Saul. That's why we have to be careful we don't anger God to the point of rejection because when God is done with an individual, God allows them to kill themselves, and suicide is the best example of God's rejection of mankind. It's called judgment!

Stay with me here, please…God did not reject Saul outside of his position, and the verse makes it clear of his rejection, but so many of us walk away from God altogether, insidiously, yes, walk away from God because we want our position or title to remain, even after our rejection of the life and the sacrifice such a position requires from our part, a position we squandered. One we despised by our actions.

Saul could have continued walking with God even if he lost his title as king; it was God who rejected him after setting him up as king, meaning this did not take God by surprise, no!

We see that his son Jonathan, who was next in line for the throne and the next heir to the crown, actually took a back seat to the throne and allowed David to become king. But we are fixated with the idea that we can live an unproductive life as believers and not compromise our position or title in God's kingdom whatsoever, and that's the wrong approach on our part because it leaves no room for repentance due to *pride* and the false sense of humility and the arrogance of entitlement.

A degree is not an anointing!

There are way too many people walking around with earned academic, ministerial accolades but no spiritual power whatsoever.

Superficial knowledge puffs up, as Paul said (1 Corinthians 8:1). They mistake the fruits of the Spirit for the power of the Spirit, and the two are not the same.

The fruit of the Spirit is what we do outwardly as believers and as a result of our walk with God. We then retain these superb qualities as we practice them more, ones that show we are His, and they are also a part of a sanctified life—they are exemplary of our conversion. But these qualities are self-attainable (love, joy, peace...). Spiritual power is entirely different. It's Spirit-led. Therefore, only God knows why He chooses to give some such gifts and not others. Just as it's stated in the parable of the talents (Matthew 25), God will never give five talents to a one-talented believer.

What I do know is this: God will not give you a gift you don't believe in. Including salvation!

Take a look once *again* at what real Christianity is supposed to look like according to Jesus:

> And these signs will follow those who *believe*: In My name, they will cast out demons; they will speak with new tongues; they will take up serpents; and if they drink anything deadly, it will by no means hurt them; they will lay hands on the sick, and they will recover.
>
> Mark 16:17-18 (NKJV), emphasis added

This is what spiritual power is all about; this is what it looks like, a power that is unattainable by human means, one that can only come by the implementation in the anointing of the Holy Ghost and His overwhelming presence and direction.

If you've never cast out a demon from someone, that does not make you unsaved; it only makes you saved and powerless because we have all power over Satan and all authority as well over the enemy, just as Jesus stated in Luke 10:19.

Taking up serpents does not mean, "Go around grabbing

poisonous snakes and provoking them to action," to prove you're anointed, kind of like that church of old that went around handling snakes, no! Not like that because handling a deadly snake for show is tempting God and very much a death wish.

It's more like in case one does bite you when unprovoked, of course. Then, you are protected as we see it in Acts 28:3-5 as Paul was bitten by a viper in Malta.

I recall one time in my early walk with Jesus as my kid brother and I were doing some spring cleaning in our mom's garage; somehow, in the reduction and condensation of things, he grabbed a big bottle of muriatic acid that was almost empty and emptied its small contents into an empty bottle of lime Gatorade that I was drinking but had finished it. One he did not relabel.

As I got thirsty later, I went for my Gatorade bottle, not paying attention it was already gone, and being that the muriatic acid is similar in color to the lime-flavored Gatorade, I took a huge gulp, only to find out it wasn't Gatorade.

My teeth began to bubble and should have deteriorated immediately, and my stomach and esophagus as well; I mean, this stuff clears drains, for God's sake, but nothing happened to me. I remember my brother being the nerd that he is when he looked up the chemical reaction after advising me to brush my teeth, only to return after to announce baking soda and fluoride were the last things I needed to mix with the acid. I was living out that promise of drinking poison and being unharmed by it, and this because it happened *that way*, as a surprise, so God covered me.

My brother wasn't trying to poison me, or at least I hope not… (ha-ha!). But my point is this: I was protected. Just like Paul was protected from that venomous viper in Malta.

I can sit here and tell you about the many people I've had the privilege of laying hands on. People who have recovered from sickness and some from their death beds, and I prayed for them because they were sick and in desperate need of a miracle, I might add. Some were at the point of death, but God intervened!

We have our marching orders, and every now and then, God tests our faith, and we are compelled to answer the call because people need the God you and I know and trust. But once I understood who God is and how I reacted to the call of the Holy Spirit in my life when I was instructed to cast demons out of people, I simply asked God for His guidance…I happen to live and believe exactly how Jesus said it should be at the end of Mark, chapter sixteen. Too many denominations are not Spirit-filled for such gifts to operate as a tool for the lost as well as for the fold, and the reason why is because they don't believe!

I believe God's Word is alive, and, well, it's not just a storybook about a once-upon-a-time nice guy named Jesus. God on Earth is called the Holy Spirit, and He arrived on the day of Pentecost with autonomous power, and that power came with Him, and that power is available to those that believe, just as Jesus said.

The Holy Spirit is God of very God. He's no lesser than the Father or the Son. He's equal and has been part of Scripture since the beginning of creation. Genesis 1:2 is a perfect example of that reality.

We saw the first king of Israel's dramatic transformation took place once the Spirit touched him, and we also saw the unfortunate transformation he underwent once the Spirit left him. He went from prophesying one day (1 Samuel 19:24) to asking a witch and a demon to prophesy to him on God's behalf (1 Samuel 28:14). The draconian expression of such a bipolar decision is unfathomable.

The Bible is clear that once someone dies, they cannot come back to life unless God does it through the resurrection, and it comes with an ultimate purpose, as in the story of Lazarus and the many who left their graves when Jesus resurrected; in other words, if dead people had the power to come back to life, they should have had the power not to die.

When Samuel asked the witch of Endor to bring up someone from the underground for him, he did so because God wouldn't answer him anymore (1 Samuel 28:6). The mediums were enemies of God; there was an instruction to excommunicate them from all Israel (Deuteronomy 18:10-11) or put them to death (Leviticus 20:27). God said, "Give no regard to mediums and familiar spirits;

do not seek after them, to be defiled by them" (Leviticus 19:31, NKJV).

Unless we take God seriously on every issue we come across in life, we can perhaps find ourselves picking and choosing what we like or don't like about Scripture, and there is a great danger with such beliefs. We can argue that the dead can come back because there were a few instances when they did do just that, like 2 Kings 13:21, where a man died and came back to life.

We see it happen daily in emergency rooms all over the spectrum, but that's not what I'm talking about. What I mean is when people are long gone, not on the fourth day like Lazarus, but months, or perhaps years of being dead.

I believe that when Jesus was resurrected and the tombs opened as stated in Matthew 27:52-53, the most recent dead were the ones who got up from the grave, but that's just me, and I'm sure I have a great chance of being right. I also believe that the radiation levels in the area were off the top when it happened.

The witch asked Saul, "Whom should I bring up for you?" (1 Samuel 28:11, NKJV). Not only was this a bad idea as we read from the Scriptures themselves, but Saul's curiosity made him numb to the idea that God had departed from Him, which is the point I'm trying to make: God does not exist in a person's life if that person embraces another god and is at a witch's house.

In this case, Saul's continuous disobedience led him to this point of lunacy, and perhaps a person can gauge themselves if there is a hint of Saul inside of them as well.

The metaphysical definition of Saul is this, "The action of the will in attaining that which it desires."[10] Saul is anyone who falls under that definition; that's why the Bible discourages coveting.

Saul answered the witch of Endor, "Bring up Samuel for me" (1 Samuel 28:11, NKJV). Why would God allow the dead to rise, especially after a witch is the one who summons the dead, and by that, I mean the twice dead, physically and spiritually, because witches are twice dead!

The reason why Samuel's name is mentioned is that it's who the subject was, and the writer couldn't have been Samuel because he was dead. Now, remember that Saul is lost, God is no longer with him, and you can bet your bottom dollar that God was not with the witch of Endor either.

So how can the prophet come back from the dead? Well, he didn't! What did come back from the grave was *a familiar spirit,* as the Bible mentions in Leviticus 19:31. "Give no regard to mediums and familiar spirits" is a written commandment. And God is not in the business of violating His commandments!

The two are a team. The witch contacts a familiar spirit, and the familiar spirit uses information collaborated by another familiar spirit. What is a familiar spirit, then?

Well, a familiar spirit is a spirit who is familiar with the current and past situation of an individual not covered by God or someone who's walked away from God. Kind of like Saul and Judas, which both were lost, but in this case, the rebellious king is fascinated by the silence from above and thus jumps off the spiritual cliff, hoping to be caught by God, but to no avail, as he summons the powers from beneath!

In essence, what took place was that a spirit from the grave communicated with an already evil spirit lodged inside king Saul as we read it took place, and the witch as well had a spirit of divination. Witches only contact demons, not God. "But the Spirit of the Lord departed from Saul, and a distressing spirit from the Lord troubled him" (1 Samuel 16:14, NKJV). The evidence of Saul's loss of salvation is evident, to say the least.

This is parallel with what Jesus said in Matthew 12:43 regarding the unclean spirit departing from a person who has accepted Christ and deflected thereafter.

Jesus said that when an unclean spirit leaves a person after conversion, it goes through dry places and finds no rest, then returns to where it once was, "finds it empty [without Jesus], swept [you can't tell they are lost, still look saved and sanctified, but their sin is secret], and put in order [attend church regularly]" (Matthew 12:44, NKJV; brackets added). What takes place next is what's scary for that individual or should be! Take a look: "Then he goes and takes with him seven more spirits, more wicked than himself, and they enter and dwell there, and the last state of that man [woman] is worse than the first" (Matthew 12:45, NKJV; brackets added).

Some Bible commentaries deal with spirituality in ways that avoid the truth of the matter. They tend to run circles around what they don't understand or are afraid to touch on the subject because the truth that shows OSAS is a lie. Yet, the Bible is full of supernatural accounts throughout its pages. God is a Spirit, and so is Satan, for that matter. Selah!

For example: in verse twenty-two of Matthew, chapter twelve, we see that a man who was demon-possessed brought over to Jesus. Jesus cast the demon out. The Bible says that the person was blind and dumb. Now, these conditions are spiritual in nature only here in the Bible. If you ask for a similar explanation today, you will get a medical condition answer. The last thing anyone in the medical field would admit to in such a diagnosis is that it's an evil spirit causing the mental condition and blindness in an individual. But we know the reality of these unfortunate accounts, and we should never allow carnality to suppress the reality of what Jesus admitted to, and that's demons are among us.

WHAT IS THE SPIRIT REALM?

This is such an important chapter for us to see. In God's Word, spirituality that deals with the reality of a fallen race goes on ignored due to lack of spiritualism. We know that before Adam was in the scene, Satan and a third of the angels were already here, perhaps for millions of years. So the spirit realm was affixed before the natural realm was. What do you suppose "let your will be done on earth as it is in heaven" is really telling us?

When they brought Jesus a demon-possessed man who by today's standards would be addressed as having a medical condition of some sort, and I mean by the church's consideration, not the medical field, can you imagine what took place that day in Israel as Jesus ended the unwelcomed stay of a blinding demon?

How about this: demons who were inside the man were right there next to Jesus. How is that possible? How can demons come within an arm's length of the Son of God and inside the church?

Yet, some believers have qualms about demons showing up in church services as people get delivered from evil spirits because, according to them, only God is present. These churches feel as if all churches should be like them: powerless or dead. Spiritually speaking, they can't handle spiritual warfare with real evil spirits. Therefore, they'd rather ignore the reality of today's evil presence and not allow the Holy Spirit to move in the name of, "let's not take the attention away from Jesus." This means they don't believe in the supernatural. Yet, they claim they know God. Who is the epitome of what is the supernatural?

The Bible also says that Satan entered Judas as he was sitting next to Jesus at the Last Supper, which means that Jesus and the twelve had unwanted company: Satan!

Jesus could have cast Satan out of Judas at once, and He could have spared Judas from the demise that followed. But He didn't.

After all, Jesus did do it when it came to Peter, right? And that's exactly why God reserves the right to have mercy on whom He wants to have mercy on. Only God knows what Judas would have done had he been spared the unfortunate turnout. As it is, he was already a traitor and a thief. Now we know that the spirit realm is as real as our reality, a reality we experience with our very own eyes, day in, day out. A reality we heard with our ears and one we can tangibly touch with our very own fingers. Maybe we can also accept the spiritual reality as we should, especially as believers! None of us can deny we've seen or felt something in the paranormal realm at some point in our lives.

Though we can't see it, touch it, or hear it at times, nevertheless, it's there. The spirit realm is very real.

WHAT IS THE SPIRIT REALM?

Whenever an individual with "supposedly" biblical principles denies the very existence of such a realm or perhaps admits it could be there yet, has never experienced that tangible reality of it, that individual is perhaps a follower of the wrongful OSAS doctrine.

People, who teach eternal security, often have a disconnect with the spirit world, which means that they have never laid hands on the sick and they've recovered immediately. For certain, they have never cast out a demon from a demon-possessed individual because of unbelief. Some believe demons were left behind in biblical times and also confuse the fruit of the Spirit with the gifts of the Spirit.

A few years ago, I attended one of the nicest churches you can find in the South Bay area. It was literally on the water, the parking lot was full of boats and yachts, and the Pacific Ocean wrapped itself around the back of the church.

I remember one particular Bible study where someone approached me about a supernatural incident that took place at another churchgoer's home. As I was made aware of it after service, I learned that it was about a young couple fairly new to the church, and they were having some paranormal issues back at their home. They were looking for volunteers to see what was taking place at the couple's home. The issue had been placed on the back burner for a while, but the situation grew even direr for the family who was experiencing this unfortunate situation.

I volunteered to take a look along with one of the other pastors, and we decided to look into the matter as to what was happening in their home. We went over right after Tuesday night service. The senior pastor had approved our visit to the couple's home, and that's very important: we must always check with our leaders when doing anything that requires permission from our spiritual leaders in any perspective. It's called *submission and divine order as well.*

We arrived at the couple's home briefly after Bible study; they were less than ten minutes away from the church, so we decided to get into prayer while driving there because you never know what you will encounter when it comes to such matters. And once we arrived at their home, they briefed us as to what the situation had been for the past few months, and there was room for concern, according to their testimony.

Now, I had experienced some similar situations before, so I kind of knew the process, not that any situation is alike and the approach is always the same, but that at least I wasn't clueless to what potentially could take place when such spiritual situations arise.

This family had a home in one of the nicest cities in the South Bay, which was only minutes from the beautiful Pacific Ocean, near Bolsa Chica. They both worked very hard to buy their dream home and have something nice to raise a family in, but to have evil spirits come and ruin the blessing of homeownership and family life was enough to rid these evil spirits from the home at once, and the couple's lives for that matter, or at least try.

They had two infant children, one was months old, and the other one a toddler, both were boys, and also, a young lady friend of theirs rented a room from them. This trend is quite populous pretty much anywhere in California because of the almost unaffordable rents there.

They all slept in the same bed (the couple and their kids) because they believed the baby would protect them from evil spirits since he was innocent and somehow felt that the evil spirits would not go near the baby. It was a heartbreaking situation, to say the least, and obviously, they were babes in the Lord as well, which made it much more difficult to ignore, and they were almost clueless on how to address such issues on their own.

We found out that it was several spirits manifesting at different times. One was that of a little boy who ran up the stairs and locked himself in the bathroom, yelling and laughing out loud and pounding on the door with tremendous force before quietly opening the door and simply evaporating into thin air. I know it sounds creepy, but wait, it gets worse: the other one was a man who would go into the bedroom next to theirs, which is the kids' bedroom, and the spirit would walk in, slam the door, shake the bed, and then scream. This was routine around the home. My first question to them was: Are you involved in witchcraft or the occult? The woman said, "No!"

I then asked if there were any items in the home that might have had spells, curses, or anything of the sort. I asked if they had been out of the country lately and perhaps purchased a souvenir of some sort, something that would have been an idol in another country perhaps, and after thinking about it, the woman brought a few items she bought in Portugal. Items that her aunt had given her during her last visit with her family.

I took possession of the items and took them with us when we left. I asked that because a great deal of witchcraft goes on in most countries outside the US, especially where Catholicism is prevalent, not that it doesn't happen here, because it does, but get me, and because of Scripture, we know these items tend toward being tangible bodies for demons to hide in, being that they are idols.

We began anointing the home with anointing oil; we did so to stay consistent with Scripture, as the anointing was always done with oil in the Bible, except for the Passover, and also because it's a sign of the Holy Spirit in Scripture.

We anointed the doors and windows as we prayed throughout the home. After about an hour or so, the air began getting very thick inside the home. We went upstairs after anointing the first floor, and since all the paranormal activity took place upstairs, it got very suspicious (spiritually speaking). I could definitely sense a manifestation of some sort.

We walked in the bathroom and literally felt a presence there, but we continued as we proclaimed victory while rebuking the spirits. We had pumped the woman up to encourage her not to fear because God was with her, and as we prayed, we had her follow us as a form of training for future incidents, if you will, and to assure her that no devil in the world can contend with our mighty God!

Then we walked into the kids' bedroom, and I asked my pastor friend if he could pray in tongues, and he said, "No!" I asked him to kneel by the side of the bed and pray but not to close his eyes as he prayed, and he nodded. And as I was walking around the room, praying in the Spirit, the woman was reading Scripture out loud from her Bible. The temperature dropped dramatically in the room; the window opened wide, all on its own; the windows were swinging windows, not up and down ones.

My pastor friend pointed to the window, and I looked…we saw the screen get covered with dust from the outside, as if we were in the Mojave Desert in the middle of a sandstorm, rather than South Bay.

Suddenly, a small handprint appeared on the window screen, perfectly shaped and that of a child. I then poured anointing oil on my own hand and placed my hand over the small handprint on the window screen; then, the window slammed shut violently, almost breaking the glass.

We continued praying until we felt the peace of God in the room. It was my friend's first encounter with demonic manifestation, and after a few hours of intercession, things seemed to have improved, and we left but exchanged numbers with the couple just in case they needed us to intercede for them again.

The following week after he reported to the senior pastor what had happened, I asked if we could go back and check on the couple and pray with them some more. Then my pastor friend said it wouldn't be necessary and that those people didn't know what they were talking about!

I thought to myself, *really?* I mean, he saw what I saw and experienced what I experienced. I was flabbergasted at his response. Later I found out the leadership did not want for any of that negative spirituality to make its way to the church and somehow disrupt a service! I couldn't believe it!

I mean, they could put together a drama about spiritual warfare and make it look intense and very real, but the reality of that real drama was shunned because of fear of being labeled radical or for fear of anything manifesting during service, and that would have perhaps ruined the happy-go-lucky atmosphere they're so used to. Harps and choirs of angels may very well be nice, but there are other angels out there as well (demons), and they are very serious about their agenda, and we need to step up to the plate every time they show up to disturb the peace of God's people, especially the new believers.

That's exactly what we're dealing with in these denominations who don't believe in what Mark's last chapter commanded us to do (Mark 16:17). If we claim we are Christ's, and if so, then these signs must follow us.

We can pretend to be spiritual and not allow the supernatural into the church setting because of fear of spiritual manifestation, and that's exactly why Satan is running circles around such church settings today.

Just look at California and its ultraliberal edicts, while 80 percent of the population claims they are Bible-believing Christians, hmm?

Notice how Jesus addresses demon possessions to be something tangible, during, prior, and in the future as well, as in Saul's case. I'm talking about when it comes to manifestations and dealing with them altogether. Saul was clearly infused with spiritual power at some point in his conversion.

We know he prophesied when he was sent among the other prophets, which tells us that if the anointing is thick in a particular place, there's the resolve of an expectation as well, an expectation of the manifestation of the Holy Spirit, and whoever comes near the anointing will definitely be overtaken by His presence. He is God!

This is why you see the manifestation in some church services; it's impossible for God to be in a place and not minister to the needs of the people. Whether it be a conversion, healing, or deliverance, the bottom line is, something will happen if God shows up in a place. Take a look: "When they came there to the hill, there was a group of prophets to meet him; then the Spirit of God came upon him, and he prophesied among them" (1 Samuel 10:10, NKJV).

At this point, Saul was still in good standing with God; he was under the direction of Samuel. So, to submit that the Holy Spirit came and went in Old Testament believers is incorrect. The Holy Spirit comes and goes when we walk away from God or when we sin, and no other time.

How can we make the claim that God is the same yesterday, today, forevermore? And if God is the Holy Spirit, then how can He change from one testament to the next?

It's not biblical to assume that the Holy Spirit came and went in Old Testament believers. That would mean He is limited and has no direction. When, in actuality, the Holy Spirit was always present in the lives of Old Testament believers. Activation of the supernatural only happened when needed, as is the case today. And the Bible only highlights the necessary accounts for us to see; otherwise, the Bible would be a kazillion pages.

Spiritual power is the difference between Christianity and other religions. Radical Islam, for example, uses the radicalization of its members to carry out acts of terror. Today, Islam makes up about 15 percent of the European Union's population, that's over twenty-five million Muslims in that demographic area, but in cities of renown, Islam can make up to over 30 percent of that city's population. That's double.

Germany alone has over six million Muslims. France over eight; even without immigration, Islam is entrained of conquering the EU due to population growth, and this by being primarily a minority, and, because of the astonishing birth rate compared with the Europeans, which is no comparison at all, it won't be long before it happens.

Most of Islam's success has to do with acts of terror, inflicting fear in its spread, and that is not to say that all Muslims are terrorists, but that most terrorists are Muslims. Besides your oddball liberals here and there creating domestic terror for leftist political reasons. Radical Islam has become such a cancer that the EU wishes there was a cure for, and what if the Pope decides to turn Catholicism over to Islam, and the possibilities are not far-fetched now?

That would give the already terror-infested globe a tremendous blow of tumultuous proportions since that will tally almost four billion souls in both false religions! Imagine that?

So, to conclude that spiritual power comes by simply knowing Scripture is preposterous, and that's an understatement. Spiritual power only comes by the anointing of the Holy Spirit, and it's up to the Holy Spirit to decide who and how much of the anointing He will impart, and not some Christian education professor who has never had an encounter with God himself.

The parable of the workers in the vineyard of Matthew 20:1-16 is clearly a message contrary to that of eternal security. It begins by telling us what the kingdom of heaven is like the landowner, and the landowner is, of course, God.

He made a verbal contract with the first hires; He then went and hired another wave of laborers. Then went out again a third time and did the same. Yet again, He went and hired some more workers for His vineyard.

They were all bearing fruit, which they were all getting paid for. The last wave, though, were the forgotten ones, the ones everyone was passing up for whatever reason, but nonetheless, they were hired in the end, though they barely got in, they got in. Then the workday finally came to an end, and it was time to pay up.

The ones who worked the longest thought they had a bigger paycheck because they were there the longest, and they gauged their earnings not on their contract, but on the contract of others… as if serving God for many years can somehow give your salvation some kind of sticker of approval.

They complained about the newcomers who labored way less than they did, but the Owner simply reminded them that it was His vineyard, His money, and they had agreed on their pay from the beginning.

How is that unfair?

Jesus said that they made a deal to work for that amount of money…Why complain now?

So much division has come about from the first hires: they slander those who did not get a PhD in divinity, just like the slander is taking place to the success of most televangelists, or televangelists who have mega ministries and are actually doing Mark 16:17-18 ministry and believe God for the impossible, like staying on the air, as expensive as it is, which is a miracle in itself.

I have yet to hear a televangelist slander a radio preacher, but I can tell you this, radio preachers are slandering someone they disagree with daily, and the slandering comes from none other than the pulpit, and that's why you see so many individuals slander these televangelists on social media, as some *feeding frenzy of sorts.* Divisive is what it is!

I find it distasteful and unrealistic, at best disenfranchised. These preachers on the radio are teaching their congregants to do likewise. I was so upset to read negative post after negative post about Joel Osteen when hurricane Harvey hit the Houston area a few years ago. How dare they use a tragedy to add insult to injury to a man of God they disagree with!

As if Greg Laurie did not live in a multimillion-dollar home, or as if he didn't make several million dollars a year at Harvest? Think about all the Lakewood church members that lost everything in the devastation of this killer hurricane?

Think about how they felt to log onto Facebook or Twitter and see their pastor being dragged through the mud yet again by well-renowned pastors who abundantly tweeted attacks on Joel Osteen. Men who put out videos blaming the news media rather than feeling conviction for such vicious attacks on another believer. Is this what we've come to in Christianity?

Especially those in the LA area, who have no business mentioning the word "shelter," since the homeless population is at a staggering almost twelve thousand and growing each day in downtown Los Angeles, in the infamous area of Skid Row and LA County's surroundings, which have nearly sixty thousand homeless people within the county itself. Adding Riverside and annex counties to LA, we may have over one hundred thousand homeless people just in those few counties.

With sixty thousand in LA county alone living on the streets, I honestly don't understand how Maxine Waters and Adam Schiff keep getting reelected in that district. I mean, downtown LA is worse than a third-world country, and that's not an exaggeration. This, while there are over a hundred megachurches in LA County alone, while dozens of pastors make over a million dollars in salary in this area alone. How can this be? Jesus said we would always have the poor with us, not the government would, but us, the church.

Do you mean to tell me that having over a hundred mega-churches in LA and the homeless population being as high as it is is because these pastors have opened their churches as *shelters* to the very unfortunate? As what they slandered Osteen for!

I think you know the answer to that! In Matthew 21:28-32, Jesus gave us the parable of the two sons; one quickly jumped on board to do His Father's will but didn't. The other said no but did! Then Jesus told the religious leaders that they knew the answer to His question when He asked, "Which one did God's will?" but what good is it to know and not put to good use that *said* knowledge?

Jesus went on to say to the religious pundits of that day that "harlots" and "tax collectors" will enter the kingdom of God before them (verse 31). Is that not an insult to the "Hey, we were here first" trendsetters?

Think about what a harlot is, and think about how someone like that could get ahead of an individual whose religious knowledge never suffices for a place of humbleness (heaven), and then ask yourself, "Was He talking to me as well?"

Now, the parable of the wicked vinedressers in verses 33-44 is another example of the erroneous misconception of eternal security.

The landowner (God) rents the vineyard to the renters; they don't own the vineyard, but sure act like it, though, and also do some cruel acts toward others while at the helm. The landowner dug a press (left it all set up for production) and built a tower (for protection against enemies). Yet, they utilized both of these gifts to promote evil rather than good and used them against Him.

He trusted them with His possession, and notice that it wasn't a freebie, but they had to put something on it. In other words, keeping a productive sense requires work and investment.

So many people feel that ministry has no financial needs and that it requires no financial responsibility to keep it going and operating for the benefit of the body but ask any pastor with a small congregation how frustrating it is to have to beg for an offering just to keep the doors open. Now imagine a megachurch. I sense people forget big churches started as small churches. I know this because we started a church with a handful of people, and to God's glory, we're near thirty thousand eighteen years later.

The parable is all about responsibility and a business sense of provision at harvest time. He sent agents to recover His part. Now, remember that He equipped them for the harvest. When the agents (the Old Testament prophets) arrived to collect what was His, they were beaten by them and also stoned them and killed one of them (Zechariah, Luke 11:51).

Lastly, the Owner sent His Son; He did so by thinking that by giving them the benefit of doubt, they would respect Him. But when they saw Him from the watchtower, of course, they plotted to kill Him as well, so as to keep the vineyard for themselves, just as what the High Priest Caiaphas said to the rest of the Pharisees, when faced with the valley of decision, that One Man should die for the people, rather than a nation perishing altogether (John 18:14).

Jesus was predicting His death: they took the landowner out of the vineyard the Bible says, and that's why the reference of placing a hedge, or a fence, or a border if you will, signified Jerusalem and how they would take Him out of the city to crucify Him, just as it happened.

Then, Jesus dropped a bomb on them in His response. There is another parable in the Old Testament, and that's that of allowing the perpetrator to incriminate themselves subconsciously, thus bringing such judgment on themselves thanks to self-righteousness as a form of reverse psychology, if you will.

I'm speaking of where the prophet Nathan allowed David to pass judgment on the man who took the ewe lamb from a man whose love for that ewe lamb was unequivocal and who treated it like it was family (2 Samuel 12:7). David wanted the man executed until Nathan said, "You are the man."

Jesus asked them in verse forty, "Therefore, when the owner of the vineyard comes, what will He do to those vinedressers?" (Matthew 21:40, NKJV). Their response is astonishing, to say the least:

"They said to Him, 'He will destroy those wicked men miserably, and lease His vineyard to other vinedressers [Gentiles] who will render to Him the fruits in their seasons'" (Matthew 21:41, NKJV; brackets added).

Jesus goes on to tell them of their rejection of Him and that what they had been entrusted with (the vineyard, or the Law) was about to be transferred to another, just as they themselves had said. This is exactly what led to the adoption of the Gentile ministry, which is done through confession unto salvation in Christ. He concludes with this, "Therefore I say to you, the kingdom of God will be taken from you and given to a nation bearing the fruits of it" (Matthew 21:43, NKJV).

How much clearer than this can it get?

They were told they were about to *lose their salvation,* and it happened just like Jesus said it would, but that didn't mean ministry would end, no! The gifts of God are irrevocable. He simply takes His presence away, but the gifts remain.

It meant it would now open the door for another remnant to advance the Gospel since Israel refused to continue doing so and to carry forward the message and reach the lost for Christ. God found it necessary to do things this way because eternal plans belong to the Lord.

In verse forty-five, the religious leaders admitted He was talking about them. *The significance of the loss of salvation hap-*

pens when a sinful lifestyle is embraced after conversion. In their case, they had made the Law their god, and not the God of the Law, who gave them the Law through Moses in the first place.

I've always said that God forgives sin but never sinful lifestyles after conversion, and I'm saying if I remain in them to the grave, of course!

Moving on to the next parable, the one about the wedding feast found in Matthew 22:1- 14. Here, Jesus sets the wedding of the Lamb in motion. He talks about a wedding arrangement for a King's Son (God the Father and Jesus the Son). It begins by inviting to the wedding some who are unwilling to come; these, of course, are people who have knowledge of the times but did not believe it was necessary to attend. They were "in" because of their race (Jews), so they thought it was automatic salvation (privilege)!

Then He sent a second invite to them and made this one a lot more interesting. Now, He told them what was at the table, but they were not trying to hear it; they were too busy with their stuff (stuff can also be an idol). Then, they went on and shot the messenger (pretty much).

The king then sent out an army and killed them (Pharisees) and burned their city (Jerusalem), just as predicted by Jesus…He is prophesying to them with these parables, but they had no clue because their phylacteries were too big to understand parables, though parables were also a prophecy from Psalm 78:2. How they missed it is unbelievable, to say the least?

In verse eight, He said, though they were invited, they were not worthy, and why? Because they treasured possessions, positions, and titles (idols) more than Him! Then, God makes an open invitation to *whosoever* (John 3:16). Now even the bad are invited, *the bad*—do you understand what that meant to the elite? The uneducated in theology 101 are *in* now. Why them?

The place was packed with bad people, but wait…when a king gives a feast, especially a wedding feast, the king tends to provide the wedding garments. Now, they were about to get some new threads for the occasion. Tux time, if you know what I mean.

But when He came to see the guests, verse eleven, which was customary of the King to do before the banquet got underway, He greeted them with an array of the underline feats in store for the rest of the festivity, the itinerary if you will, and kings are known to hold it down for days, but not this King, this King's celebration will go on forever!

But wait: He found one without a wedding garment! Did he not like the garment? Did he perhaps take it off? Not putting on Christ is not the same as Christ walking away. Because of the simple fact that he was *at* the wedding (OSAS), was it why a garment had been given to him?

Keeping the wedding garment on was a requirement (just like today), as we will see.

This wedding was a "proper attire required" kind of wedding but provided by the King because the poor could not afford a tux.

The man did get inside. Meaning that a garment was given to him, and the King asked him, "Friend, how did you come in here without a wedding garment?" (Matthew 22:12, NKJV). And the man was speechless; the Bible said so because he did have a garment at the point of entry; otherwise, he couldn't have gotten in. Did he get past security without a garment? This is heaven we're talking about here, the same heaven Lucifer was kicked out of.

How is it that someone can make it all the way into the wedding, get dressed, and to top it off, get in front of the King [Jesus], and know that he definitely is not right with Him (God) because he has taken off the clothes provided for such an awesome event as the wedding of the Lamb (which is sanctification)?

Beloved, all of us will see the King in the end, and if Christ is in us and we in Him, we will be this man if we take off our wedding clothes too. The white garments are mentioned in Revelation 7:9, but in verse six of the parable, Jesus lays out how they have treated God's messengers over the centuries, and that's why God changed His mind about Israel.

In verse seven, we see that the end of the Old Testament wrapped up with the city under the Greek and Roman empires, as well as the Crusaders that followed. God sent armies to clean up the act of Israel.

Pride set in on God's people; they thought they owned the covenant and felt that an automatic pilot would suffice the rest of the way to enter the promised land without hesitation, but not so!

We must work out our own salvation with fear and trembling, just like Hebrews tells us.

In verse eight, He deems the first guests unworthy, unworthy! Meaning that you cannot take for granted the open invitation from the Lord. That invitation may very well change the course of one's life, and the destruction we once were in because of our sinful nature can go away by accepting the sacrifice provided to end that judgment, or we can continue playing Russian roulette with life; the choice is ours.

Once we receive a garment change, we must keep that garment clean, and that only happens by confessing our sins daily. Yes, we must keep track of our own sanctification; that's our responsibility, not God's, that's why we have 1 John 1:9. God will wash your clothes, but it's your job to call for pick up.

How can you stand in the King's presence without the proper attire and without a white wedding garment, just as it's required for the wedding banquet of the Lamb?

Here is where God must turn His back on you; you don't get in because of a confession you made once upon a time, no! You get in because of a lifestyle that validated that confession!

Verse twelve says that He asked the man how he got into the wedding without a garment, and the man was pretty much speechless! How can you defend yourself against the truth, especially when it's Jesus talking with you? The parable states that the person was invited, he was called a friend, just like Judas was called a friend as he was about to have Satan enter him at the Last Supper. The man was in the wedding hall, or court, if you will. He was given an invitation. Therefore, he accepted Jesus and was given a garment, which was forgiveness of sin. When he was approached by the Bridegroom, he was asked how he got in, meaning at the entrance, not the banquet itself. He had no defense because he no longer had a wedding garment. This person thought he could get in because he accepted Jesus, and obviously, at some point, he took off his garment, or his salvation. The message to work out your salvation with fear and trembling is clear in this parable!

He finishes the parable by ordering His servants (angels) to bind him hand and foot and cast him into outer darkness, which is the lake of fire (the black hole), or the second death. All these parables have one thing in common: they teach that eternal security is a lie!

Not convinced yet?

Well, then take a closer look at what Matthew 25:1-13 has to say regarding readiness.

The parable of the wise and foolish virgins paints a precise peculiarity of descending overtones deriving from obedience and participation while enacting wise council, and it's done due to an understanding and believing of the command simultaneously. Therefore, readiness paid off in the end for the five wise virgins, and it instructs us to do the same.

Five wise and five foolish virgins, now, kind of remember the 50 percent similarity here because I personally believe this ties the analogy to the rapture already in the works as described by Jesus in chapter twenty-four of the Gospel of Matthew. I'm speaking about the two men in the field, where one is left behind, and the other one is taken, as well as the two women grinding at the mill as is described in verses forty and forty-one.

As I understand it, only half the body (the church) is getting in. There are similarities to when Jesus expresses repetition of a thing, like when He says, "verily, verily I say unto you." We understand the priority of repetition here, and it is no different when He speaks of verses forty and forty-one.

There is not only urgency in repetition but also the warning of fellowship, as we all know the two women at the mill were not only coworkers but also friends who once held similar ideologies, i.e., religious convictions. The two men were equally so in their description as well. But let's get back to the five-and-five-virgin parable, shall we?

"Then the kingdom of heaven shall be likened to ten virgins

who took their lamps and went out to meet the bridegroom" (Matthew 25:1, NKJV).

In this particular verse, the setting is about ten female individuals who began a journey of inexplicable joy and did so simultaneously, but then, as they continued with the same agenda in mind, and that was to meet the Bridegroom, both parties were offered the same opportunity to accomplish the end result, and that's to get into the wedding, which was presented to them all in equality. But somehow, five of them didn't take the matter seriously enough *in the end,* and they were left behind for lack of preparation, sort of like trusting equity as if the entitlement has precedence.

They felt as if the invitation would suffice, but it didn't. Jesus clearly said, "But those who endure to the end will be saved," meaning an invitation is never enough, and that's because enduring takes great effort and, most of all, *self-denial* in a lifelong journey underlining Christianity as an action. To the very end of it!

As believers, we must follow through in our faith journey and try to get better at the things of God as we continue to grow, and as we mature in Him progressively, we are not to become worse, as it's the case with so many believers today. "But if anyone draws back, My soul has no pleasure in him" (Hebrews 10:38b, NKJV). There are way too many scriptures to discourage a believer from walking away; though the enticing is legit, we are not in the wilderness for forty days with the devil, if the truth be told. In fact, James says we are tempted because of our own desires (James

1:14), and not merely tempted but *drawn away by our own evil desires as is the case* always.

What did he mean by that?

Well, if you like the nightlife, chances are your temptation awaits you at a nightclub, not at church, or local bar and grille, if you will. But if you're in love with chocolate cake, chances are that the 2 a.m. bathroom visit won't disapprove of a detour to the refrigerator just to see if the chocolate cake is safe and sound. You get the picture: yet we see it take place daily as we set ourselves up for self-disappointment, and what's worse is that the disappointment of it is directed to our God. People who we know and love are doing it, just as we were too at some point in our lives.

The parable goes on to note that five of the virgins were wise, and five were foolish. Now, what was it that made the foolish virgins foolish?

My take is not bringing oil for the journey. The oil is a representation of the anointing of the Holy Spirit throughout Scripture, but unfortunately, today, there are way too many *Christians* doing life outside of God's will and, what's worse, without the Oil. And the truth is that there cannot be a conviction in our lives without Oil. The Holy Spirit will show up to convict us of sin as Jesus declared in John 16:8, but He will not beg or twist our arm for us to repent from it.

They took their lamps! Yes, they did, but no extra oil was

found. It's like having a Bible you don't read. Let's face it, the Bible will not read itself, and to add insult to injury, they slumbered because the Bridegroom was delayed. Meaning that they were perhaps up late the night before, so all ten made the same mistake, but five recovered from it and five didn't at the end when it meant the most. The foolish used up the oil in their lamps. Perhaps they left them on all night and then fell asleep with the lights on. Who knows, really? But the bottom line is they had no oil.

Doesn't it remind you of today's church? But before you excuse your feelings or judge me, may I remind you how the book of Revelation begins with a command to the seven churches to *repent.* God doesn't ignore the good we are doing, but rest assured He doesn't ignore our wrong either. Jesus didn't end the seven churches' discourse stating all their wrongdoing by saying, "It's okay, you're eternally secured," but did say their lamp would be removed unless they repented!

Oh, they have lamps as well (countless ministries, titles, positions, wealth, and education) but no oil, no substance, or desire to make it to the wedding either and are slowly slipping into apostasy undetected. Some because of racial motivation, some because of doctrinal error, and some because they simply can't stand to lose popularity and thus succumb to rebellion.

The thing is, we have had ample warning, and just as Jesus said in the parable of Lazarus and the rich man, "They have Moses and the Prophets," so do we: we have the same instructions, plus the

Gospels and the New Testament letters.

In verse six, the announcement was made to meet the Bridegroom. He was finally there, and the moment of expectation finally came. In verse seven, we see the five foolish virgins go through the motions; they trimmed their lamps (but without oil in them) and leaped for joy as well; in other words, they raised their hands in church, they cried at the altar, scores of crocodile tears, they even put in the offering or the proverbial two mites, but they only did it out of mere habit, kinda like how Bathsheba went through her customary religious ceremonies after committing adultery with the king, and that's all it is, religiosity…and that's what religion is, a good, bad habit and nothing more, or less!

In verse eight, they *demanded* some of the oil of the wise virgins. In other words, an entitlement surfaced because they felt preparedness wasn't required, and equity is a must, and they wanted someone who had Oil to fork it over to them, or better yet, to chance missing out on their own way into the event by such distraction…but wait, it gets deeper than that because it was Jesus talking here, it's the red letters.

At what point are we to take full responsibility for our own shortcomings so that we don't repeat them repeatedly and not have to always rely on someone else to pray for us because we've been in church all their lives, but sometimes our prayers can't seem to make it past the ceiling, being that we don't really have a true relationship with God? With the pastor maybe, but not with God, and we become lukewarm, willingly or not, may very well be the case, but the result is the same!

What happens when you're in dire straits, but there's no one around to help, a time when you need the entire army of God to pray for you, but you can't access them? Did it ever occur to you that when no one is around, we still have God next to us, and He knows exactly what we're going through every single time!

A few years back, I was at home waiting for a brother in Christ to come by because we were supposed to hang out later that day, and I had been very sick that week. Now, I'm the kind of guy who doesn't get sick very often, and when I do, well, I'm a big baby, but this time I was really sick, and I began spitting up blood when I coughed. Congestion, discomfort, you name it, I had it. As I greeted my then friend at the door, he right away asked if I was sick, and I said I wasn't feeling too good. He then suggested we hang out another day; well, before I could get a word out, I began coughing again, and it got really bad. He left kind of worried and suggested I see the doctor.

But stubborn me decided to wait until morning, hoping I'd wake up better. But in the morning, I woke up feeling as if a Mack truck had run over me while I slept, which wasn't much because of the cough. And I decided to get my stubborn self to the emergency room, which I did. They asked what was wrong, and I explained while coughing and was immediately quarantined. Well, next, they sent me to get chest X-rays and said I had pneumonia. The doctor told me I wasn't going home for a while; of course, I panicked. I tried going on my phone and texting my pastor and other pastor friends but had no reception. I also tried going on Facebook and posting a need-for-a-prayer post, but nothing. I was lining up with the diagnosis, and I don't mean you should ignore the reality, but what I mean is don't agree with it and accept it as your state of mind so as to keep faith and hope alive and line up with the miracle-working power of the Holy Spirit. And stay consistent with Romans 4:17.

I began to lay hands on myself as I remembered the Scripture about David encouraging himself in the Lord (1 Samuel 30:6). I reminded the Lord that He had given me an assignment that wasn't yet complete, besides this book. I pleaded with Him about it, and then I thought about the disciples when Jesus told them to go with Him to the other side of the lake in Luke 8:22, as a "we will get there regardless of the storm" kind of deal. I remembered that there was a storm and that the disciples panicked, and Jesus was asleep in the boat, but then He woke up and rebuked the wind; they ended up making it to the other side despite the storm.

This actually boosted my faith back up; I had fallen into a momentary depression because of the bad news coming from the medical field (the storm) and realized that I had to get to the other side of the lake (my destiny) because of the negative thoughts that were going to my mind; working against my faith were thoughts of famous people I knew had died from pneumonia, like the late Bernie Mac, which had me at a standstill.

WHAT IS THE SPIRIT REALM?

By now, I was already praying in the Spirit and fighting my own thoughts, and about ten minutes later, the doctor walked into the room and told me to put on a robe, and someone was going to come in and do blood work, and that also a colleague was coming back later with him so to reassess the diagnosis to the lead physician. Now I knew I was in serious trouble, but I refocused my efforts on praying. I remember the nurse walking in and out getting things ready, but suddenly, I looked at my X-rays *and began rebuking the wind* as Jesus did (pneumonia) and for a few minutes, I felt the warfare was intense, my chest was collapsing, but I spoke against it and began commending every blood vessel, every fiber, every sinew and every bone in my body to line up with God's perfect will and beat of life for myself, and then finally a breakthrough took place. As the doctor came back in with another doctor, and a few minutes later, the head physician also joined, they were all looking at the X-rays, and then at me, then they would pin them on the white lighted board and grab them again, and then dumbfoundingly put them to another light, then back on the board.

Finally, the lead doctor came to me and said I didn't have pneumonia; he said it was bronchitis and that I was being released. He gave me an inhaler, which I didn't use, and in a matter of hours, I went from spitting blood to spilling hallelujah on my way back home. I went in coughing up blood, and all symptoms were gone by the time I got in my car. I took pictures before and after, which I ended up using in a social media post and gave God the glory for it.

Not that storms won't come because they will, not that we

won't find ourselves alone and vulnerable at times because we will, but that despite the situation, we will always have access to God, who is a present help in our time of need, just like Scripture says. I'm not telling you to believe something I don't believe in, and as I testify of God's provision in my life at all levels should be enough to let you know I live what I believe. I pray till I'm blue in the face, and for whatever reason, God does not do the thing I'm asking Him to do; it will not be because I didn't pray till I was blue in the face!

Notice that at the end of verse eight, the foolish virgins make a remarkable statement after their demand for oil, they said, "Give us some of your oil, for our lamps are going out" (Matthew 25:8, NKJV). This can only mean that if their lamps were going out, it was because they were once on, and now something has happened, and no oil was available for them, and let's ask the question of "Why did God allow the oil to run out, and why did He not supply them with someone to give them oil?" Because we read that the wise said no, and once the foolish left to get more oil, they not only did not find any oil but came back and were rejected by the Groom who initially invited them to the wedding as He did the five wise!

The obvious is that they did have some oil initially, enough to be a light, but what happened to them? Why did they not prepare for the end? Because they believed they could not lose their salvation, and oil is to be kept in our lamps until the Bridegroom shows up. Did not 50 percent of the virgins get in? We see that five of the ten did prepare, five did go after the Oil (Holy Spirit) and thus, had enough Oil to complete the journey to the wedding (heaven).

All ten virgins were given a lamp filled with Oil. That, my friends, signifies the initial acceptance of Jesus as Savior. At such a point of conversion, God gives the Holy Spirit (the Oil) to us all who accept Him, and our lamps are lit, and we become the light of the world (Matthew 5:14). This parable clearly teaches that our light can go out if we do not prepare as we're supposed to. We have five wise virgins as a reference, who did retain the ability to receive more of the Holy Spirit due to reinvesting in a personal relationship with Him. In fact, they had enough oil to make it into the presence of the Bridegroom, as required. And not what Lutzer teaches that they did not get accolades but did get in on the coat-tails of their inability to remain saved!

In verse nine, there is a shrewd reality at play, and that's the fact that this relationship with God has to be personal. We are fooling ourselves if we think that God owes us anything just because once upon a time, we went through the motions, the religious rituals, if you will, to accept Him as Savior.

God owes us nothing; on the contrary, we owe Him. The answer to the five foolish virgins was "no."

The best possible thing the wise virgins could do was to send them where the foolish could get the oil. But it was too late. Can we miss the boat if we're not careful?

In verse ten, the foolish virgins did another foolish thing; they went back. There it is again: they drew back. Remember the passage in Hebrews about drawing back? God has no pleasure in that, none whatsoever. The end of verse ten says, "The door was shut." Wow! (Noah's ark, all over again.)

In verse eleven, they are called "the other virgins." They came back, but when they came back, the door was shut. There is such a thing as enough is enough, even with God. We saw what happened to Saul and Judas, but for some odd reason, people believe that God is this white-haired jolly old man sitting on a fluffy cloud, just smiling at us all the time, and that is not the case. When Jesus returns, He will return as a righteous Judge, not as Savior.

The foolish virgins begged Jesus to open the door, "Lord, Lord, open to us!" they said. "But He answered and said, 'Assuredly, I say to you, I do not know you'" (Matthew 25:12, NKJV).

THE DIRECT ASSIGNMENT OF THE TIMES!

Let's begin with a closer observation of this controversial edict of transitional biblical fluctuation. When developing a more accurate medium of scriptural interpretation, and after doing so by looking at Scripture with an open heart and mind, asking God for a revelation of His word, it's exactly how we need to approach the study of God's Word on a daily basis—doing so by analyzing our very lives through this filter.

In the Gospel of John, the Lord addresses the disciples in prayer. He's praying specifically for them. Meaning, it's not intended for anyone other than the twelve disciples.

Too often, we make the mistake of misinterpreting the Word of God because of the lack of recognition of the times it was intended for, and that's in whatever scripture setting it may be. In this case, it was directed to a special group of people: Jesus's disciples.

The Bible has four stages of biblical timetables for interpretation that need to be examined as we confirm its application.

- Some teachings are for biblical times.

- Some are for today.

- Some are for *then and now.*

- Some are for future events, i.e., are prophecies!

And we must respect and recognize those four stages of biblical timetables in order to understand our place in Scripture so that we do not misconstrue the meaning of such critical events as intended by the Lord. Take a look:

> While I was with them in the world, I kept them in Your name. Those whom You gave Me I have kept; and none of them is lost, except the son of perdition, that the Scripture might be fulfilled.
>
> John 17:12 (NKJV)

The obvious is that Jesus was praying only for His disciples, the twelve. The ones who walked with Him daily, that is. In other words, this prayer was exclusive to them. But what's important here is that Jesus was addressing the loss of one of the twelve. Judas in particular.

What you get from most teachers who take to the OSAS doctrine is that Judas was never saved. This is an easy way out of not losing ground on their perspective and the erroneous belief system they have adopted. Also, not compromising doctrinal conjecture as a means of evading the issue is very intentional in their adaptation of misinterpretation. Thus, by making Judas unsaved, they make for error a perfect situation in admitting Judas was the only apostle who wasn't saved.

That would mean that giving us the great commission to make disciples of all nations is something He missed the mark on in choosing Judas, who, according to OSAS, was perhaps a nonbeliever, one who kept the purse for the Lord. Imagine that?

It's like saying you lost twenty dollars, but you never did have twenty dollars in the first place. How then can someone lose what they never had? In Judas's case, the Bible is very clear he was one of the twelve!

But was Judas saved? Let's look at Judas's arrival from the first mention of his appearance according to the Gospel of Matthew:

> Jesus called His *twelve* disciples to Him and *gave them* [all] *authority* to drive out impure spirits [can only be done by the Holy Spirit] and to heal *every* disease and sickness. [All Twelve had such powers.] These are the names of the twelve apostles: first, Simon [who is called Peter] and his brother Andrew; James son of Zebedee, and his brother John; Philip and Bartholomew; Thomas and Matthew the tax collector; James son of Alphaeus, and

353

Thaddaeus; Simon the Zealot and Judas Iscariot, who betrayed Him [after the fact]. These twelve Jesus sent out
with the following instructions…

Matthew 10:1-5 (NIV), emphasis and brackets added

Without a doubt, Jesus equally empowered the twelve apostles
before sending them out to preach the Gospel, heal the sick, and
cast out demons. They were also setting up churches; that is what
the apostolic ministry is. He didn't single out Judas saying, "I'm
giving you all power except Judas." As we saw Him single out
Judas earlier in John 17:12, speaking about whom He had lost.

How is it that some teach that he was never saved or that he
didn't have the power to cast out demons like the others, and this,
without being saved? Knowing that Jesus said, "If Satan is also divided against himself, how will his kingdom stand?" (Luke 11:18,
NKJV).

That's exactly what OSAS doctrine does: it manipulates every
scripture to fit its erroneous agenda, but how can an apostle be an
apostle and not be saved? Is the Bible not clear of what the great
commission is? Isn't it to go and make disciples of all nations…?
Can you make an unsaved disciple? Furthermore: Did Jesus make
one? Jesus said we cast out demons by the Holy Spirit in Matthew
12:28, meaning that the disciples were empowered with the Spirit;
otherwise, they could not cast them out, and the misconception of
the Holy Spirit not yet given can easily be rebutted since Elizabeth

was filled with the Holy Spirit when Mary entered the room as she was pregnant, as well as Mary for that matter, and let's not forget John the Baptist who was filled with the Spirit inside his mother's womb.

It is leaving us no doubt whatsoever that Judas was indeed saved and filled with the Holy Spirit.

We read in 1 Timothy 3:6 that one of the requirements for a bishop is to not be a *recent convert*. How then, can an apostle, which is a greater calling than a bishop, be labeled unsaved as is the case of Judas, according to OSAS that is, especially when a bishop can't even be allowed to be a recent convert, how can an apostle, and one handpicked by Jesus at that, be labeled unsaved by the OSAS frenzy, after walking with Jesus three and a half years and along with the other eleven?

We must be careful not to fall into the demise and trap of undermining Scripture in order to fit doctrine. That would be the equivalent of making *doctrine* an idol, or a god, if you will. In this direction, we know that Judas was present while Jesus addressed the apostles altogether. He was obviously giving even Judas's power over the enemy as well as all the others. Otherwise, Jesus would have said, "Hey, you eleven," excluding Judas.

Look at how the Bible reiterates Judas's role as one of the twelve: "While he was still speaking, Judas, *one of the Twelve*, arrived" (Matthew 26:47, NIV; emphasis added).

It's undeniably noted that Scripture wanted us to understand and identify the role of Judas as one of the twelve disciples. Furthermore, Judas, unlike the others, held an extra office of ministry than none of the twelve did. He kept the purse according to Scripture (see John 13:29).

Jesus trusted Judas (Psalm 41:9). No one places the responsibility of finances in the hands of an untrusted and unreliable source, let alone that the person was Jesus!

This emphasizes Jesus's limited ability as a human (John 5:19). The Bible tells us that after three and a half years of walking with Jesus, the disciples were operating in the anointing Jesus imparted onto them.

Jesus sent them out two by two to do ministry (Mark 6:7), and this included Judas as well, and that makes six pairs, and if He sent them out two by two having only eleven, well, we would be looking for answers on that. He (Judas) was just like them: he went out and cast out demons, laid hands on the sick, and the sick recovered and perhaps won many over to Jesus in this three-and-a-half-year journey of walking with the Master and in His power.

If Judas was casting out demons as the other twelve were, who was he casting them out by? By Beelzebub, perhaps? Just as Jesus was wrongly accused of doing when the religious pundits hinted, He was casting them out by the lord of the flies (Matthew 12:24). Furthermore, the Bible is very clear about when Satan entered

Judas (see John 13:27).

Before this, it was a mere temptation that Judas was dealing with as he was plotting to betray Jesus because of the kingdom Jesus proclaimed, which differed from Judas's own mindset of doing things and not what they were used to in those days. A violent overthrow was what everyone was expecting. Not so this time!

But today, so many Bible scholars solely repeat what they've learned in seminary and or Bible college, conveying others' revelation and not their own. What they teach in some of these theological institutions is textbook theology, but none of these pupils have personal, spiritual experiences intertwined with Bible knowledge. At least those that speak of real spiritual accounts, that is. Those only come by belief and faith in God's Word. God will never give someone a gift they don't believe in!

Though acceptable, some of these believers go through life without ever having an encounter with God, a real, one on one if you will, and perhaps have never experienced the supernatural either or ever will. If they continue relying on books alone, they'll be book smart at best, but outside of biblical spirituality, they are clueless of the spirit realm. Yet, God and Satan are both spirits. Go figure! The reason why prophecy was uttered when it was uttered in those days was that God has a window into the future, and that's why the things predicted about Judas actually came to pass. God is not making things happen; God sees into the future. God pushed the *play* button in eternity past. We can all pretty much agree that

God is not restrained by time or space.

Yet, most of the time, we don't allow God His time or His space, and when it comes to spiritual matters, we are clueless about what each prophecy was intended for. We only pretend to know. There are at least ten different Bible commentaries that are almost identical to each other. I have no idea why, why we need so much of the same, and those commentaries who disagree with them are, of course, written by *heretics,* or so they're labeled. And since God has this window into the future, He can pretty much predict what will happen in a certain situation. Like that of Judas. Take a look at Acts 1:16 (NIV):

> ...and said, "Brothers and sisters, the Scripture had to be fulfilled in which the *Holy Spirit* spoke long ago through David concerning Judas, who served as a guide for those who arrested Jesus."

> emphasis added

Here's where most people become numb to the idea of the prophetic application. An analogy of prophecy here can be summarized as perhaps that of watching a movie, one that you've watched over and over, where you can pretty much predict the next move and even repeat the next line as it's playing itself out. If you were watching a movie with your child, and you knew the movie like the back of your hand, you would mute bad words to spare your child's ears, or if there was violence or some sort of indecency, you would skip a frame or two. God gave us His Word for that purpose. We are sheltered from His wrath to come, but we must obey to the end! Except that God is way more awesome and more sophisticated at this than we could ever be or imagine; of course, we can pretend we know, but the truth is we don't—unless it's revealed unto us.

Now let's look back at what Luke was writing concerning David and the psalms: "Even *my close friend,* someone I trusted, one who shared my bread, has turned against me" (Psalm 41:9, NIV; emphasis added).

The simple fact that the book of Acts tells us that this scripture was a description of Judas should be sufficient for us to take it in as intended, right? We know Jesus was God in the flesh but limited to what the flesh would allow Him to see, or better yet, to what God the Father would allow Him to see. Speaking of when in the human nature He found Himself, i.e., in the flesh.

He was limited, nonetheless. Jesus gave up a lot of His Godhead attributes when he transitioned into humanity (John 5:19).

The fact that Judas was one of the chosen twelve is no mystery at all (Matthew 10:1-5). But how can some characterize his role in Scripture as that of an unsaved man and not express a limited cliché of doctrinal error because it would be impossible to be a disciple and not be saved? (Therefore, OSAS is a lie.) How many pastors have you seen walk away from God in your life? I bet too many to count! Were they ever saved?

If Judas was not saved because he committed suicide, then why not say the same about people who claim to know Jesus and then kill themselves? Why portray them as saved and not Judas? Why instruct them to take their lives and reassure them of eternal security, just as Lutzer puts it? In my view, we must apply everything said about Judas in the chronological stages it took place in and also display the many events pertaining to such incidents, and yes, even the ones prophesied about him. But what about the ones that never made it into the New Testament at all?

We should not manufacture a new and perhaps applied revelation from what we already know but rather synchronize what we already established in the texts and in conjunction expound on where and when it was assigned for by keeping up with the times and places in Scripture, which can stay true to its concurrent revelation.

I say this because of the "quick to judge" Christian fringe that labels heresy to anything they simply can't or won't understand or something they find written in the Bible for that matter, which was perhaps read in the redundancy of one of the many commentaries that say the same.

Remember my earlier statement that God will not give you a gift you don't believe in (like the revelation of His Word); this is very crucial in order to understand the Bible. Remember Paul's frustration with *meat* and Christians living off baby formula? (Hebrews 5:12). We have to grow and stay grown; otherwise, we can undermine what we don't understand because of the lack of revelation and knowledge of Scripture. And get this…get away with it as well, just like those who teach eternal security. At least on this side of eternity!

Let's begin the biblical breakdown of the infamous apostle named Judas; some say he wasn't an apostle but only a disciple, which means an admission of salvation either way. Unless, of course, a disciple of Jesus is somehow a possibility allowed without the necessity of being saved, and what a joke that would be, but back to what was expounded from the psalms and the prophets about him, and also what wasn't, for that matter!

The apostle Peter stood up and addressed 120 believers in Acts 1:16, saying that King David had insight into Judas's arrival in the first-century church.

Peter addressed the situation by pointing out that Judas was the *aid-and-assist* to the arrest of Jesus in the garden of Gethsemane's betrayal. But what's confusing here is that Peter mentions that Judas was included as one sharing in the ministry with them, an apostolic ministry.

and said, "Brothers and sisters, *the Scripture had to be fulfilled* in which *the Holy Spirit spoke* long ago through

David concerning Judas, who served as a guide for those who arrested Jesus. *He was one of our members* and share in our ministry." With the payment he received for his wickedness, Judas bought a field; there he fell headlong, his body burst open and all his intestines spilled out. Everyone in Jerusalem heard about this…

Acts 1:16-19 (NIV), emphasis added

What we have here is a prophetic word that was awaiting much-needed fulfillment, and it also helped the fact that Peter and the disciples somewhat knew Scripture, not in a Pharisee-like way, but in general knowledge as in being a Jew. Remember when Judas was called by Jesus back in John 1:40-42. Andrew, Peter's brother, introduced Peter to Jesus. Andrew was a disciple of John the Baptist once upon a time. But when he decided to follow Jesus, he brought Peter into the mix and said, "We have found the Messiah." Obviously, a biblical term.

Philip found Nathanael and told him, "We have found the One Moses wrote about in the law, and about whom the prophets also wrote about—Jesus of Nazareth, the son of Joseph" (John 1:45, NIV), which asserts that the disciples weren't clueless about Scripture, though uneducated, as some would have you to believe. They knew the signs, and they sounded like they were expecting this season.

Judas was one of them, no doubt, but he was the one God had

looked into in eternity past by writing what his lot in life would be once it all began to unravel. Not because God made it happen, no! But because God allowed it to happen; therefore, preparation for the outcome comes from God's wisdom on how to align everything else to the occasion to outwit the adversary. Otherwise, free will is nonexistent, and that will make us all robots. How many people have done perhaps even worse things than Judas?

Clearly, God allowing Adam and Eve to eat from the tree of knowledge of good and evil in the Garden's undimmed setting is very much proof of God's reluctance to intervene when free will is implemented, but the fact that God inspired the prophets and psalmists to pen such events before their time is what most believers are bollixed about when it comes to their writings' proper interpretation. And you know this is true!

God doesn't force anyone to act out situations any more than Satan does. James was pretty clear when he said that we are drawn away by our own evil desires (James 1:14). Therefore, Judas acted on his own evil desires, and the fact that it was all predicted was because God saw it happen before it took place, yet, without manipulating the situation one bit. And because He didn't have to: He simply prepared for it and used it for His glory. Thus, *packaging* salvation in the death of the Messiah (for lack of a better word) was instrumental, and why? Well, because Satan was a murderer from the beginning, according to Jesus (John 8:44), and a very predictable devil at that.

We saw Satan have Abel killed by his brother Cain, thinking he was the Messiah. We see it in the curses discourse of Genesis, chapter three. God knew that Satan would kill the Messiah, and that's why our salvation was implemented in His death. This, due to the predictability of the evil one, who was a murderer from the beginning.

Although everyone who embraces Judas's idea of not being saved very much enjoys quoting his infamous betrayal from some of the psalms, I'm pretty sure that if they were to include everything said of Judas in the Old Testament, they would probably make a better case of promoting him as never saved, or any chronological history pertaining to him for that matter. Of course, you know that the reason they believe he wasn't saved is to protect the OSAS erroneous doctrine. But was he?

"Even my close friend, someone I trusted, one who shared my bread, has turned against me" (Psalm 41:9, NIV).

David perhaps was clueless about what he was writing when he wrote this verse of Scripture, but we know that the setting here is none other than the Last Supper's turn of events, where Satan was the uninvited guest.

Jesus turned to Judas, called him friend, and then He told him to do what he had to do and to do it quickly. Not a word to Judas to not do such a thing. So, Judas, of course, obeyed. But those who want to portray Judas as an outsider who was never saved do so from doctrinal error without a doubt. Jesus called him His close friend!

Look at what the psalmist says once again, "Even My close friend." How would you like to interpret that? How about this one: "Someone I trusted"? Remember that we are talking about Jesus and Judas here. Did Jesus really trust Judas? He must have because Judas was His treasurer. Or that would make Jesus a liar to say what He didn't mean. And I'm not one to suggest that idiocy!

Let me ask you this question: Would you give your money to someone you didn't trust?

I hope the answer is no! What pastor you know places the church's money in the hands of an unbeliever? Then why would anyone in their right mind think Jesus would? Jesus, though being God, agreed to leave most of His attributes behind to experience humanity in its fullest, yet, without sin, and He only knew revelation as it was given to Him by the Father.

He stated that He only did what the Father showed Him. Why is that so hard to believe? In Psalm 109, we see the prediction, or the rendering of Judas's life, just as it took place in the aftermath of his betrayal of Jesus. And this presentation is implemented substantively in the scope of things, which perhaps has never been displayed before in such an undimmed way of presentation in complete error, suggesting that he was never saved.

No commentary or biblical writing has, for that matter, presented itself in a clear view of validity on the subject at hand (except for Dake's), that's without referring to some obscure revelation from centuries ago that suggests Judas was the only unsaved disciple of Jesus.

Reaching such a conclusion because the Holy Spirit wasn't given yet is also wrong, but wait, we know that John the Baptist was filled with the Spirit before He was born (Luke 1:15). How then can anyone argue Judas did not operate under the Holy Spirit's anointing when Jesus empowered all his disciples? Not only eleven! Furthermore, that Judas wasn't saved?

Psalm 109, verse six, says, "Appoint someone evil [The High Priest] to oppose my enemy [Judas]; let an accuser [Satan] stand at his right hand" (Psalm 109:6, NIV). When Jesus decided to reveal His betrayer, the Bible clearly states that at that moment, Satan entered Judas, and it happened at the Last Supper (John 13:27).

Not while he did ministry for three and a half years alongside the disciples, but exactly at the time he took a piece of bread from the Lord and dipped it simultaneously. Jesus is about to have the last supper with His disciples. He announces that His time was at hand and that one of them was going to betray Him.

They perhaps looked to one another in dismay and asked, "Is it me, Lord?" But when Jesus said it would be the one who would take the bread after Him, dipping it, and be that as it may, it turned out to be none other than Judas Iscariot. Jesus saw Satan in the room. Jesus saw Satan walk up close to Judas, Jesus saw Satan enter Judas, and that's because Judas was next to Jesus!

What's amazing to me is that right after Judas takes the bread, the Bible says that "As soon as Judas took the bread, Satan entered him." Now, Satan didn't enter Judas while he was out fornicating, no! He didn't enter Judas while he was doing witchcraft or idol worship or any other physical or spiritual offense. We all know sins are portals for demon possession, and let's not ignore the fact that it wasn't a demon that entered Judas but Satan himself!

Satan entered Judas as he was sitting next to Jesus! How close was Jesus to Judas that the devil had the audacity to inherit one of Jesus's disciples literally in the presence of the second member of the Trinity, and at arm's length, or perhaps closer?

Well, it seems to me that the Bible is quite clear on how close Jesus and Judas were at the point of possession. You mean to tell me that Satan can show up at the Last Supper, uninvited, unwelcomed, and knowing full well that Jesus is in the room and yet, possess one of the apostles?

Well, yes!

Maybe we need to look at Genesis, chapter three's account of Adam and Eve's Garden of Eden debacle where Satan once again showed up to possess someone God had entrusted humanity and eternity to. And I don't mean the serpent, though it was the first to host the evil one.

This time, Satan possessed God's only creation with redemptive power, a human, and did it by invitation on their part. Satan merely was the waiter at that table, he presented the menu, and they decided on the meal themselves. The devil did not force-feed them the DNA altering fruit, or first RNA vaccine, if you will. They were drawn by their own evil desires, the lust of the eyes, the lust of the flesh, and the pride of life!

What about when Satan showed up in the presence of God along with a host of angels back in Job 1:6 and 2:1? It seems to me that the Bible didn't bother leaving out of the confines of Scripture such information that could be deemed contradicting, but scholars do like to skip over such concrete observations, and for a good reason (lack of revelation, or to protect erroneous doctrine, such as OSAS).

But let's enter into the last time the devil showed up to make trouble yet again, and before the Last Supper took place back in the New Testament's "close encounter of the evil kind," found in Matthew (4:1).

Here, the Bible tells us that Jesus was led by the Spirit into the wilderness to be tempted by the devil.

In verse three, the Bible says that the *tempter* came to Him. It seems to me that this devil had clear-cut access to God's presence several times, and I don't see God intimidated by it whatsoever or attempting to hide the evidence that somehow the devil keeps popping up in all these intense conversations of deity.

Why is that? My take on this is that God is not worried about what Satan is doing, not at all. God is God, and Satan is not. Period!

How humiliating it must be for Satan to have lost his power to mere humanity because that's why he hates us so much, a power he can't get back unless he causes us to fall for the temptation and we then sin and turn over power back to him. Thus, the need for confession, which snatches that power back from Satan, immediately!

Now call me crazy, but why didn't Satan enter Judas...perhaps while he was cutting a deal with the Pharisees?

Why did Satan enter Judas as he was literally taking a piece of bread from Jesus's hand? We know that Jesus taught that light and darkness don't abide in the same place simultaneously.

We know that God and Satan can't be inside a person at the same time either. But how is it that the devil jumps inside of Judas at the moment of taking the bread from Jesus's hand? *Appoint someone evil to oppose my enemy,* said the psalmist. And here's Judas being placed in a tough spot after attempting to give back the money he was paid for betraying his Master. Money that was given to him by the chief priests.

When Judas, who had betrayed Him, saw that Jesus was

condemned, he was seized with remorse and returned the thirty pieces of silver to the chief priests and the elders. "I have sinned," he said, "for I have betrayed innocent blood." "What is it to us?" they replied. "That's your responsibility."

Matthew 27:4-5 (NIV)

Evil men opposed him, as the psalmist predicted, after they influenced him to betray Jesus. But wait a minute…he acknowledged his sin! He was filled with remorse. Furthermore, he gave back the blood money, and that's restitution or the purest form or sign of repentance, if you will.

Why then wasn't he able to get his right mind back? *Let an accuser stand at his right hand.* Of course, this is speaking of none other than Satan, the accuser of the brethren (Revelation 12:10). Remember that at this point, Satan was already inside Judas; we learned that from Jesus's *dipping of the bread event.*

I thought that once we feel remorse or conviction and attempt restitution after confession that we are all good, just as Judas did, then God has to take us back. After all, none of us are perfect, right?

That's why the OSAS frenzy placed Judas as someone who was never saved, and again I say: How can Jesus lose Judas if He never had him?

No one could claim losing twenty bucks if they never had twenty bucks, to begin with. Jesus clearly stated that out of all the disciples, He lost none, except Judas, the son of perdition.

> While I was with them, I protected them and kept them
> safe by the name You gave Me. None has been lost except
> the one doomed to destruction so that Scripture would be
> fulfilled.

> John 17:12 (NIV)

What kind of destruction should follow the man responsible for betraying the Son of God? Because some may read this verse and think that God planned the destruction of Judas, as someone God wanted to end up in hell, a hell we are told was reserved for Satan and his demons, and if God wants anyone in hell, then He clearly contradicts His entire being, as well as the purpose of sending Jesus to die for the sins of the whole world for that matter.

The Lord is not slow in keeping His *promise*, as some understand slowness. Instead, He is patient with you, not wanting anyone to perish but everyone to come to repentance (2 Peter 3:9).

This, of course, included Judas as well. Otherwise, the word *everyone* could not be applied in the verse above. What then can we make of Judas's tragic end of events? Is it possible for God to, at some point, give up on someone? Perhaps because He knows their latter end (2 Kings 20:6). Because so many people are under the impression that God is always there no matter what, especially the OSAS individuals who subscribe to such erroneous theology. King Hezekiah was given a fifteen-year extension on his life, all to walk away from the God who gave him that extension through the healing of a deadly disease. I think we better leave God's things up to God!

When you tell people daily that they can't ever lose their salvation, then why are so many of these pastors leaving their churches and families for extramarital affairs? As is the case in most denominations with such beliefs nowadays. Is it may be part of what the Great Apostasy from Thessalonians that we're seeing taking place in our midst?

"When he is tried, let him be found guilty, and may his prayers condemn him" (Psalm 109:7, NIV).

Can we observe this verse in the Psalms with an open mind, furthermore, with a spiritual eye?

Judas admitted his sin in Matthew 27:4. He admitted he betrayed innocent blood. The Pharisees pretty much told him, "So!" But then, Judas threw the money back at them. I'd say that's an act of repentance and restitution, don't you?

Verse five says he went and hanged himself. ("May another take his place of leadership" [Psalm 109:8, NIV]). His demise was foretold because God knew exactly how it was supposed to go down, but one thing we cannot ignore is the fact that Judas attempted to repent but couldn't.

Maybe this is what inspired the writer of Hebrews when he wrote it is a fearful thing to fall into the hands of the living god (Hebrews 10:31). There is no better explanation to underline the loss of Judas's salvation than that of Hebrews 10:3. Judas clearly fell into the hands of the living god. And what exactly does that mean anyway?

When an individual falls into the hands of the living god, there is no longer a cure for that man or woman once this event takes place, as they acquire such a state of spiritual disconnect that it has to have broken God's heart and angered Him in the process, but without turning back the clock this time. There is an "enough is enough" with God as well, or do we ignore the flood of Noah's day?

A disconnect because this verse is speaking to the Judases of today, as well as those in biblical times, of course. God has made it evident for us that He will have mercy on whom He will have mercy, as He made it clear to Moses in Romans 9:15.

In other words, God's mercy cannot be attained outside of confessing Christ as Savior because outside of that, every single individual who refuses to accept Jesus as Lord by being born again is condemned to God's wrath automatically.

Falling into the hands of the living god is when someone who once was in a relationship with God (like Judas was) somehow embraced a relationship with the enemy of God, and that's regardless of the reason. Once things go south for them, they attempt to return to God by exercising religion or going through the motions, if you will, by then, it's no longer a two-way street, and that is the end for any Judas!

DO WE LEAVE GOD, OR DOES GOD LEAVE US?

God has left them as they once left Him. We saw it in Esau's failed attempt to repent (Hebrews 12:16-17). We saw it in King Saul's demise as he also was once indwelled by the Holy Spirit in 1 Samuel 11:6, then later ended up in the home of a witch in 1 Samuel 28, asking her to inquire of Satan to speak for God.

Saul was clearly rejected out of God's will because of his sin. We also know that Saul eventually took his own life after being injured on the battlefield, as did Judas, and yes, both were filled with the Spirit at some point in their lives. Though many may want to minimize the Holy Spirit's presence in the Old Testament, that He leaves and returns on Old Testament believers periodically, it is the wrong approach, and there's no biblical support for it unless one makes it up for lack of understanding of the Bible.

We know that God does not change, and the Holy Spirit is God; therefore, He does not change either. In New Testament times, we receive Him as we accept Jesus as Savior, and He leaves us as we leave Jesus as Savior as well. In all fairness, that's what happens, and that's why confession of sin is necessary daily.

It happens all the time, yet some people can fellowship with others in the Lord and do so for years, but as soon as that person rejects their faith and embraces a sinful lifestyle, they're quick to say that they were never saved. It happens all the time when someone is seared to protect the OSAS doctrine and the proverbial solecism in its regard.

In Psalm 95, verses ten and eleven, God held back His rest and His promise to a people He brought out of Egypt, a people He considered His own, but because of rebellion, they did not enter the promised land as planned. Two out of two million (Joshua and Caleb) got to see the promised land. Not even Moses was able to get in. And to think we have it made in the shade because Jesus said, "It is finished"? And now somehow, we're in? I believe He was referring to His assignment, not yours or mine!

What I have encountered in my twenty-year-plus walk with Jesus is that many who believe OSAS tend to dismiss anyone who once was on fire for God to simply conclude that they were never saved, that's if they defaulted from the faith and right back into the world. The punch line is always the old cliché, "I never knew you"; that's what they refer to when they unsaved the saved amongst themselves (Matthew 7:23). But watch what Matthew 7:22 (NIV) says: "Many will say to me that day, 'Lord, Lord, did we not prophesy in Your name and in Your name drive out demons and in Your name perform many miracles?'"

In verse twenty-one, the conversation is centered on entering heaven. Of course, we know that there are two stages by which we enter God's kingdom. One is by death if saved, and the other will be at the rapture. The understanding we face here is that upon dying, we step into the presence of God.

According to Jesus, these individuals He's referring to have passed on. They are at the judgment seat. It is obvious that at some point, they walked in the anointing. The fact is that being gifted by the Spirit only happens to converts of Jesus. We know that the driving out of demons is done by individuals with that kind of power (Holy Ghost power).

When the Pharisees suggested Jesus cast out demons in the name of Beelzebub, Jesus made it clear that Satan is not in the business of casting out Satan (Matthew 12:25-27). Therefore, people who prophesied and cast out demons were once saved by that premise alone.

In Hebrews 6:4-6, the Bible speaks about someone who once was enlightened by the Spirit, and unfortunately, concluded in want! Take a look:

> For it is impossible for those who were once enlightened, and have tasted the heavenly gift, and have become partakers of the Holy Spirit, and have tasted the good word of God and the powers of the age to come, if they fall away, to renew them again to repentance...
>
> Hebrews 6:4-6 (NKJV)

The Bible is very clear on what the different stages of

Christianity are.

People who operate in God's anointing are people who have been gifted due to either the level of faith they once operated under or the length of time of their spiritual walk with the Lord. But God is certain about giving all believers according to their faith or what they believe (Romans 12:3).

Sin, on the other hand, is the ugly thing we all wish was never there, but boy does it taste good! Some people have literally walked away from God to experience that tasty trifle over and over again. Although we know its end result is death, some do it anyway (Romans 6:23), and spiritual death is still tearing down marriages and individuals who embrace it, and what's worse, ministries! Especially high-profile preachers and televangelists.

I have personally experienced close friends and family who once were on fire for God but unfortunately are no longer walking with the Lord, and that's because of shame and condemnation that comes with such bad decisions, as both are without a doubt the byproduct of sin. Some people just never get over their sin, they never recover, and some just don't care to. But how do we know if someone lost their salvation?

We don't! Plain and simple. That question is answered at the fulfillment of Matthew 7:23, "I never knew you," and no sooner than that. One must die first in order to know where one will end up for all eternity. In other words: Did you die with Jesus as

Savior, or not? That will tell the story!

What's taking place in the OSAS community is that a great number of believers begin to abuse God's grace, thinking it's the gift that keeps on giving. Perhaps many are utterly clueless about what grace means, or some just don't care. My interpretation of grace is the time from when we first sin to the time when we get judged for that sin unless, of course, we repent before judgment begins.

Grace is that span of time allotted by God for us to come to our senses. If the believer remains unrepentant until that day comes, then it is up to God to either exercise grace or mercy on such individuals, and of course, also judgment.

God does not forgive unconfessed sin. That's 100 percent biblical. Grace is not getting what we deserve. Mercy is not getting anything at all that we should. But that's entirely up to God. We see it in the story of David when he went there with Bathsheba; it's found in 2 Samuel 11 and 12.

If we were to estimate the time from beginning to end in David's sin with Bathsheba, and afterward when he repented as Nathan the prophet showed him his sin thanks to a colorful story of a man and his ewe lamb, we can probably conclude it took him months to repent.

Chapter eleven tells us that it was in the spring of the year when kings went out to war, and David stayed behind. Obviously, that's between March and June. And it takes at least a month to figure out a woman's pregnancy. But for the sake of argument, let's say it took two months before David repented once he fell into adultery.

Imagine a man after God's own heart ignoring his sin, perhaps because of complacency, or maybe it was sheer rebellion, but the Bible does describe Bathsheba as being "beautiful to behold." How beautiful? Beautiful enough to make David forget about his God, and I'm sure David is not alone in this one. I'm sure there are many Davids and definitely plenty of Bathshebas out there.

When Nathan approached David in chapter twelve, he told him a story, or a parable, if you will, to get David's attention since David perhaps thought everything was peachy and thought he had cleaned up his mess undetected. But what's important here is that David came to the point of embracing his walk with God as something common. Something he hadn't done in the past. And we must never attain such a delusion of making our relationship with God a common thing. God should be our all, always.

Isn't it just like some of us, how we can believe that God will never leave us or forsake us, and then, we too begin to treat our relationship with God as something common, just like David did? Leaving Him and forsaking Him as well. David spent a great deal of his life writing about God's grace and mercy, as we can see in most of the psalms he wrote. But in those months of spiritual hiatus, David allowed for comeuppance to build against himself because of his secret sin.

That's because sin somehow makes us conveniently ignorant to the reality of our current situation, thus, implementing a shutoff in the conviction department…where we ignore all the signs God presents to us when in sin.

How can we attempt to converge on what happens in the spirit realm or make sense of it at all but without believing it exists? Especially as we abandon our proper abode with God, and of course, that's because of sin and its desires, just like the angels did as they lost their place forever when they experienced perpetual detrimental ousting from heaven due to rebellion (2 Peter 2:4).

In the first letter of John, chapter one and verse nine, the Bible says that we have to confess our sins in order to be forgiven and also that God is just to forgive us of our sin. Of course, the word "just" means He has to exercise justice for that sin. Being that God is a just God. And what exactly is that allusion?

It means that God must judge sin in order to be God. But you may say, "He already has; Jesus died for the sins of the world!" And the answer to that is: yes! And only if you confess Him as Savior. In other words, there is no redemption for nonbelievers (John 3:18) but only self-condemnation.

Yes, He did die for the sins of the world, but just as an individual who comes to Jesus at the point of salvation dumping their prior sin by way of confession as informal as it may be, likewise, one must continue confessing one's sin in order to advance a right standing with God, and a right standing on a daily basis, and thus, in order to continue to get closer and closer in one's walk with the Lord, confession is necessary on a daily basis.

Doesn't Luke 3:8 tell us to bear fruit worthy of repentance? That's what the verse is telling us to do, but when OSAS presents its error of interpretation, it suggests that confessing our sin is no longer a prerequisite. And it is. At least that's what I pick up from most of Jesus's parables. Jesus laid down a crystal-clear explanation in bearing fruit. He also stated the *pros and cons* of taking either approach. Watch what He tells us in John, chapter fifteen:

> I am the true vine, and My Father is the vinedresser. Every branch in Me that does not bear fruit He takes away, and every branch that bears fruit He prunes, that it may bear more fruit.

> John 15:1-2 (NKJV)

Jesus tells us that God is the vinedresser, meaning He is engaged in the process of our growth on a personal level.

"Every branch in Me that does not bear fruit" means someone who is connected to Him has stopped producing fruit, and He says that these branches are in Him. In other words, they are Christians who are saved but have no desire to serve after some point in their conversion. Probably because of sin.

Then, the Vinedresser (The Father) takes them away. Then what? Well, they are thrown into the fire…

"You are already clean because of the word which I have spoken to you" (John 15:3, NKJV).

It seems to me that Jesus is very clear about His part; He has made them clean by His word. Now, He was speaking to the twelve apostles here, and if anybody was saved, these twelve were. After all, they were all handpicked by an all-knowing God, right? If eternal security was real, then John 15:3 would have no need for John 15:4.

"Abide in Me and I in you. As the branch cannot bear fruit of itself, unless it abides in the vine, neither can you, unless you abide in Me" (John 15:4, NKJV).

Verse three gives the impression that the disciples were eternally secured, that is until we read verse four, where Jesus made it clear that unless they abide in Him, they could bear no fruit. You may say, "Well, not bearing fruit does not prove you can lose your salvation?" Really? Let's see what Jesus had to say about that.

"I am the Vine; you are the branches. He who abides in Me, and I in him, bears much fruit; for without Me you can do nothing" (John 15:5, NKJV).

Although this verse is self-explanatory, I'd like to reiterate the notion at play and perhaps explore it one more time if I may….

We are the branches. And it's important to remember that because He continues to unveil the meaning of this address to the branches (Christians), and that's to abide.

In verse six, Jesus warns us of the consequences of not only the refusal of not bearing fruit but the disconnect that it eventually creates once it takes place.

> If anyone [He generalizes this beyond the apostles] does not abide in Me [or continue a connection of bearing fruit], he is cast out as a branch [this branch was connected to the Vine at some point but dried up] and is withered; and they gather them and are thrown into the fire, and they are burned [this exemplifies hell].

> John 15:6 (NKJV), emphasis added

A branch that is part of the Vine is, by all means, a Christian who is saved. We have made that clear as Jesus spoke about it in the verses above. Now, what happened to that branch for it to wither? What went wrong? The "why" is irrelevant, I might add, but what's important is that it stopped bearing fruit, so it's the "what" that matters, and the only culprit I can think of that could cause such a disconnect is a sinful lifestyle, not just sin. Also, that branch gets cut off from the Vine by the Vinedresser, who is the Lord Himself. Dry branches are cut off. Furthermore, it is thrown into the fire, or hell, if you will.

This explains why Jesus cursed the fig tree when it didn't yield fruit, but OSAS insists that since Jesus said, "It is finished" when at the cross, that for some reason, that meant we need to just relax and enjoy the ride…and cruise-control Christianity is not at all what the Lord had in mind when He went up on the cross.

To think that our salvation is secured is not at all what Jesus meant when He made that agonizing statement of victory before He breathed His last breath. What Jesus meant was, *it is finished* for Himself.

In other words, the day you and I can utter those same words is when we ourselves prepare to meet our Maker, and only then can we say, "It is finished."

In essence, it means we have completed the task the Lord has entrusted to us in our journey with Him. In other words, that our ministry was fulfilled. Paul puts it this way in his "It is finished" moment: "I have fought the good fight, I have finished the race, I have kept the faith" (2 Timothy 4:7, NKJV).

What will you and I say when our "It is finished" moment finally comes? In John 15:7 (NKJV), as the Lord closes out the Vinedresser discourse, He once again reaffirms the need to *abide* in Him: "If you abide in Me, and My words abide in you, you will ask what you desire, and it should be done for you."

The conditional clause, "*if,*" is by all means without a lack of substance…It ignites results from both spectrums: "if" you do, you will have the right to ask for anything, and "if" you don't, you have absolutely no right whatsoever, other than being cut off from the Vine. That's why it's imperative that we understand that unless we abide in Him, we cannot advance in kingdom business one *iota* outside of His perfect will.

The Christian life is a life of constant challenges; it's somehow a contrast of liability loaded with pain and suffering with, sometimes, no end in sight and betrayals at the forefront that are all too common, so it seems, and at times from trusted sources, or perhaps family members—disappointment after disappointment can surely be the norm for a season of despair—we will definitely experience episodes of lack and perhaps heartbreak as well, and taking on all those issues without Christ is a sure recipe for agony and disaster. It can lead to depression, stagnation, discomfort, and/or discouragement in our faith walk, but *if* we hold onto God, the outcome will make the process a procedure rather than cortege. That's "if"?

We need Jesus every single day of our lives since our very next breath depends on Him, especially when times are hard and bearing fruit by serving God is not an option dictated by current conditions, and to take a break from producing fruit while we're hurting is at least questionable and perhaps permissible, but we must rise to the occasion time and time again. He said we must pick up our cross and follow after Him. What cross are you carrying?

Sometimes we must fight and build at the same time, just like Nehemiah had to when rebuilding the wall (Nehemiah 3); sometimes there are no breaks in our walk with Jesus, and even though we may feel spent and undoubtedly overwhelmed, remember that in our weakness, He is strong.

God's grace has to be sufficient for us when we are at wit's end...but know that the Lord has promised that He will never leave us or forsake us, and He will not put on us more than what we can handle—these are promises we must hold onto in order to continue with our heads up high. We know persecution is coming, and therefore, we must grow a thick skin, or else?

The events described by Jesus in Matthew, chapter twenty-four, are events that we have to undergo because the Lord has found it necessary to convey this message to a generation who has everything it needs from a biblical standpoint to understand the times we're in and to efficiently tackle the task when it arrives. We are not the first but may very well be the last generation of believers to endure such persecution by wicked individuals sold out into ushering destruction and chaos perpetrated by the enemy of our souls.

Whether we like it or not, an end-times systematic approach has been implemented for at least one hundred years, but that shouldn't stop us from continuing strong in the Lord but encourage us instead.

Many believers will walk away from God because they are not rooted in the Word as they should, and some will be beheaded for their faith, according to the book of Revelation. Although many will not succumb to such apocalyptic suggestions of rejection of faith, others will—to keep their own lives—but will rather deny Christ and live. Anybody has the opportunity to take their life back, and Jesus knows exactly who those people are; they'd rather live without Christ through the apocalypse and spend eternity in hell than die with Him and experience the culmination of their confession (salvation).

If the book of Revelation is a book of prophecy for the end times, then we must treat it as such, and the message to the church of the last days, which begins this apocalyptic book, is to *repent.* Therefore, we are then obliged to analyze what is said to us here so that the rest of the eschatological writings can unfold uniformly and give us perspective on where we are in biblical prophecy and in readiness as well.

Therefore, the revelation of biblical proportions is a complicated subject that's accompanied by great tribulation unlike anything we've seen in past disasters, and that should give us as believers some perspective of where to be as on the side of truth, to say the least. Therefore, we must carefully connect the dots so as to have validation when it comes to God's warnings of things to come. The players in these roles, for lack of a better analogy, have to fit the narrative in order to unfold the truth. And they are already lining up, as you see today.

A PANDORA'S BOX IS OPENED

Either we pay attention to Scripture, or we don't? Either we believe it, or we don't? But it will come to pass regardless of which side of the coin we stand on.

"And He said to them, 'I saw Satan fall like lightning from heaven'" (Luke 10:18, NKJV).

This is Jesus speaking here, and His words are the eternal Word of God. Therefore, Jesus must be deemed as the final Word!

And just what did the final Word say to us in this scripture?

Well, He identified an event dating back to the fall of Lucifer back in heaven. It is clear that He was telling us Satan fell fast like lightning, or as if he had no choice, and if we are to reason within a common-sense framework to determine what took place, we would understand that lightning did not occur until rain and precipitation began simultaneously, and that's because we need a cloud and a hot ground with substantial positive energy that will absorb heated moisture and cool it as the cloud thickens and grows in size to disperse a bolt of lightning as a result of atmospheric electric discharges that concentrate a negative charge in the clouds—to anything standing tall on the ground with a positive charge, i.e., trees or even people.

But that explanation goes nowhere in biblical terms until we ask ourselves why Jesus said what He said to describe Satan's fall, which is well documented in the prophets as his name comes up numerous times (Satan). For example: "How are you fallen from heaven, O Lucifer, son of the morning! How you are cut down to the ground, you who weakened the nations!" (Isaiah 14:12, NKJV). Does this not resonate with what Jesus was saying in Luke 10:18? And considering what COVID-19 has done to the nations, I think this is something worth highlighting in your memory bank— given where the virus began and who funded it?

This is a prophetic verse that takes us back to day one of Satan's fall, and just think about the distance between heaven and earth, which is mega light years away…just as Luke 10:18 is a verse that looks at what happened in eternity past, and what we do know is that rebellion and sin did not originate on Earth, but heaven.

> Therefore rejoice, O heavens, and you who dwell in them!
> Woe to the inhabitants of the earth and the sea! For the
> devil has come down to you, having great wrath, because
> he knows that he has a short time.
>
> Revelation 12:12 (NKJV)

Luke, Isaiah, Ezekiel, Job, and John the revelator all took time to inscribe in our Bibles a reference to Satan's origins and destination, as well as his expected end by different writings, which are lapsed by thousands of years in between origin. It's humanly impossible to pen such accounts that the writers had absolutely no idea would connect in the end. Furthermore, Luke quoting Jesus saying He saw Satan fall makes it quite personal on the part of Jesus. And those who dwell in the sea are referring to islanders, not fish. Since we know animals are not God's concern, but humans!

Isaiah wrote about it but wasn't there, and John wrote about it but wasn't there either. In other words, Luke, though not a part of the original twelve, actually placed Jesus in heaven the day Lucifer was thrown out of heaven, and that's pretty amazing if you ask me. To have such a revelation is by far one of the greatest attributes a believer can have when it comes to the anointing.

We now know that Satan fell from heaven like *lightning* (Luke 10:18). We also know what causes lightning to appear. And that's a storm, but let's see what the word used for lightning means in Greek?

According to Strong's, *astrape* is the word used in the translation in New Testament texts, and of course, God is not limited to language barriers like we are. But this translation explains that lightning, which stretches out through the stratosphere as it's used in this text, also means *bright, dazzling, transformed,*[11] but it seems that these are characteristics of an individual rather than a jolt of translucent electric discharge of sorts.

What's interesting is that the word "lightning" in Hebrew is the word *baraq (k), (ck)*.[12] Now if we were to replace the word lightning in the Luke 10:18 entry with the Hebrew word *baraq*, it would read as follows; "I saw Satan fall like *Barak [ck]* from heaven." Dazzling, *bright,* and transformed describe the word *barak* and are characteristics worthy of an individual named Barack, at least according to Joe Biden's personal opinion. I think he is also called articulate by Joe.

Why is it important to connect these verses? Because we are all waiting for the man of lawlessness to be revealed at some point! But do you really think that that man is going to announce *he is the one?* I mean, didn't Oprah Winfrey shout from the rooftops, "Barack Obama, he is the one"? Was she revealing him then or just announcing his entrance into the prophetic theater?

What about his pastor of twenty years, Jeremiah Wright, did he not say, "No, no, no, God, bless America, God, [fill in the blank] America…America's chickens are coming home to roost." How did you perceive this statement? I personally saw this as a prophecy, not as a statement. If he knew Barack for twenty years, he said what he said because he knew Barack intimately. I think that would be an educated guess. This was a warning to America of what was coming our way, prophetically speaking, and not only to America but the world itself.

Wright knew what Obama was about, and that's because he watched his actions for two decades and knew he was one driven by racial payback, just as he hinted in his first book, *Dreams from My Father*. And we see it on our city streets today thanks to him. The product of racism's many insurrections is playing out right before our very eyes like a well-thought-out plan from some community organizer with ties to a well-known terrorist of Bill Ayers from the terror group Weather Underground, and it's hard not to miss, though a complete opposite of what Martin Luther King did when his time came to step up to address racial injustice. But the riots that are ongoing is what Jeremiah Wright was aiming at when he spoke, and of course, validated by Kamala Harris, who went a little further with her prescription of "They're not gonna to let up and they should not, and we should not," in regard to the riots as she spoke to Stephen Colbert on the *Late Show*, which makes one wonder if she belongs in the big house rather than the White House.

We as believers understand that we are in a battle between good and evil, and unfortunately, because of racial tensions, many have called good evil and evil good. Something the Bible warns us about in Isaiah 5:20. Matthew, chapter twenty-four, has an amazing way of beginning the discourse: it says Jesus left the temple (the church?).

In Matthew 24:7, Jesus said that "nation will rise against nation," but He used the Greek word *ethnos* to describe nation, not meaning the same as a country, but an ethnic group instead, and this is the word we use for a particular *race,* and in today's standard it would read, *race will rise against race,* or ethnicity against ethnicity. And "race" is where we get the popular word racism from. How accurate is God's Word? Very!

It seems Satan is throwing everything he has at this world, and I believe the last-day church will have the opportunity to accept or reject the mark of the beast because Revelation 13:16 is very clear that he will cause many to receive the mark, but Revelation 14:9-11 tells us that anyone receiving the mark will not get into heaven, which means the mark is permanent.

It's 2021, and technology is here. The man of lawlessness, as described in 2 Thessalonians 2:9-11, is an individual, not a mere concept. Take a look:

> The coming of the lawless one is according with the working of Satan, with all power, signs, and lying wonders, and all unrighteous deception among those who perish, because they did not receive the love of the truth, that they might be saved And for this reason God will send them strong delusion, that they should believe the lie.
>
> Thessalonians 2:9-11 (NKJV)

Isn't it a coincidence that the many riots disguised as protests are somehow warranted and considered a first amendment, right? The passage above concerns me because it's too accurate in my view. I mean, the first amendment is clear about peaceful assembling, but arson and violence are crimes, and no crime is protected by our constitution. Furthermore, it is elevated and praised as righteous while people are attacking law enforcement and law-abiding citizens all over the nation, as leftist public officials allowed it and championed it as well, in line with 2 Thessalonians 2:9-11.

Now, does that strike you as normal? Because it's not. The recent "pandemic" has shut down first amendment rights for religious organizations, funerals, schools, and a lot of nonessential jobs as well, while rioters and high-profile funerals are allowed to break CDC protocol in its entirety. And furthermore, it is applauded by the lawless.

Even congressional hearings have taken to the delusion of their fabricated truth, and that's okay; evil is evil, but when we have Bible-believing Christians subscribe to such a lie, it's when, in my view, Scripture literally fulfills itself. I expect the wicked to be wicked, but not the church! Looting was righteous when it happened in downtown Chicago, but once it moved to black neighborhoods, then it wasn't, okay? I remember watching on Facebook live the Latin Kings on Twenty-Sixth Street barricaded their streets so as not to allow the mom-and-pop shops to get looted. I was amazed that the street thugs cared about their local small businesses. And I'm sorry, but I can't say the same about Blacks and how they handled the looting. I heard a pastor on IG live validating the Chicago looting until they ransacked his local grocery store the next day, then he complained and addressed the looters by saying that now Blacks have to go out and buy groceries at *their* stores, meaning white suburban grocery stores because Blacks looted their own grocery stores. And this was a pastor, for God's sake!

There is a clear delusion taking place in America's cities, in fact, worldwide, and why?

I was watching like everyone else the unfortunate death of George Floyd that captivated the entire world's attention thanks to the news media who had a financial stake in this demise in prompting the violence by calling the protests peaceful while buildings burned behind reporters as they were reporting, literally, and that's when the Lord prompted me to get my Bible. He revealed that the incident would fulfill Scripture, and I don't expect you to understand or believe what I'm saying at face value. Perhaps you will, I'm not sure, but from my standpoint, I'm convinced. A best seller for left-wing media.

Not only did this man's death happen to be mourned across the entire globe, but somehow even as I'm writing this today, August 1, 2020, riots are still taking place at this very moment, and the death of this man is supposedly the cause of it all. I don't believe that for a moment because the police bodycam did not show a single hint of racism, but what I do believe is that his death drew more attention than Jesus's death, he had three funerals, and one was overwhelmed with mourners, at least ten thousand people came to pay their last respects to a man who became famous overnight because his death happened at the hands of the police and a White cop at that. All by committing a misdemeanor.

A PANDORA'S BOX IS OPENED

The man was high on drugs (fentanyl) when he died—twice or three times the amount it takes to overdose. He had an extensive criminal background, which included pointing a gun at a pregnant woman of color as he burglarized her home but received a hero's farewell; police bodycam footage showed that he clearly resisted arrest, and this incident was definitely not racially motivated, but it was used to set America's liberal cities on fire with zero proof of racism in the police bodycam, and thus, fulfilling 2 Thessalonians 2:11-12. All based on a series of lies.

Also, there were scores of politicians in attendance at this funeral which was bigger than Jesus' funeral. As well as movie industry people, professional athletes, and of course, the proverbial activists, whom some suggested he was messianic, and perhaps that's why his mural was struck by lightning thereafter? Here is when this worldwide event fulfilled Scripture, and this is what the Lord put in my heart regarding this funeral: "Wherever the corpse is, there the vultures will flock together" (Matthew 24:28, AMP).

I know you think it sounds mean-spirited, but this was a funeral that violated the very reason the nation went on lockdown in the first place. Where the pandemic somehow took a break while Black Lives Matter wreaked havoc on our streets as they were championed by Washington's leftists, and furthermore, violating the much-worshipped social distancing rules, which were put on pause—not only here, but every day riots surged all over the fruited plain. Then, to now, and for a special group of people (rioters), the pandemic protocol was not active, which is not only hypocritical but also criminal, to say the least!

We all saw the agonizing death of a man whose life expectancy quickly evaporated into eternity, and seemingly, Floyd did not once mention, acknowledge, or call on his Maker. That was the worst part of the whole incident: so many could address the police brutality and broadcast it to Facebook live stream but never mention their Maker either. I mean, at least the thief on the cross had the presence of mind to get right with God because he knew his life was about to end, and George Floyd knew his hour had neared because he said several times that he was going to die. He could have repented, but fentanyl was calling the shots by that time.

Scripture was meant to be fulfilled to its fullest, and that's exactly how we will conclude the end of the ages. If you want it to make sense, then you're going to be disappointed.

For example, the time Obama gave Queen Elizabeth a certificate of appreciation supposedly from the American people on his first visit to the palace, back in 2010. The date on that document was the right day and month, but from 2008, now it was spun in the news media as cute, and as an innocent mistake when they decided to run it as "Poor Obama, he is so stressed-out being president that he wrote down the wrong date," except that Obama did not fabricate the document as he met with the Queen, no! Obama had someone write it beforehand, thus fulfilling Scripture found in Daniel 7:25 (NKJV), "He […] shall intend to change times and law." Of course, we know he changed God's law of marriage years later, but by him changing the time, and as the Lord revealed to me to notice these two events that were years apart and directed me to Daniel, chapter seven, I was awaiting the end of the verse to be fulfilled, which was to change the law, and when that happened, I no longer treated that certificate *mishap* to the Queen, as an innocent *oops* from Obama's part, but a well-calculated effort and a sheer act of rebellion.

Therefore, when it comes to accounts that affect the body of Christ, we must be bold and attain such decrees. That's why it's important to understand the times we're living in and to screen all accounts under a biblical filter that breaks down these events as they develop in their awaited fulfillment, and fulfill they will, without a doubt.

One of the things I noticed about our former president was that he signed an executive order to obtain control over the internet with his executive power, way back in 2012. I noticed he kept saying that he wanted a third term and complained how the constitution didn't allow it but remained politically connected even after finishing his second term. Why was he engaged to that degree as it is to this day? I wish I knew!

Well, I believe Barack Obama may very well be one of the three individuals in the unholy trinity, and only time will tell, but he comes up too many times in the realm of *coincidence*.

For example, Jesus also said in Matthew 24:27 (NKJV), "For

as the lightning comes from the east and flashes to the west, so also the coming of the Son of man be." Earlier, we looked at the word *lightning* to be the word *barak* in Hebrew and Greek, and we also know that Barack (Obama) came from Indonesia, an island in the far east, and he later went to Hawaii, another island, and that's in the west, of course, but wait, today he lives on an island again, Martha's Vineyard.

Among other words, we can trace the word *barak* to "flash." We know he is a flashy individual; I mean, Peter Jennings once drooled over the crease on his pants. I believe he was talking with Tom Brokaw about it. Another word is *gem,* which is a characteristic of Lucifer himself as described by the prophet Ezekiel. He was adorned to the teeth with gems. Well, you get the picture.

The reason I brought up the George Floyd situation was that we saw half the country jump to the conclusion that this man's death was the product of racism, and it clearly wasn't. According to the released police bodycam video, which sat on Keith Ellison's lap for months, which is suspicious enough of itself since he's a self-proclaimed Antifa member and is the district attorney in Minneapolis.

We are led to believe America is racist seemingly after America elected a Black president twice, which was perhaps the worst mistake in American history, and don't take my word for it, just YouTube Jeremiah Wright's curse to America; he told us the chickens were coming home to roost! Well, it looks like they are.

But why aren't most pastors preaching on the end times of which we are in, and why aren't they trying to figure out who the players of the unholy trinity are? I mean, doesn't that call for wisdom? You can see the play-by-play developments taking place in America today simply by rewinding one hundred years and reading Manning Johnson's book, *Color, Communism And Common Sense*, and you'll be shocked how predictable the Democratic Party is in pushing communism in the proverbial socialist agenda, which leaves God out of the picture indefinitely.

The relevancy of opening the controversial George Floyd Pandora's box was to display what Jesus said about believing the lie, that He will send them a delusion to believe the lie. And if God sends someone the ability to believe a lie and perish, it's clearly an indication that God knows those people will never repent.

After all, He is omniscient!

THE GREAT APOSTASY!

The idea that once you're saved, you're always saved steers attention away from a truth already established in the Bible, which is the *Great Apostasy*!

The correlation between the start of the end-times discourse in Matthew, chapter twenty-four, the letters that touch on eschatology, and the letters to the seven churches' message, which is to *repent*, clearly make a case for why these things were said if one cannot lose one's salvation. Especially in the way Matthew, chapter twenty-four, begins:

"Then Jesus went out and departed from the temple [the church]" (Matthew 24:1, NKJV; brackets added).

If this verse does not catch your attention to what it could mean once we tie it to the seven churches' discourse of the book of Revelation, seemingly so, then you can clearly understand what Jesus meant in the next verse when He said that the rock-solid stones that keep the church together will eventually fall. If He is called the Rock on which the builders build and is later rejected, then the stones He refers to are church leaders!

An apostasy has leaders, church leaders. Apostasy is a movement that insights watered-down Christianity, and the sheep simply follow because of the simple fact that it insists we all need that little white lie of "God knows your heart." One from a trusted source tells us, "We're gonna be okay because we are secured in our salvation." Kinda like Eve and the serpent—remember that little white lie? "You should not surely die" (Genesis 3:4). God knowing our heart is not a compliment since He also says that the heart is desperately wicked above all things. Let's not ignore the elephant in the room.

And the caveat was to be like God; of course, the very thing Lucifer tried to do while he was an angel was to entice others with empty promises. That's exactly what got him thrown out of heaven by failing miserably at staying in his lane, and guess what eating from the tree of knowledge got Adam and Eve? You guessed it, be "thrown out of Eden" and thrown out of Eden for good!

The introduction to the book of Revelation's first three verses can be summed up to just one sentence at the end of verse three. So, get your highlighter and please highlight these words: "And keep those words which are written in it." The focus is on keeping the words, or better yet, doing them!

There is one keyword to the last-day church, and that's to repent! Notice that every church had an issue within them that screamed, "Get right, or else?" And as we look at them individually, we can see why Jesus addressed each shortcoming with the notion of "Get it right or get left behind." Period! kind of attitude.

The first church that is addressed by John is the church of

Ephesus, and probably because it is the closest to the island of Patmos where this revelation took place, and as John was serving a life sentence for his faith in God, Christ revealed not only why he wouldn't die like the rest of the apostles but of old age instead. What was said about this church is that it had some rather peculiar instances we can identify within today's Christian circles, which makes this message relevant to our times.

In essence, the seven churches are not seven buildings or seven congregations in biblical times, no! These are seven churches in the last days—being that the Bible clarifies that these are not only churches but seven spirits of seven angels, which tell us something most want to ignore, and that's the fact that it's speaking of the last-day church: us!

To the angel of the church of Ephesus write, "These things say He who holds the seven stars in His right hand, who walk in the midst of the seven golden lampstands: I know your works, your labor, your patience, and that you cannot bear those who are evil. And you have tested those who say they are apostles and are not and have found them liars; and you have persevered and had patience and have labored for My name's sake and have not become weary. *Nevertheless, I have this against you,* that you have left your first love. Remember therefore from where you have fallen; repent and do the first works, or else I will come to you quickly and remove your lampstand from its place—unless you repent. But this you have, that you hate the deeds of the Nicolaitans, which I also hate. *He who has an ear, let him hear what the Spirit says to the churches.* To him who overcomes I will give to eat from the tree of life, which is in the midst of the paradise of God."

Revelation 2:1-7 (NKJV), emphasis added

The basis for the seven churches being addressed as examples to end-times Christianity is simply to reconnect them to the initial fundamentals of first-century Christianity. One that was willing to die for their faith. Jesus is coming to pick up a perfect church; therefore, there has to be an evaluation on a denominational level as well as a personal one, and He is not ignoring our good deeds by any stretch of the imagination, no! But definitely not shying away from observing any shortcomings we may have encountered either.

Thus, the opening statement is centered in pointing out directly to the *angel* of the church individually, not the church itself, or if it is, it's done so indirectly. What did Jesus mean by directing the focus to the angel in such a statement as that?

I believe it was to refocus the attention on what was taking place, spiritually speaking, in that particular denomination, which is what I believe took place, and it wasn't good, to say the least. In verse one, the Lord is not addressing the angel as if he had anything to do with what the church was doing. Jesus was introducing

His authority over the angels, and He was also projecting the message that needed completion on the part of the Ephesus-like church or denomination.

They hated what the Nicolaitans did, and as verse two commences, Jesus tells them He hated it too, which was being lukewarm, one day in, and another day out. I guess they thought, *A little immorality couldn't kill you.* And although the Ephesus church saw the wrongdoing of the Nicolaitans, Jesus was quick to point out their own plank in the eye issues.

In verse four, Jesus gives them something to think about, and literally, right after elevating them from all their good deeds before He said, "Nevertheless I have this against you"!

Jesus accused them of leaving their first love, and that pretty much meant Him! But in verse five, Jesus tells them to remember where they have fallen from, which means a disconnect from God, and whether it means individually or corporately, that was the case regardless. If anyone loses their connection with God, God will not forget what you've done for His kingdom, and that's why He encourages them to repent, but He had no qualms telling them that unless they returned to their first love and repent, He will remove their lampstand from its place.

In other words, the angel will be missing from a denomination, or territory if you will. Daniel talked about territorial superpowers existing in the spirit realm. Read it for yourself; it's in Daniel

10:13. Spiritually speaking, angels and demons have assignments just like we do; we don't belong just anywhere; we belong somewhere, and that somewhere is where the anointing of our calling is more prevalent, centralized, and more efficient, which will leave no other suggestion than the replacement of another angel, in this case, it's replaced by a fallen one, and not one from God anymore since it's removed completely. Therefore, if the body of believers Jesus was speaking to does not repent, an exchange of a spiritual atmosphere will disguise itself as legit when it isn't, just like it happened to King Saul. Here is where most church bodies accept what the Bible refers to as doctrines of demons!

Verse seven speaks about an event to take place in the paradise of God, and that's to partake of the tree of life, and that can only be offered to those who overcome and no one else. Once Adam and Eve sinned, God kicked them out of Eden because He wanted them not to eat from the tree of life. If they had eaten from the tree as a fallen race, they would be eternal sinners and could no longer die. Can you imagine a human race of immoral immortals?

I believe the same thing is taking place now, and what I mean by that is that the fruit that was on the tree of knowledge was tainted with RNA particles that had the power to alter human DNA. Now human DNA can only be sequenced by the Creator, but the perversion of DNA comes from Satan, and he created a tree with RNA and its fruit, which perverted DNA which God created.

If God created every tree for food and said it was good, and if

He told Adam not to eat from a tree that would potentially kill him, then God could not create such a tree because God created life, not death (Genesis 2:9). And if the tree of knowledge was created by God, then the tree of knowledge was created by Satan because God only creates good things. God then had to put them out of the Garden because they could potentially eat from the tree of life and live forever as sinners. That would end the plan of redemption, which was underway immediately thereafter in chapter three.

The same RNA used to introduce death in the Garden of Eden through the consumption of fruit deriving from the tree of knowledge is the same RNA that is introduced in the recent mRNA vaccines. At some point, these vaccines will attempt to do what God stopped by evicting Adam and Eve from the Garden. They will, as Elon Musk believes, reshape modern medicine, introduce the fountain of youth, and stop not only aging but also death at some point (Revelation 9:6).

This could potentially usher the mark of the beast, with COVID-19 coming from China and China being the Red Dragon, which gives power to the beast that comes out of the sea or an island, and as we all saw the church shut down by the virus, which gave power to the beast thereafter, and as you read this book, you can see how this makes sense even now. You'd understand why it is imperative not to take the mark of the beast because it will leave you out of the fold, and the last-day church will, in my opinion, be faced with the opportunity to take or deny the mark. Persecution awaits thereafter for the default believer!

Satan and his demons cannot eat from the tree of life because it's guarded by angels (Genesis 3:24). Satan is breaching it through RNA in a bypass of incendiary tactics using his minions to do so, and him being a spirit, he could not eat from either tree; he could only create a tree and only to mock God, which was the tree of knowledge of good and evil. God planted it (maybe), and Satan perverted it. I believe the fruit is what altered their and our DNA, which introduced death in humanity as warned.

If they ate from the tree of knowledge, they ate from it because they believed the serpent, and God made it clear He was not about to let them eat from the tree of life, which would have been the next step to accomplish by Satan in order to be God. If he can fool them once, he could fool them twice, and he wants to create his own race.

I say Satan created the tree of knowledge of good and evil or perverted it rather, because Genesis 2:9 says God created every tree that is pleasant to the eye and good for food, thus eliminating the chances of Him creating a tree that would destroy humanity before it had a chance to begin. God gives us the best example of free will in the Garden of Eden. He simply told Adam not to eat it, or he would die, and why would God create a perfect human being, just to kill him? That would make no sense, right?

We also know Adam told Eve because Eve had a conversation with the serpent about the forbidden fruit, but that didn't matter; Eve believed the lie and influenced Adam to partake of it as well.

Both lost their initial relationship with God, and if God's first humans can lose their place in paradise, what makes you think you're special?

But Satan's intention was to have Adam and Eve eat from both trees; that's why eating from the first tree was important. The first tree was to have access to the second tree, the tree of life. And just what is required to eat from the tree of life? Read what He said: "To him who overcomes I will give to eat from the tree of life, which is in the midst of the paradise of God" (Revelation 2:7b, NKJV).

We read Adam and Eve were responsible for the fall of man, yet they passed the buck when asked about what they had done; they both blamed someone else for their mistakes, but when Eve blamed the serpent, God immediately announced what the price was for disobeying His command.

The serpent was given an enemy, and that enemy was the woman's seed; therefore, Cain's relationship with Satan being one in good terms was perhaps Satan's assurance Cain wasn't the one to crush his head as the curse went out of the mouth of God in regard to the serpent, and the focus shifted to baby number two, Abel, who manifested when Abel's, and not Satan's friend Cain's, sacrifice was accepted by God.

God went to Cain before he killed his brother Abel and found his facial expressions to be out of order; in other words, someone else was already operating inside of Cain. Someone he befriended and perhaps admired more than God.

Cain was a host for the first recorded murder in human history, and that's why Jesus referenced the fact that Satan was a murderer from the beginning (John 8:25) because Satan had possession of Cain as he cowardly murdered his brother, perhaps while Abel wasn't looking, but after Cain (Satan) killed Abel, God allowed him to repent, not sure it would have changed the outcome of the punishment, but just like Adam and Eve did by passing the buck, Cain also showed a remorseless attitude to the reaction of his actions, ones that were the result from his parents partaking from the tree of knowledge of good and evil. Does it sound like the tree was more evil than good?

God told Adam and Eve that if they took from the tree of knowledge, they would die. In other words, Adam and Eve were created perfect, they were immortals, and the day they ate the fruit, it altered their DNA forever, and ours for that matter. What was in the fruit that brought death to an otherwise perfect immune system? My guess is RNA synthetic application.

God only knows, but what we do know is that the fruit gave birth to death, and something inside their immune system changed. Although death was not instant, death was born out of that simple yet, complicated act of disobedience from the two humans ruling their own lives from the beginning.

Then once their DNA changed from immortality to mortality, it changed from morality to immorality. Their own son Abel was taken from this world to the land of the dead, and he was there alone. Unfortunately, his death came at the hands of their firstborn, and even though Abel did absolutely nothing to deserve death, he died because his brother was tempted by Satan to kill him, and he also died because his parents were tempted by Satan and allowed death to be born because they ate the forbidden fruit, therefore altering their DNA forever. And now the possibility of instant death was born, through murder, but what's amazing is that it was their offspring who primarily paid the price of eating a simple harmless good-looking fruit that was masqueraded with enticing looks and as venomous as a rattlesnake would be on an infant, if you will.

God said Abel's blood was crying out to Him from the ground; think about that.

The second church addressed is the persecuted church. Jesus again addresses a message to the angel in charge of the church in Smyrna. Jesus begins to acknowledge their good deeds once again, and He is speaking to this denomination or body of believers, if you will, about the things they did right (Revelation 2:8-11).

The centric evaluation of what this body of believers has to go through does not appear to look any better for them, but in fact, worse. Yet, the Lord tells them to "be faithful until death. and I will give you the crown of life" (Revelation 2:10, NKJV). That's because salvation takes place the day we meet our Maker, and not a moment sooner, think about it He promises the crown of life if you're faithful until death. Shouldn't the crown of life be given while we live?

Jesus goes on to say, "He who overcomes shall not be hurt by the second death" (Revelation 2:11, NKJV), which means you are saved only if you overcome. And in order to enter into the second death or avoid it, you have to first die the first death. Essentially so, salvation is escaping the second death altogether, but in order to escape the second death, you have to die the first death first, unless, of course, you are raptured.

What took place here in this instructive truth was that Jesus addressed the angel in Smyrna first. He addressed the body of believers next, and as you see at the end of the text, Jesus made it personal. That's exactly what I've been telling you. But what amazed me the most was that Jesus did not hold back when He related a message to the next body of believers—Jesus literally mentioned where Satan's throne is and where Satan dwells. In other words, Satan's headquarters reside in this place, and this place is called *Pergamos.* Pergamos was pretty much a hub for almost every religion imaginable under heaven. It seems it housed just about every deity and temple for it, but what's important to assess is that the more religions there are in a society, the less unity and the more division there is. Of course, politically speaking, this would have no balance, but when addressing the many faiths in today's societies, it all makes sense. This relevancy continues to have an impact, and whether we like it or not, that's just how the cookie crumbles!

Take a look at Christianity alone; there are so many denominations just within the body itself, and each denomination has adopted its own doctrine to conform to its own agenda. In other words: it's nothing but a recipe for division and chaos among the body, and the seven churches are seven Christian denominations at the end. Jesus gives Pergamos a message of where they needed to be, and it goes like this: "I know your works, and where you dwell, where Satan's throne is. And you hold fast to my name and did not deny My faith" (Revelation 2:13, NKJV).

By now, we can clearly see that the Lord led with a message to angels, or spirits. Then, a corporate message to the intended body of believers, and eventually it becomes personal again as He ends every letter with the conditional clause of a sentence, "he who has an ear," which means you and me.

Imagine being a believer knowing Satan has his headquarters in your backyard—would that not put a damper on your faith walk? But as we see here, Jesus lets them know that they have something tangible to build upon despite their past shortcomings, which needed accommodation in a confrontational manner, and their immediate attention was required as well. But only in order to have a future with Him, which was the caveat, but then He highlights where they needed to be as a body, individually, and, as He encourages them to step up their walk when He shifts the narrative to what needs to be improved. A laserlike focus on the real issue: "But I have a few things against you because you have there, those who hold the doctrine of Balaam, who taught Balak to put a stumbling block before the children of Israel" (Revelation 2:14, NKJV).

In other words: *to prophesy for hire!*

I don't think Jesus was pulling punches here. I think Jesus was conveying a message that resonated with a lifestyle of holiness for the entire duration of the journey regardless of whether Satan lives next door, as the case was here, and not just when it's convenient. Verse fourteen was way beyond Balak and Balaam's account. Verse fourteen is also about sacrificing to idols and sexual immorality, which is today's most prevalent issue in Christianity as a whole and not prosperity preachers by a long stretch.

In the next verse, Jesus tells them they have the wrong doctrine. They were practicing the doctrine of the Nicolaitans, which He hated and admonished them to stop and repent. But what we see taking place in every directive to the seven churches is not only the acknowledgment of good deeds but also where they needed to improve as a body of believers. Otherwise, He would end His relationship with them. In other words, Jesus was handing down ultimatums, and they weren't up for discussion, a thing most who take to OSAS doctrine have an issue with because it contradicts their core beliefs of error.

When it comes to the compromising church, Jesus continues to first highlight their good behavior, but just like the rest of them, He puts an emphasis on the irregularities within as He tries to reconnect them to Himself because they have issues to correct, and repentance is the only alternative conduit by which to do so.

Even the church titled the corrupt church as the header appears in most Bibles is given a second chance to return to normalcy in Jesus.

> I know your works, love, service, faith, and your patience; and as for your works, the last are more than the first. Nevertheless, I have a few things against you because you allow that woman Jezebel, who calls herself a prophet-ess, to teach and seduce My servants to commit sexual immorality and eat things sacrificed to idols. And I gave her time to repent from her sexual immorality, and she did not repent. Indeed, I will cast her into a sickbed, and those who commit adultery with her into great tribulation unless they repent of their deeds.
>
> Revelation 2:19-22 (NKJV)

The problem is highlighted by Jesus Himself, and it is sexual immorality, and unless they, and us, repent from it, then the relationship ends, and that's Jesus speaking, therefore placing a limit to His grace and what grace really is! Remember that this is addressing the last days!

I guess the million-dollar question would be, when does the grace period expire?

I think most people don't understand or perhaps ignore the fact that sin has consequences. Either that or they don't think the punishment is for the believer, though the Bible clearly states He punishes those He loves (Hebrews 12:6) and that judgment will begin in the church (1 Peter 4:17). Seemingly, sin has not only consequences but also seasons. What that means is that sin has levels in the offense, and that includes both ends of its origin.

For example, sin that is premeditated is something like talking to someone about perhaps meeting at a hotel to engage in adultery, or perhaps fornication, and fornication pretty much covers all sexual sin outside of God's will, including homosexuality, and I'm talking about Christians here. That sin is a planned sin. I know two people inside a car allowing their emotions and feelings to get the best of them by ending up doing something they have no business doing in the back seat of a car may very well be the same sinful action, while the hotel couple does it in style, which is the same exact sin, and yes, adultery is adultery no matter where it happens, but think about how you would punish that sin if you were the judge?

Doesn't premeditated murder carry a harsher prison sentence than second-degree murder? Premeditated sin is by far the worst kind of sin in my view, and I believe in God's view as well. Peter was told he would deny Jesus after swearing up and down he was ready to die for Jesus; Jesus simply saw what would happen before the rooster crowed. And that verbiage did not come out of Peter's mouth, but Jesus's mouth. Peter did not say, "Wait till I deny you three times before the rooster crows!"

418

Judas, on the other hand, went to the enemies of the Lord and asked for payment for his betrayal. He premeditated his sin, and Peter fell into it. Big difference!

There's also a stage in sin called *grace,* and grace is a period of time between sin and the judgment of that sin. Think of it as being out on bail. Sometimes crimes have an opportunity of having the accuser drop the charges during the period of time while out on bail. When it comes to sin, God, being a just God, has to punish that sin, or else He cannot be God!

He is holy, and He expects holiness from us, and that is why He has given us a chance to repent. Most people have that opportunity to make things right with God, but some don't: like Judas, Cain, and King Saul types, and only God knows why. But for the most part, we all have a chance to come to our senses and eventually repent and restore our relationship with God once again. Though some things cannot be restored when it comes to ministry, our relationship with God can mostly find common ground once again.

So, what happens when we don't repent? Let's just say that the "heaven's in the back seat of my Cadillac" couple didn't repent after a heated and forbidden affair. Let's say they both feel like there should be more to it than a cheap thrill in the back of a car and in the middle of a dark, deserted road, and if they go ahead, plan an escape out of their nine-to-five routine, end up in some fancy hotel a little more dignified than the back seat of a car, and *plan* their sin, wouldn't that be different than the previous mess they put themselves in? Of course, it would!

We are talking about two Christians here, and this scenario is, more often than not, too close to home. But that's what sin is, and that's what sin does. It confuses the individual into thinking that there are better thrills ahead because this one did not hit climax as it should, so they think, and you just must work the kinks out and try again, then it all comes together when in reality, there is never a "better" if you're in sin.

Once two individuals have forbidden sex, the Holy Spirit has to leave them immediately because there is no way the Holy Spirit is going to live inside someone who just allowed a demon of adultery inside their inner being. And if we have the keys to heaven, guess what…? We also have the keys to hell!

Therefore, repentance is needed immediately after sinning! In the back seat of the car, the couple reengages their affair soon after its origin, even if it's in a more modest and respectful way, according to them, i.e., a motel. It's a clear sign they didn't repent.

The amount of stress that comes with affairs is overwhelming, to say the least. I say that because you have to lie about everything just to cover it up. And fooling your spouse may become a vendetta of some sort to justify the affair. In other words, you manipulate your home life to excuse the affair, and that's because repentance is nowhere near you, and justification is on deck for its continuation. Let's not forget David and Bathsheba's story, which validates what

I am saying here to a tee.

What happens when the grace period ends? Living in an adulterous lifestyle will end in an unfortunate event like divorce. A broken family is in the making during the affair, not only after the divorce as some would think, and all because of an unrepentant heart. What are the chances the adulterer gets married to the person they had an affair with? Perhaps slim to none!

Ugly divorces are mostly the product of illicit affairs. And Jesus was warning the church of sexual immorality as you saw in the letters to the seven churches, and there is no way we can ignore what's taking place in our midst. Scores of pastors are turning to homosexuality because having a man in your room is easier to hide than having a woman who is not your wife and walking freely in and out of your quarters and always undetected.

If the grace period expires, you will be judged by God. Don't believe me? Well, look what happened to Bishop Eddy Long: he died months after trying to deny his homosexuality of which he was caught red-handed, and that judgment depends on God, of course, but by that time, you have accumulated way more unrepentant sin than just the simple love affair in a steamed-window, midsize car, or as it happened to the bishop, covering it up seems easier than coming clean.

Now you have the cards stacked up against you, and you know you did it willingly. Just think of it as your Garden of Eden experience, and God is calling your name just as He did Adam's, "Adam, Adam, where are you?" and I think He meant spiritually speaking when He asked, "Where are you?" The opportunity to repent had arrived but came and went. This means there is a grace period between our sin and our acknowledgment of that sin. Also, the ability to recognize our wrong and feel conviction, then henceforth, repent. But God reserves the exercise of mercy or judgment, and I think that depends on our state of mind and heart, of how we feel about getting caught. In Adam's case, he blamed the only person in the room other than him, "The woman, you put her here." Do you see where his heart was? Well, that heart got him kicked out of paradise!

Therefore, since the aftermath of *sin* is having a grace period for believers to see if repentance will follow through, and so to gauge our conviction levels in order to help restore that broken relationship with God, and now that the reflection of that person's heart is monitored to a personal spiritual state in acknowledging God and His presence, we can conclude that our love for God will either bring us to our knees, or our love for sin will isolate us from our God. In which He now has to punish that sin, and the punishment is His prerogative. God can exercise mercy or judgment, and that depends on where He sees you and me as in the future in Him.

You'd ever wondered why Jesus didn't beg Judas to stay or to not do what he was about to do? "Then Satan entered Judas, surnamed Iscariot, who was numbered among the twelve" (Luke 22:3, NKJV).

This scripture is somehow hidden from the reality of the consequences of an unchecked and unrepentant life. Judas walked with the Lord the same amount of time the other eleven did. Satan entered Judas, who was one of the twelve disciples, and of course, you know that the definition of a disciple is a disciplined follower of Christ.

This means Judas was casting out demons like the other eleven. He was healing the sick like the other eleven, just as we learned earlier. But Judas had an extra office (coincidentally, so did Lucifer). Judas handled the purse, and if you think for a moment that Jesus was going to put a thief in charge of the money, then you may conclude Jesus was a buffoon (just like believing God would trust Lucifer with two ministries in heaven forgetting His own power's limits), and you know that's impossible. This means that at some point, temptation came to Judas just like it came to Lucifer, Peter, and just as it came to the disciples who walked away from Jesus in John, chapter six, and just like it will come our way today, tomorrow, and perhaps every day thereafter.

Judas being an apostle, did not have a whole lot of time to repent. He tried to, but by then, it was a little too late. These were times of almost instant judgment. Jesus was on planet Earth: meaning God was on planet Earth in the flesh. This, regardless of Him not exercising His attributes while in the flesh, and by flesh, I mean alive amongst us.

During the last supper, we see that once again, Satan entered

Judas. This time it happened while Judas was sitting next to Jesus. Selah.

That pivot point meant only one thing: that an apostle had had an encounter with the enemy of God, and that his early temptation to betray Jesus for a price was right on the money with prophecy as is read in the Gospels and being that it was about the thirty pieces of silver, which, according to the Psalms, was bound to happen, and thus, Judas continued to feed into this forbidden relationship with the enemy of God, just as he premeditated Jesus's betrayal.

Jesus did not say anything to Judas about his wrongdoing. He simply said: "Friend, go and do what you came to do and do it quickly." He didn't beg Judas to stay either! Selah. Judas, on the other hand, was not seeking the counsel of the disciples regarding his curiosity, no! Judas sought counsel from Jesus's enemies, the religious leaders, and of course, they were to encourage Judas; it's almost textbook betrayal!

After Judas figured out what he had done, there was no place for repentance, and that grace period came to a halt in such a steadfast and speedy fashion. Because of his office, or should I say, *offices, that unfortunately led to* the reason why grace was shortened.

Then Judas went and simply killed himself because he went past the redemption point, and that's the outcome of every single suicide outside of unplanned overdoses, where redemption point has its limits and eventually time runs out.

THE GREAT APOSTASY!

Let the words of James resonate within you if you happen to be high up in the mountain of God, e.g., ministry (James 3:1). Circumspectly, Judas became the seventh and last suicide in the Bible!

And I know most would want to be numbered in the faithful church, but the reality is that we are probably more like the Sardis church, if anything. At least it describes us best: "Be watchful, and strengthen the things which remain, that are ready to die, for I have not found your works perfect before God" (Revelation 3:2, NKJV).

Call me crazy, but if that does not describe the last-day church to a tee, I don't know what does. I mean, the divorce rate is no different than the secular world; most denominations are now pro-choice and have conformed to the idea of gay marriage as the norm. So, if that description of today's church isn't on point, then just sue me for thinking the obvious!

Not too long ago, I had a social media conversation with one of Chicago's most popular pastors. He had posted a live video during the George Floyd riots and gave some misinformation about a police shooting in a high-profile case that the leftist media decided to cover, and that conversation somehow led to Donald Trump being racist. Laughable, of course, but what came out of this pastor's heart is what left me at *hello*!

I said to him that for the first time in a long time, we finally have a president who has given the church a place at the table, and

425

his response was, and I quote, "There is more to an election than just abortion and gay marriage." Wow! I was stunned to hear a pastor pretend those are not the top two laws that make the difference between righteousness and wickedness, but I held it in nevertheless!

Over twenty-four million babies have been aborted since Roe v. Wade, sadly passed abortion law, and it takes place mostly in minority communities, and to pretend that this law shouldn't be on our radar to change if we saw an opportunity, or Defense of Marriage Act for that matter, but abortion law is what literally broke my heart because I've known this pastor for twenty years. He did come out against gay marriage when it first happened, but now somehow, that or abortion was not a priority now, and I'm talking about a man I admired prior to the woke mentality of today's takeover of the church of color (Isaiah 1:4).

Sardis is told in verse three that it received and heard the message, and after that, it is told to repent, and in my view, at some point, we must take inventory of our individual walks, and when it's all said and done, we just put two and two together, and the outcome has to be four, as simple as that. Success in ministry means absolutely nothing if we are against Scripture at any point and for whatever matter!

Just look at verse two of Revelation chapter three,

"Wake up!' [this is because the church is asleep, of

course] Strengthen what remains [meaning weakness is detected in their midst as a whole] [...] for I have found your deeds unfinished [In other words, the church is growing, people are getting saved, the community is improving, but they are okay with abortion and gay marriage and the woke-wicked culture) [...] Remember, therefore, what you have received and heard; hold fast, *and repent. But if you do not wake up*, I will come like a thief, and you will not know at what time I will come to you. [If a thief comes but to kill, steal, and destroy, well, you do the math. He becomes your enemy is what He is hinting at].

Revelation 3:2-3 (NKJV), emphasis brackets added

Interestingly enough, as we move to chapter three and verse seven, the church of Philadelphia resonates with America today because well, Philadelphia is the center of attention not only because of the past presidential election but because of the overwhelming voter fraud investigation that is underway and because Kim Clement prophesied so much about the Trump administration before his death, and some of it has already been fulfilled. In fact, Kim Clement prophesied in 2011 and 2014 pretty much everything revolving in American politics, from Hillary trying to get into the White House after her own criminal fiasco, as Clement describes her as a witch trying to usurp her way into the White House, and he referred to Donald Trump as God's David.

Clement not only prophesied the impeachment twice, which was an impossibility until it happened because no president has had that happened, but also that they would fail to impeach the president in the Senate twice, and yes, Clement prophesied Ukraine by name, and even to what's heading down the pike. He mentioned Trump, or God's David, to be a two-term president, though he never said back-to-back and that both parties would experience a shameful moment, an embarrassment, if you will. I can only think of one thing, God pulling the covers from all the corruption in the past ten years of these Washington politicians.

The current chaos in trying to figure out voter fraud is also stamped by Clement as an upcoming shameful day for the democrats. Also, Clement promised that a new Snowden will arise, and that means someone with a tech background like Snowden will use his ability of the trade to expose fraud in some spectacular way. My guess is regarding Dominion voting systems and their affiliates. We shall see, and of course, that has nothing to do with how the justice and judicial branch will receive or even accept such evidence, especially after we read in second Thessalonians 2:11 that God Himself will send a strong delusion to believe the lie.

But since the book of Revelation is a book for the end times, then we can surely apply these prophecies to current events and filter them with biblical authenticity in their own fulfillment.

...these are the words of Him who is holy and true, who

holds the key of David. What He opens no one can shut, and what He shuts no one can open. I know your deeds. See, I have placed before you an open door that no one can shut. I know that you have little strength, yet you have kept my word and have not denied my name. I will make those who are of the synagogue of Satan, who claim to be Jews though they are not, but are liars—I will make them come fall down at your feet and acknowledge that I have loved you. Since you have kept My command to endure patiently, I will also keep you from the hour of trial that is going to come on the whole world to test the inhabitants of the earth.

Revelation 3:7-10 (NIV)

Kim Clement said God was going to set His *David* in the White House; he said that God's David would flip the Supreme Court, all of which already took place, and the death of Ruth Bader Ginsburg came and went at a perfect time for the fulfillment of this prophecy though as tragic of a loss as that it was. Is it because the 2020 election was supposed to be decided in the Supreme Court, as Bush Gore's was? If they were to accept such evidence, maybe so. Sadly, they passed on the idea, and perhaps as part of the lawlessness agenda being put through in our nation.

Look at verse seven above as it speaks of a door that opens that no one can shut. I believe it is a prophecy to the political spectrum of current events and that eventually, Kim Clément's long-awaited prophecy of God's David (Donald Trump) will indeed be fulfilled. I said that because prophecy and true prophecy usually encounter extravagant opposition.

Why would God bring to pass so much regarding Clément's prophecies just to leave him out to hang dry in the end? That wouldn't make much sense, in my humble opinion. But whether we like it or not, God will fulfill His Word, and we can't ignore what took place in 2020!

The key to the connection between the correlation of the Philadelphia church, King David, and Donald J. Trump in today's spectrum of incidents is simply tied together in the written Word and Kim Clément's prophecy without the hypotheticals as a waiting game. This means every word in the Bible will be fulfilled just as Jesus said it would. He said, "Heaven and earth will pass away, but My words will by no means pass away" (Matthew 24:35, NKJV).

God tells us that He will make *the Jews*; I believe He is speaking of the *media giants* who own all the networks, as well as Hollywood and all those finding themselves to be the enemy god and are number one of all things anti-God, like George Soros, who is a Jew. Thus, making these players candidates of *end-time* prophecies the key components of submission unto God's David according to Clement and Revelation, chapter three. And why would they bow to this David? Well, because he was faithful and waited on

God. The truth does not need to be defended, the truth has truth, and the truth is its own defense.

One thing you need to know is that if the media makes you, then that very same media can break you at some point. Don't believe me? Ask Andrew Cuomo!

God will reveal all the lies fed to the American people and the world, not just about politics, but the W.H.O., the CDC, and federal law enforcement. Also, the COVID-19 manipulation handbook and everything in between. The perfect storm may have given the wicked an edge, but don't go thinking God is by any means fooled by it all or asleep behind the wheel!

Faithfulness has its many rewards (Hebrews 11:6), and at the same time and in the same way, just like unfaithfulness has its many judgments and downfalls, they both are brought to fruition at some point. And we will see soon, but nevertheless, we win!

What's interesting about the book of church-friendly messages for the church in general in the first three chapters of Revelation is to repent. Here we have a president that has been the most church-friendly and unapologetic to all things Jesus in the history of the US in former President Trump, and half of the church has abandoned him on the premise of false accusations of racism, i.e., the church of color, and in case you were wondering why, well, the deception was prophesied, and I hope that's enough reason for you to believe repentance from such deception. After knowing our Bibles like the backs of our hands, it definitely comes at a price, or are we that calloused? Jesus told the Pharisees they would have gotten a pass, but since they knew the Scriptures, they get no pass…we call that accountability. And politics have always tied themselves one way or another into religion pretty much throughout history.

Verse ten of the church of Philadelphia tells us that a test is underway for the church. Will the church pass the test? At the end of the day, we, the church, are faced with the opportunity to rise up and stand for righteousness. "Woe unto you who call good evil and evil good," said Isaiah, the prophet.

I believe Jesus has pinned us to the Laodicean church, one who is lukewarm, one who is willing to continue to see pedophilia lose its criminality, one that has seen marriage as God intended to lose its attribute, one that has turned a blind eye to the millions of babies being slaughtered daily by the abortion mandate of liberal presidents and politicians.

How can any Bible-believing Christian cast a vote for the party of genocide, the party of abomination, the party of corruption, the party of lawlessness and indignation, and the party of anti-Christianity?

The answer is in the letters to the seven churches, and the only message to those seven churches is to repent!

I know your deeds, that you are neither hot nor cold. I wish you were either one or the other! So, because you are lukewarm—neither hot nor cold—I am about to spit you out of My mouth.

Revelation 3:15-16 (NIV)

I know this is a hard pill to swallow, but He said He would rather we be cold than lukewarm, which can only be that He wishes He would never have tasted us. He said He is about to spit us out of His mouth. Does that take you as if Christianity has its many levels, or is being on fire for God the only state of faith He is comfortable with?

Verse nineteen says, "Those whom I love I rebuke and discipline." Well, here is the downside of that, if He doesn't rebuke you or discipline you, He doesn't love you, and He is speaking to believers. Now, do you believe that the Great Apostasy is Christians leaving Christ for Satan and what he has to offer, or that God also has left them simultaneously because, in apostasy, there is no room for God any longer?

Is America ready to be judged for her godlessness of past and recent days, or is the entire world ready for the final judgment since it is the measuring stick?

Has Christianity as we know it has ended, and has the age of the church ended along with it? Matthew 24:1 (NKJV) begins with these words: "Then Jesus went out and *departed* from the temple," i.e., the church. Blue Letter Bible's first metaphysical definition of the word *departed* is "to go out of an assembly, i.e., forsake it."

Think about that for a minute, the church around the world was shut down for a virus that has a 99.7 percent survival rate. Never mind that it was instrumental in rigging the election, but that the church age perhaps ended by such a feat. And that the church leadership decided to keep people from dying rather than keeping people from going to hell as expected by God by closing the local church for close to a year, thus stopping the lost souls who would be walk-ins as has always been the case if the doors were left open. Something happened to Christianity during the COVID-19 era; like it or not, this was a test of tests, and since COVID-19 is the gift that keeps on giving for leftists worldwide, don't expect your freedom anytime soon without a fight.

In Matthew 24:7 (NKJV), the Lord said, "Nation will rise against nation, and kingdom against kingdom." What's interesting about these two statements is that the word "nation" used here is the word *ethnos* in Greek, and it means ethnicity. Well, I don't need to tell you what a scam racism has turned out to be since every single day, the corrupt leftist media has a way to remind us how racist simply being White is. As if people could pick their skin color.

We are supposed to be a different kind of breed as believers, a remnant, if you will, and to ignore the elephant in the room is to ignore our belief in the Scriptures.

THE GREAT APOSTASY!

We have experienced the lawlessness of corrupt politicians and corrupt media outlets in the past, but today, social media, along with these powerful entities, have decided to unite and create their own agenda-driven reality, and I, for one, am glad it's finally here because I am looking forward to the culmination of the matter.

From federal law enforcement, as well as the Supreme Court, to your cable and local news, we are experiencing lawlessness almost daily, and in the words of John the revelator in chapter twenty-two and verse twenty: "Amen. Come, Lord Jesus."

NOTES

Endnotes

1 John MacArthur, *The MacArthur Study Bible* (Nashville: Thomas Nelson Bibles), 1905.

2 Finis Jennings Dake, *Dake's Annotated Reference Bible* (Lawrenceville: Dake Publishing), Hebrews 6 commentary, 434 NT.

3 Chuck Smith, *Chuck Smith Bible Commentary*, "Commentary on Hebrews 3," as quoted in Studylight, accessed September 02, 2021, https://www.studylight.org/commentaries/eng/csc/hebrews-3.html.

4 John MacArthur, *The MacArthur Study Bible. NKJV* (Nashville: Thomas Nelson Bibles), 1400.

5 Chuck Smith, *Chuck Smith Bible Commentary*, "Commentary on Hebrews 3," as quoted in Studylight, accessed September 02, 2021, https://www.studylight.org/commentaries/eng/csc/hebrews-3.html.

6 John MacArthur, *The MacArthur Study Bible* (Nashville: Thomas Nelson Bibles), 1706.

7 John MacArthur, *The MacArthur Study Bible* (Nashville: Thomas Nelson Bibles), 1706.

8 James Strong, *Strong's Concordance*, "Strong's #3877:

parakoloutheo," as quoted in Bibletools, accessed September 02, 2021, https://www.bibletools.org/index.cfm/fuseaction/Lexicon. show/ID/G3877/parakoloutheo.htm.

9 Erwin W. Lutzer, Moody Media Church, "Suicide And Salvation," accessed September 02, 2021, https://www.moodyme-dia.org/articles/suicide-and-savation.

10 Charles Fillmore, *Metaphysical Bible Dictionary* (North Chelmsford: Courier Corporation, 2013), 575.

11 James Strong, *Strong's Concordance*, "Strong's #796: astrape," as quoted in Bibletools, accessed September 02, 2021, https://www.bibletools.org/index.cfm/fuseaction/Lexicon.show/ID/ G796/astrape.htm.

12 James Strong, *Strong's Concordance*, "Strong's #1300: baraq," as quoted in Bibletools, accessed September 02, 2021, https://www.bibletools.org/index.cfm/fuseaction/Lexicon.show/ID/ H1300/baraq.htm.